JULIE SHAW

OUR VINNIE

THE TRUE STORY OF YORKSHIRE'S
NOTORIOUS CRIMINAL FAMILY

HarperElement
An imprint of HarperCollins*Publishers*
77–85 Fulham Palace Road,
Hammersmith, London W6 8JB

www.harpercollins.co.uk

and HarperElement are trademarks of
HarperCollins*Publishers* Ltd

First published by HarperElement 2014

3 5 7 9 10 8 6 4 2

© Julie Shaw and Lynne Barrett-Lee 2014

Julie Shaw and Lynne Barrett-Lee assert the moral right
to be identified as the authors of this work

A catalogue record of this book is
available from the British Library

PB ISBN: 978-0-00-754224-6
EB ISBN: 978-0-00-754225-3

Printed and bound in Great Britain by
Clays Ltd, St Ives plc

MIX
Paper from
responsible sources
FSC® C007454

The Canterbury Warriors

We are the Canterbury Warriors
We stay out late at night
If anybody dare come near us
There's sure to be a fight
Last night we were in trouble
Tonight we are in jail
We're doing six months' hard labour
For pulling a donkey's tail
Way back whoa back
Come and get yer money back
Pea and pies for supper
Our old lass has plenty of brass
And we don't give a bugger!

(Anon.)

Note by the Author

My name is Julie Shaw, and my father, Keith, is the only surviving member of the 13 Hudson siblings, born to Annie and Reggie Hudson on the infamous Canterbury Estate in Bradford. We were and are a very close family, even though there were so many of us, and those of us who are left always will be.

I wanted to write these stories as a tribute to my parents and family. The stories are all based on the truth but, as I'm sure you'll understand, I've had to disguise some identities and facts to protect the innocent. Those of you who still live on the Canterbury Estate will appreciate the folklore that we all grew up with: the stories of our predecessors, good and bad, and the names that can still strike fear or respect into our hearts – the stories of the Canterbury Warriors.

ANNIE AND REGGIE HUDSON

Married 1919

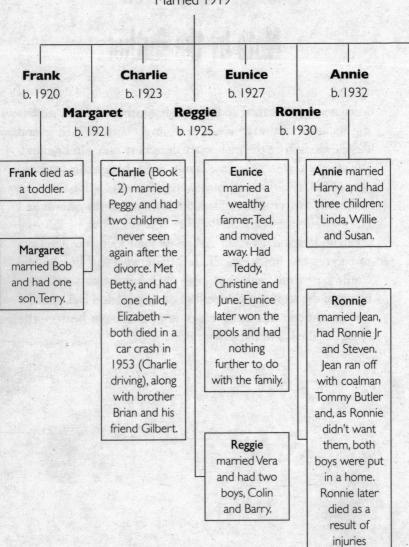

Frank b. 1920

Margaret b. 1921

Charlie b. 1923

Reggie b. 1925

Eunice b. 1927

Ronnie b. 1930

Annie b. 1932

Frank died as a toddler.

Margaret married Bob and had one son, Terry.

Charlie (Book 2) married Peggy and had two children – never seen again after the divorce. Met Betty, and had one child, Elizabeth – both died in a car crash in 1953 (Charlie driving), along with brother Brian and his friend Gilbert.

Eunice married a wealthy farmer, Ted, and moved away. Had Teddy, Christine and June. Eunice later won the pools and had nothing further to do with the family.

Reggie married Vera and had two boys, Colin and Barry.

Annie married Harry and had three children: Linda, Willie and Susan.

Ronnie married Jean, had Ronnie Jr and Steven. Jean ran off with coalman Tommy Butler and, as Ronnie didn't want them, both boys were put in a home. Ronnie later died as a result of injuries sustained in the car crash.

Hudson Family Tree

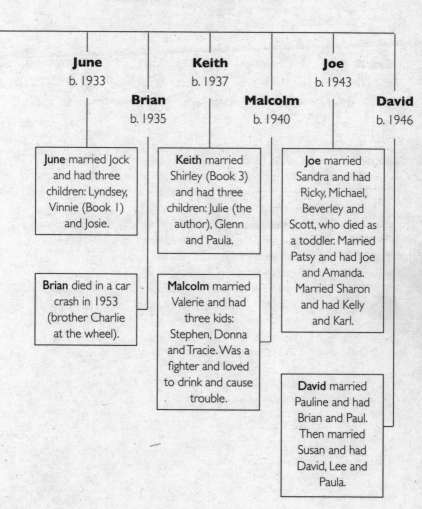

June
b. 1933

Brian
b. 1935

Keith
b. 1937

Malcolm
b. 1940

Joe
b. 1943

David
b. 1946

June married Jock and had three children: Lyndsey, Vinnie (Book 1) and Josie.

Brian died in a car crash in 1953 (brother Charlie at the wheel).

Keith married Shirley (Book 3) and had three children: Julie (the author), Glenn and Paula.

Malcolm married Valerie and had three kids: Stephen, Donna and Tracie. Was a fighter and loved to drink and cause trouble.

Joe married Sandra and had Ricky, Michael, Beverley and Scott, who died as a toddler. Married Patsy and had Joe and Amanda. Married Sharon and had Kelly and Karl.

David married Pauline and had Brian and Paul. Then married Susan and had David, Lee and Paula.

1970

Chapter I

Bradford, October

June McKellan was standing in front of her chipped-tile fire-place, skirt hitched up slightly at the back. She was warming her backside from the last of the embers that were sizzling out on the coal fire. Her husband, Jock, was slouched across the brown moquette settee in his favourite position – bottle of cider in one hand, cigarette in the other. His eyes were glued to the television as he squinted through a cloud of fag smoke to watch the last race of the day. June stared at the sight she had married. 'Are you gonna fucking move today, or what?' she asked him. 'And if you've won fuck all on the horses again, you better get yourself out on the tap. We've no coal, and I'm off out tonight!'

Jock dragged his gaze from the TV and looked up at her. 'Shut your cake-hole, June,' he said. 'You're going no-fucking-where till you've got me another bottle of Joe Rider and some twifters.' Jock turned his attention to his wife then, his gaze full of animosity as he looked her up and down, and she could tell exactly what he was thinking. And knowing none of the thoughts were nice – the contents of his head rarely were – she jabbed him in the shoulder to reinforce her orders.

'I've got your cider and your fags, gob shite,' she snapped. 'Now move your arse off that couch before our Vinnie gets in for his tea. Fucking social worker's coming at half five.'

'What?' Jock said, alert now. 'What the fuck for?'

'Been to see Moira,' June told him irritably. 'Needs to talk about something apparently. And, no, I don't know what, because I haven't spoken to her yet, have I?'

'Moira?' he said again. 'Why Moira?'

'Because I was fucking asleep, okay?' *And hungover, same as you were*, she thought but didn't add. 'Anyway, get up and get out, will you? I don't want you sitting here pissed as a fart when she gets here. Go on – go round your Maureen's and borrow some coal and a few quid till we get your dole.'

Jock dragged himself up and pulled his woollen cardigan closer round his bloated stomach. 'I'm getting a bit sick of this, June,' he said, crushing out his cigarette. 'Our Maureen thinks I should give you a fucking slap and make you stay in.'

June threw her head back and laughed at him. 'Your Maureen's coming out with me, idiot! And I'd like to see the day you give *me* a fucking slap!'

Jock slammed the door as he stumbled out of the house, and into the sooty late afternoon light. Little twat! He was a good foot and a half bigger than her, and one of these days he would knock her out, never mind the slap. What a fucking cow bag she was, stood there like that, all bleached hair and lippy. Oh, all his mates had thought he'd cracked it when he copped for June – five foot fuck all, and a waist you could get your hand around. Well, they didn't know what he had to put up with, did they? Gobby little cow that she was.

He meandered down the path and into the street, scowling as he dodged the dog shit on the pavement. He could do nothing right in her eyes. Not these days, at any rate. The three kids, on the other hand, could do no wrong. Fucking twat. He'd slap her proper, one of these days.

* * *

Her feckless hulk of a husband out of the way, June resumed her position by the fire, shivering but happy now. She would be down at the Bull with Maureen in a couple of hours, and she couldn't wait; the blokes down there wouldn't dream of talking to her like that. Let the miserable bastard stew, she thought. She wouldn't be dwelling on it, not after a couple of halves, anyway.

Jock had only been gone five minutes when 13-year-old Vinnie burst through the door, a big smile on his face for his mum. 'Warming the old man's supper up, ma?' he joked, pointing to her skirt. June laughed. He was a case, was her Vinnie, and no one understood him like she did. And all the neighbours were just jealous bastards, that was all – accusing him of every little thing that went down on the estate. Yes, he had gotten himself into bother now and again, but so what? All kids got into fights or went out robbing, didn't they? Why always blame *her* son? It wasn't fair.

'Quite funny for you that were, son!' she told him drily. Then she nodded towards the kitchen. 'Go on,' she told him. 'There's some sarnies in there for you and a biscuit on top of the cupboard. Don't tell your dad where they are though,' she added. 'Greedy bastard's fat enough as it is!'

Vinnie grinned. Then his expression changed. 'Mam,' he said, not quite looking at her, 'you know when the social worker gets here? Well, whatever she says is a load of shit. A few on the estate are saying the youthy got robbed last night, so no doubt she'll try and fit me up for it, you know, to the bizzies. I swear I wasn't there, Mam, honest I wasn't. But you're gonna have to say I was in all night cos they're not gonna believe me when I say it, are they?'

June looked sadly at her son. With his wild, shoulder-length ginger hair and his bright blue eyes he looked the picture of innocence. Okay, so 'innocent' was pushing it, but he wasn't the evil twat that everyone made him out to be. He had a smile that could melt her heart and a sense of humour that could have an audience in stitches. She sighed. Now it seemed she was going to have to defend him *again*. He'd better not have done anything; she was off out tonight, come hell or high water.

As if on cue, the letterbox rattled and the front door was pushed open. 'Can I come in, June?' they heard a voice say. 'It's only me!'

Sally, the social worker, waddled into the front room, puffing and panting as usual, as familiar a presence in the McKellan household as most of the furniture. She flopped down onto the place on the settee Jock had only just vacated. 'Hiya, Vinnie, love,' she said, smiling up at him as she settled into the sagging seat cushion. 'It's brass monkeys out there, mate, isn't it? Get the kettle on!'

Vinnie gave an obligatory smile and went off to fill the kettle. June knew from the absence of banging and clattering that he'd be trying to listen in. He hated his social worker and not without reason; she was always trying to have him sent away. And June knew part of the reason was the same as the reason she did – because it always felt like Sally could see right through him. Not that he'd hear much of interest. June was too busy staring malevolently at the interfering witch. Not grassing up her son when he wasn't there.

But he was as quick as a whippet coming back with Sally's tea, so there was no time to say anything anyway.

'There you go, Sal,' said Vinnie as he handed over a pint pot. And then, obviously deciding to really take the piss, he adopted his best posh voice. 'Best mug in the house, that,' he said. 'Especially for you. Now then, to what do we owe this honour?'

Sally turned to June, looking less than impressed, and June felt a prickle of anxiety. 'Hark at him,' Sally said. 'Proper little host, isn't he?'

June scowled at her son. 'Take no notice, Sally. He has got a point though; you're not due for a fortnight. What d'you want with us? It all seems a bit suss to me.'

Sally looked directly at Vinnie then. She knew how the estate operated and especially this family. She might be a lump but her brain was pretty sharp. 'Well, are you going to tell her, or should I?' she asked Vinnie.

'What are you on about, you daft cow?' he responded. 'She's off it, Mam, I swear to God. I told you I would get accused of summat, didn't I?'

June braced herself. 'What's he supposed to have done this time?' she asked evenly. 'Only, if it's about the youth club, I've heard all about it. He can't have been involved because he was in here all night with me and our little Josie.' She glared at the social worker, daring her to contradict her, although half of her knew that Vinnie probably *had* been at the scene of the crime; had most likely orchestrated the whole thing in fact.

'June, I'm really sorry, love,' Sally said, frowning, 'but he's been fingered by at least three witnesses, all of whom will say it in court, as well. Vinnie was seen smashing in the skylight, lowering one of his mates in and then –' she looked at Vinnie again, and June clocked his expression – 'jumping in himself.'

June digested this, and having done so, felt the bile rise inside her. The stupid little fucker. She sprang forward then, making Sally leap up from the couch in fright. She lunged towards Vinnie, grabbing him by the hair and punching him repeatedly in the head. 'You lying little bastard, I'll fucking kill you! When are you gonna fucking learn, you fucking simpleton?!'

Vinnie squirmed under her grip, but she held firm onto his hair. 'Mam, fuck off! I didn't do it, I swear!' he squealed. 'They're lying, Mam! Get off me, you div – you're hurting, Mam, stop it!'

Vinnie was almost hysterical by now, but it didn't appease her. She might be small but she was as nasty as fuck when she started, and boy, did she feel like starting now.

Sally was up on her feet again. 'Calm down, June,' she said, trying to get in between them and extricate June's hands from Vinnie's hair. 'Let's just sit down and talk about what to do next, shall we? This is getting us nowhere. Come on, June. Let him go.'

She succeeded. June allowed herself to be led to the fireplace, where Sally handed her the cigarettes and matches from the shelf. She lit up with trembling fingers and watched her errant son as he tried in vain to straighten his messed up hair and re-adjust his jumper. He was snivelling now, too, and shaking his head as though he couldn't believe that his own mother would doubt him. *Look at him*, she thought angrily, *playing it out to the full. Thinks he can even fool me. Me, his own fucking mother!*

'Now then,' Sally started to explain, once she was back sitting on the sofa, her boobs visibly quivering beneath her floral maxi dress as she checked her long ponytail was still securely in place. 'It's a given that Vinnie *did* do the youth club. I know for a fact that he was also involved in the bingo-hall robbery a fortnight ago.'

'What?' June started.

'It's also a *fact*,' Sally continued, ignoring her, 'that he hasn't attended school for at least two months.' She paused to let both of them digest this part too, and June could see the patronising look in her eyes. She knew what Sally thought of them: that they were lunatics of the highest order. Snotty bitch.

'Just cut the shit, Sal,' June said. 'What's the score then? My Vinnie getting blamed for the lot, is he? Just cos he's a bit of a lad?' She raised her finger threateningly, the cigarette trailing coils of smoke as she did so. 'You wanna watch your mouth, Sally, because there's a lot of us on this estate getting a bit sick of your fucking accusations!'

Sally looked pained. Looked like she could do with a slap herself. June wasn't sure who she wanted to slap most right now. Her idiot son or this arrogant cow. 'Look, June,' Sally said, 'blame me if it helps, but it's not my fault. If Vinnie chooses a life like this, he needs to know there are consequences. *If* you had turned up at court – like you were meant to – you would have heard what was decided there, wouldn't you?'

June glanced at Vinnie. Could see the fear in his face now. '*Court?*' he spluttered. 'What's she on about, Mam?'

June spread her hands. 'I didn't know I had to attend, did I? I thought it was just all the usual crap about skiving school, an' I've said it all before, haven't I?' She glared at Sally. 'I can't force him to stay in school, can I? He's not a fucking toddler, is he? I can't drag him by the fucking hand.' She turned to Vinnie then. 'And don't you look at me like that, Vin. If you stayed out of bother we'd have no need for all this, would we? *Would* we?'

June clocked Sally's frown and felt herself shaking. She could tell that she hadn't heard the worst of it yet. There was something bad coming, for definite. She steadied herself with an arm on the nicotine-coloured shelf. 'Go on then,' she said, seeing the social worker's pitying expression. 'What?'

'Unfortunately, love – and I did try to stop this, believe me – the courts have decided that he has to be sent away.'

Vinnie, who'd perched himself on the sofa arm by now, sprang up at this in dismay. 'No, Mam, tell her! I'm not going anywhere! You can fuck off, you fat bitch! Tell her, Mam!'

June was every bit as shocked as he was by this turn of events. She saw his face begin to crumple – proper, genuine tears this time, and she couldn't bear it – she could never bear to see her boy so upset. If he deserved a leathering, then, yes, she would give him one in an instant. But for someone else to be punishing him was unthinkable. Another thought smacked her in the face then – Jock. Jock was going to go fucking *apeshit*.

'Come on, Sal,' she tried. 'That can't be right, surely? It hasn't even gone to court yet about the robberies! How can he be punished for something not proven? We haven't even had the bizzies round or anything.'

'The police *will* be round, June. They are currently collecting statements about that one, but this is because of all the other stuff as well.' She raised her hands and started ticking off Vinnie's transgressions on her fingers. 'Fighting,' she started, 'robbing, mugging, smashing up cars, starting fires … I could go on. He's lucky he's lasted so long. No, June, this is the end of the line, love. It will be a week today.' She picked up her handbag. 'I'll be collecting him and we'll be taking him to an approved school down in Brighton.'

June gawped. 'Fucking Brighton? How the fuck are we meant to get to Brighton for a visit?' She could hear Vinnie really snivelling now. She could hardly bear to look at him. She concentrated on Sally. 'How long is he off for?'

Sally explained how Vinnie would be staying at the school until his behaviour improved, and that the distance didn't matter because they wouldn't be *allowed* to visit. June was open-mouthed at this and Vinnie was really crying now, his head in his hands bent over towards his knees. This was killing him, June knew. *And* her, for that matter, watching him – sobbing as Sally patted his back as she told him that after a while, *if* he behaved himself, that was, he would be allowed some weekend visits home. *Why'd she flown at him?* she thought miserably. Why hadn't she stood by him? Been a decent alibi? Fucking witnesses. What witnesses? Who knew if they weren't just out to fit him up, after all?

Sally left not long after and June tried to pull herself together. She needed to be there for poor Vin, who was obviously distressed. But no sooner had she turned back to him than he was wiping his face and grinning. '*Que sera sera*, muvver! Alter your face, I'll be okay!'

June shook her head, not sure whether to be relieved he'd been putting it on, or furious at the little git for all the play-acting. She chose the latter and went to clip him round the ear again, but he managed to dodge her. 'We'll see, son,' she snapped. 'We'll see. I hope you're right. You realise your dad's gonna throw a right mental though when he hears this, don't you?'

And he would, too. Which was no less than Vin deserved. And which she wasn't hanging about for. 'Anyway, I'm off out, mate,' she added, '*before* he gets back. I've got a few quid stashed away that he don't know about.'

Vinnie looked affronted. 'Well I'm not staying here on my own!' he said. 'He'll be pissed, won't he? I'm not having him battering me as well as you.'

June softened then. 'I'm sorry, love, you know what I'm like.' She pulled her packet of fags out from where she'd just stowed them in her handbag and tried not to think about him not being around for a bit. 'Here,' she said, 'take a couple of ciggies and a few bob for some supper. I'm off to the Bull to meet Moira and Maureen. You can go round to our Lyndsey's for the night; tell her what's happened.'

Vinnie, who clearly couldn't believe his good fortune, grinned widely. Then gave his mum a quick hug and a kiss before running out of the house.

June turned back to the mirror and quickly applied some more panstick onto the bags under her eyes, and a fresh slice of ruby red across her lips. She then changed her coal-burnt slippers for a pair of black stilettos and within minutes she was off up the road to her local, her evening back on track, at least for now. She wondered how many scratters with a few bob she was going to pull tonight. She pulled her old fur coat closer round her, to keep out the chill. And pushed all thoughts of her wayward son to the back of her mind.

Like you did. It was like Vinnie said, *Que sera sera*. What could you do?

Chapter 2

Vinnie peeped into the window, through the gap in the curtains of his sister's house, taking care not to be seen. He had vaulted the six garden fences round the backs which separated his house from hers, and he could feel his breath rasping in his throat. Squatting down then, out of sight, he shivered against the freezing wind as he ate the last of his vinegar-soaked chips. He wished he'd had the bottle to nip into his own house for his coat. Fucking old man had put paid to that idea, though. Must have heard the latest news from his auntie or something, because when Vinnie had popped his head inside 10 minutes ago, the senile old bastard had started ranting and raging. Fuck that for a lark – he was off.

He hated coming up to Lyndsey's because she lived like a pig. But right now, she felt the lesser of two evils. But only just; peering back in through the window, he could see that she was off her head already. She was slumped in an armchair that was covered in puke and chocolate stains, eyes glazed over and with that stupid vacant smile on her face as she watched the three kids playing on the ratty carpet. Vinnie frowned. Fucking 10 o'clock at night and the kids still up. They were only three, four and seven as well. The 'idiot' – her bloke Robbo – was squatting on the floor, too, smoking his weed through a milk-bottle pipe, oblivious to fucking anything. Vinnie crumpled up his chip bag and knocked hard on the window. *'Police, open up!'* he shouted.

Little Robbie, the eldest kid, looked up and smiled at him and Lyndsey, at once alert, jumped up from her chair. Seeing Vinnie grinning in at her, she relaxed and sat down again and was back slumped by the time he'd let himself in through the unlocked back door. 'Fucking divvy!' she said as the kids all ran to jump up at their uncle.

'All right kids, calm down,' he said, fending them off. 'Fuckin' hell, Lynds, you wanna tell him to give that pipe a rest – these three are high as kites!'

'Cheeky fucker,' she responded, clearly less out of it than she looked. 'You're not too old to get your arse smacked, you know.' Then her tone changed. 'Aw, put 'em to bed for us, will you, Vin?' She looked at him hopefully. 'I'll do another mix if I can get the pipe off Marty-fucking-Feldman there. Just look at them fucking eyes. Oi! Numpty – pipe!'

It was always like this and Vinnie wasn't about to say no to her. *Someone* needed to look after the poor little fuckers. Vinnie picked his nieces up, one giggling on each arm. 'C'mon then, mate,' he said to Robbie, then, choosing his route carefully over the shoes and clothes that had been left all over the floor, took them all up to bed.

Sammy and Lou shared bunk beds in the same bedroom as their brother, and Vinnie took his usual deep breath of the clear air on the tiny landing before going into the room. It never changed – it stank of piss and always made him retch.

'Will you play with us, Uncle Vinnie? Just for a little bit?' asked Robbie.

Vinnie shook his head. 'Not tonight, matey. You three need some sleep. It's late and your mam wants me downstairs. I'm sleeping on your couch though,' he added, while casting around for some wearable nightwear. 'So we can play in the morning, all right?'

Having settled the kids, Vinnie went down to join Lyndsey and Robbo. At least when they were stoned they shared the hash out. Not like if they'd been on the other stuff. He hated them then. That was the trouble with coming here, though; you either walked in and fucking floated out or you entered a war zone. You never knew what you might find.

'Don't suppose you've heard about me, then?' Vinnie asked as he sat on the couch. Clearly not. His sister and Robbo just looked puzzled. 'I'm getting sent down, aren't I?' he said. 'Next week. Fuckin' right piss-take.'

'Fuck off!' laughed Robbo. 'You're only 13. They can't fucking send you down at your age!'

Vinnie glared at the idiot. He hated him, and couldn't understand what his sister saw in him. 'Well they are. Durr! They know I did the fucking bingo hall *and* the youthy. Fucking Saggy Tits came up today, said it was all decided in court yesterday. But, of course, me mother didn't attend, did she?'

'Aw, here love,' Lyndsey said as she passed Vinnie a joint. He looked at it, smiling at her with something approaching pity. She was well gone now, her eyes just a pair of slits in her face. A far cry from the stunner she'd once been, way back. Now she just looked fucking tragic. 'It don't really surprise me about *her* though. They don't serve bitter in court, do they?' She tipped her head back and laughed at her own joke. Vinnie didn't. 'And you have to admit, Vin, you had it coming, mate.'

He lit the paper, watched the stray ends of tobacco flare and redden. Perhaps having a smoke would give him some more of the Dutch courage he needed. Was going to keep needing, in fact. 'Cheers for the moral support and all that,' he said. 'I'm not bothered anyway. Piece of piss approved school'll be.'

Robbo opened his mouth to speak but started to choke instead – either over Vinnie's words or the smoke that wreathed his face. 'Approved school?' he spluttered finally. 'That's not going down, mate. The nick is going down. Armley or Thorp Arch is going *down*. Fucking approved school?'

Robbo bent over to suck again on the piece of plastic tube, laughing. The homemade pipe had another tube next to the plastic one; a length of copper pipe that was wedged into the model milk bottle with a lump of plasticine. Vinnie watched, fascinated, as the dirty liquid in the bottle started to bubble. He hoped the arsehole *did* choke on it. Like, lethally. Who did he think he was, trying to make a cunt out of him?

Lyndsey snatched the pipe back. 'Shut it, you! Even if it's not the nick, he'll still be away, won't he? It's not like he'll be allowed out fucking shopping, is it?'

That shut him up for a bit. *Good*. Robbo thought he was still a fucking hard man but Vinnie knew the truth. He might have been a fighter 10 years ago, back when he was dealing, but as soon as he started getting a taste for it himself he had gone downhill fast, just like they all did. Now he was just a run-of-the-mill junkie who had no respect. It made Vinnie sick when he saw him queuing outside the post office with the family allowance book on Monday mornings. Using the money meant for food to buy a bit of red or black, or if they really did have to buy food, he would resort to a couple of bottles of Actifed. Fucking joke, Robbo was. Fucking cough medicine!

No matter what happened the rest of the week, the kids always got took to school on Mondays. Mondays, and every other Thursday as well, because every second Thursdays were pan crack days. The days when the big money came – the dole, the big green drug token. Vinnie knew enough to know the score there. And the score was that Robbo had soon got his sister round to the junkie way of thinking. He also knew – though he wouldn't dare mention it – that Lyndsey was on the game as well. He looked at his older sister with disgust now. The slag was all over the estate with Robbo's two sisters, fucking giving it up all week for the price of an ounce.

Vinnie noticed Lyndsey and the idiot had fallen asleep now, so he turned up the portable TV. He settled back onto the couch, resting his head on the arm and his legs, for want of anywhere else to put them, spread out across his inert sister's lap. The room felt fuggy: it had taken on the familiar sickly-sweet smell of dope and in the thick lingering smoke that had settled all around him, Vinnie could barely keep his eyes open. Though he could still make out the giant picture that took pride of place above the fireplace. It was a picture of a lad – around three was his guess – whose grizzling face stared mournfully down. It was called 'The Crying Boy', or so his mam had told him years back. And seeing what he was looking down on here, it wasn't fucking surprising.

The late night news was on – more grizzling, as far as he could tell – but he wasn't listening. His head was too full of thoughts about his impending incarceration, and what it might be like. His Uncle Charlie had once told him about the time he had gone to jail. How loads of the blokes were arse bandits and you couldn't bend over to pick up the soap if you dropped it in the shower. Charlie was hard though, a big mean bastard with hands like coal shovels. No one messed with his uncle. He didn't even live in a house. Throughout the day he was usually found outside the Boy and Barrel or the Old Crown, but at nights, unless it was proper freezing, at least, he slept on a bench in the town centre. If it was cold, though, he'd simply smash a window or start a fight so that he had a nice warm cell for the night. Trouble was though, Uncle Charlie and the rest of his uncles hated thieves. It was all right to rob a business or a bank or run some crooked gambling, but the youthy – Vinnie knew his Uncle Charlie would see that as shitting on your own doorstep. And shitting on your own doorstep was the lowest of the low. He wasn't stupid; he knew that. Just like he knew Charlie and his lot slagged him off to his mam. Fuck that, then, he wouldn't be going to Charlie for advice.

Vinnie had drifted off to sleep at last, dreaming about fighting off giant arse bandits and sharing a cell with his Uncle Charlie.

He woke up with a start some time later, unclear where he was, to feel Lou and Sammy jumping on him and laughing. 'Come on, Uncle Vin,' they trilled. 'Come on, let's play out!'

Vinnie yawned and rubbed his eyes. He got up to open the window to get rid of the smoke and the stench of weed. 'Gimme a chance, kids. I've only just woke up. Go get dressed and get your brother up. We'll go down to Nan's and get some brekkie, okay?'

'Yay, Nanny's! Nanny, Nanny, Nanny's!' sang the girls as they ran back upstairs.

Vinnie glanced around him at the filthy, stinking living room. His sister and the idiot must have somehow got themselves to bed because there was no sign of them now. He went into the kitchen and opened the fridge and the grease-coated food cupboard, just to check if there was any food in. Not that he held out much hope. Lyndsey went shoplifting at the Co-op every other day, but yesterday she had been in too much of a state. Which was a shame. Least when she went lifting she brought back proper good stuff. 'Only the best for my kids!' she would say as she brought out packs of bacon and joints of meat from up her skirt. Vinnie knew she would fill up her knickers with stuff too, but he didn't like to dwell on it – not if he was going to be sharing the spoils, anyway.

It was only eight o'clock but the kids were chomping at the bit to get out of the shit-hole. But Vinnie knew his mam and dad wouldn't be up yet and, given what had gone down with Saggy Tits Sally, he was reluctant to wake them this early. He decided to walk about with the kids for half an hour first, and then hopefully his little sister would be up for school, at least. Little Josie, or 'Titch', as she was known to almost everybody, was alright. She was only 10, but she adored her big brother and would try to kick the shit out of anybody who called him ginger nut, no matter how big they were.

The kids dressed and ready, they headed straight out. There was no point in saying goodbye to his sister and the idiot. They'd be comatose for hours yet, knowing he was there to see to the kids. Which would have to change, he thought, feeling a sudden pang of nerves. And fear – fear of being so far away from everyone and everything he knew. He had to stop that in its tracks. Snuff it out.

He vaulted the fence into the next door back garden, heading back the same way as he'd come the night before. It was the route he always used to get from Lyndsey's house to home and back. Same as everyone. Everyone fit enough to jump fences and crawl through holes, anyway. It was their private route around the place and he didn't know any different way to travel. Much less why. He thought seriously about this as he lifted the kids over Mrs Elliot's fence. Probably to make it easier running from the pigs, he decided. But he wasn't alone in Mrs Elliot's garden. As he lifted over little Robbie, he was immediately attacked by a huge, angry black-and-white cat. Which clearly had no truck with what he'd been up to either. It wasted no time in scratching him, badly.

'Fuck!' he yelled, bringing a hand up to his stinging cheek. He was bleeding. Proper bleeding. The little shit. With the kids laughing hysterically, he leapt around the garden then, trying to catch the mangy moggy who'd taken him on.

At last he managed to grab it and held it in a headlock with one arm, clamping its body under his arm, safely out of scratching distance. It squirmed and spat, but he held on tight. It was going nowhere. It had to pay for what it did.

'Robbie, quick,' he said to his nephew, 'find me some rope or string or summat!'

The kids stared at Vinnie, puzzled. 'Why?' Sammy and Lou wanted to know.

'Hurry up,' he said. 'If I let it go it will attack us all, won't it!'

Robbie, Lou and Sammy dutifully scoured the back garden, ignoring the syringes and old car tyres and crap. Eventually, four-year-old Lou held up a length of aerial cable. 'Uncle Vinnie, look!' she said proudly.

'Ssssh!' he said, conscious that Mrs Elliot might hear them. 'C'mon,' he gestured, 'Good girl, Lou … fetch it over!'

They all watched mesmerised as Vinnie fought the now writhing cat, to get the cable around its front legs. It was hissing and putting up a valiant fight, but was no match for its human tormentor. Grabbing Mrs Elliot's washing line, he flipped the end of the cable over it a couple of times, letting the cat fall – the cable straining now – strung up by its front legs.

He turned to the little ones, who were looking up at him, wide-eyed with shock. 'See, this cat's not really a cat, kids,' he explained, tying the cable off. 'It's a piece of wet washing.' He pointed to the terrified animal. 'And it can stay the fuck there all day now, till it dries.'

'It's just a big old kitty, Uncle Vinnie,' said Sammy nervously, not at all convinced.

Vinnie smiled softly and bent down to tickle beneath his niece's chin. He felt better now he could see the shock and awe in the children's eyes. 'No, Sam. It just *looks* like a kitty, but it's not really. Now, we off to Nan's for brekkie or are we not?'

'Are you just going to leave it there?' Lou wanted to know. 'Like, till it *dies*?'

'What do you think?' Vinnie asked her. 'C'mon – quick. We gotta *go*!' He hauled the kids over the next fence and told them to head straight beneath the hedge opposite. 'Go on,' he said. 'Quick. I think I can hear her!'

Then once he'd seen them all go through and knew he was safely out of sight, he quicky unlooped the cable and let the cat go, booting it up the backside as it skittered away. 'Last time you'll go for me, you big fat fucker,' he hissed at it. 'Next time you won't be so fucking lucky!'

The job done, he vaulted the fence and plunged after the younger children, pleased with having seized upon an excellent opportunity for self-promotion, proud of a good job well executed. Some things needed seeing and some things definitely didn't. Children talked. Children blabbed. Children told tales that made reputations. And he knew what it was that he wanted them blabbing. What they said about Vinnie *mattered*. Especially now.

Chapter 3

Little Josie was sitting on her dad's knee, eating her cereal, watching her mother move restlessly around the kitchen. She knew her mum was upset because she was trying so hard not to look it – turning up the radio till it was much too loud for comfort, and singing raggedly along to the song on it. 'Sweets for my sweet,' she sang. 'Sugar for my honey …'

She always sang along to that one if it came on, but her voice wasn't quite right today. 'Are you alright, Mam?' she ventured.

'Course she's alright, Titch,' said Jock. 'Eat your cornflakes.' His eyes followed June as she walked to the hallway at the bottom of the stairs. 'Where you going now?' he asked her. 'Just leave him alone, he'll be down when he's ready.'

June spun around. 'He's been ready all fucking morning!' she spat back at him. 'Now, if you don't mind, I'm bringing *our* fucking son down here, instead of leaving him up there to stew on his own!'

Josie started to cry – she couldn't stop herself – and climbed down from her dad's knee, placing her now unwanted cereal onto the floor. Why did they have to argue today? She sat on the hearth of the fireplace, pulled her nightie over her knees and sobbed. What was she supposed to do without her brother? Left here with these two – what a bleedin' nightmare!

No one understood how much she loved Vinnie – if they did, they wouldn't carry on like this all the time. Her dad started shouting and swearing about Vinnie and she clapped a hand over each ear to drown it out. Shut her eyes too, to block the whole *day* out. She loved her dad but he shouldn't talk about her brother like that. He was always saying that her mam didn't love anyone except Vinnie. Josie knew that. She knew her mam didn't love her very much, but she didn't care. Lyndsey didn't like her neither, but none of that mattered. All that mattered was that she had her Vinnie, and now they were taking him away from her. She started to sob harder as the fact began to hit home.

She felt a touch on her head. A light one. She opened her eyes. It was Vinnie, come downstairs, dressed in his flared jeans and favourite Rolling Stones T-shirt, and looking like none of it even mattered. 'What's up with your face, Titch?' he asked her, sitting down beside her. 'It looks like a smacked arse. Cheer up!'

Josie smiled as Vinnie joined her by the fire.

She rubbed her eyes. 'I don't want you to go away, Vin – when are they coming?'

Vinnie looked at the big guitar clock hanging from the wall. It was one of a batch he and his mates had stolen a while back. Half the houses on the estate now had one the same.

He gave her an odd look. Was he scared? She couldn't tell. 'About 10 minutes, our kid,' he said. 'But look, Titch, I'm not gonna be away for ages. I'll probably be back after Christmas.'

'After *Christmas?*' Josie wailed. This news was too terrible to even think about. 'But what about your presents and your Christmas dinner?'

Vinnie pulled her close and hugged her tight to him. He smelled of Hai Karate and Vosene, just like he always did, and his freshly washed hair tickled her cheek. 'Just save 'em for me, eh?' he said softly.

He then turned to his mum and grinned. 'That's right, innit, Mam? You'll save me a Santa sack for when I get home, yeah? Cos I'm sure Saggy Tits Sally won't be buying me a selection box this year.'

June frowned, her expression hardening. 'God, I hate bleedin' social workers, Vin!'

She was on one now, full throttle, and Josie watched in awe. She always did when her mum transformed from little sex-kitten June into this arm-swinging, neck-shaking, raving luna-tic. 'They're all bastards, the lot of 'em!' she railed now. 'Locking up innocent kids ...'

Then Jock kicked off too. 'Innocent? For fuck's sake, give this woman a fucking Oscar. *That's* his trouble, June. *You*!'

'Piss off, Jock,' she snapped. 'Who asked you?'

June glanced through the window, as she'd been doing every other minute for the last half hour. Josie could tell just by the way she stiffened that they must have come for him. And they had. 'Oh fucking hell, Vinnie,' her mum said. 'They're here. They're outside!'

Vinnie jumped up. This was it. Josie scrambled up as well. Did Vin feel as terrified as she did? He must be feeling shit-scared by now, mustn't he? But if he did, he wasn't letting on. The only way she could tell that he might be was by the way he licked his lips before he spoke. 'Go to the door, Mam,' he said. 'Don't have 'em in. My stuff's all here, I'm just gonna go out and get off. Don't be showing me up, all coming out.'

Vinnie then turned once again to his sister and winked. '*Never be ashamed of our tears*,' he whispered. 'Remember that?'

Josie nodded and tried her best not to start wailing. Her mum and dad wouldn't have a clue what Vinnie meant, but she did. It was a sad part in the book *Great Expectations*. That was another thing she'd miss and it made the tears well even more

– her brother reading to her late at night when he was excited about one of his books.

She remembered the words from this one very well. Pip, the hero, had been sad about leaving for London and his life changing, and sad about Joe, but after he'd cried, he felt ready to go on again. Trust Vinnie to dig up one of his favourite stories, she thought, to try to make her feel better. And it did. And she'd have to hang on to it, because now he really was leaving her. He gave her shoulder another quick squeeze and then he was out the door.

Josie dragged her dad's foot stool across the tatty linoleum, positioning it under the front-room window so she could climb up to wave Vinnie off. June was beside her, holding back the once-white net curtain, trying to put on a brave face, while Jock sat back in his armchair and rolled a cigarette.

'Stop crying, Josie,' June said gently, giving her an unexpected hug. 'You'll upset him if he sees you.'

She lowered the net, just as the black car pulled away, then walked away from the window, sighing heavily. Josie remained where she was till the car disappeared, and with it, her brother. Life was certainly going to be a lot quieter without Vinnie, she knew that. She felt strange, as though she had suddenly lost part of herself. She wondered if her mum felt the same. Like there was a hole in her stomach. She certainly looked angry as she turned to look at Jock. 'Happy now?' she asked him, waving his plume of smoke away.

Jock was having none of it. 'You can blame me all you like, you stupid mare. But we all know whose fault it is, June. If he wasn't such a little fucker, he'd be going nowhere, would he?'

'Fuck off, Jock,' she spat back. 'You've never liked him, never stuck up for him, you'll be loving this.'

Josie shook her head sadly. Was this what she had to look forward to now? These two at it all the time? As sure as she knew night followed day, she knew that her mum wouldn't settle until Vinnie was home. That this argument would grind on till he *was* home, as well. Josie wrestled with emotions that sometimes felt wrong where her brother was concerned. She loved her brother every bit as much as her mum did, but she could also see her dad's point. She knew that Vinnie had a bad streak. Was even nasty to *her* sometimes. She shuddered as she remembered some of the tricks he'd played on her, and yesterday's had been no exception.

She still shuddered as she brought it to mind. The sight, the sounds, the smell – the *horrible* smell. If Vinnie hadn't been leaving her today things would have been different. She'd still be fuming with her brother about that.

She should have seen it coming though. That was the thing. What possessed her? Him asking her if she wanted to go to the cemmy with him and his mates should have told her he'd have mischief in mind. And it wasn't like she agreed because she thought they'd include her much – they wouldn't. She'd only said yes because she didn't have anything else to do and because she liked to look at the inscriptions on the gravestones.

She always had. Since she was little and had gone to the cemetery with some nuns from her school and they'd done rubbings with paper and a pencil on some of the more ornate graves. It was on that visit that she'd come across the resting place of one of her uncles. She'd been shocked at first, to think of Uncle Brian being buried right there with all the other dead people, but after a while she'd got used to the idea. In fact, she'd often go back, after that, to see if she could find other dead relatives. The rest of the family would tease her and call her a nutter but she didn't care. She felt at ease with the dead.

And that's what she'd been doing, mostly, while the boys messed about, trying to scare each other by telling ghost stories, when Vinnie, without warning, but who must have planned it all beforehand, had grabbed his little sister and pushed her backwards. She had fallen straight into the open grave just behind her, which had been freshly dug ready to take a new coffin. Yes, it had been empty, but still she'd screamed and screamed, terrified – imagining all sorts, scrabbling down there among the worms and the maggots, while the boys just stood and laughed at her, tipping their heads back. That was typical of Vinnie, and Brendan and Pete too, they were thick as thieves – they *were* thieves – and bad as each other. It felt like forever before they finally deigned to haul her out, by which time she was out of her mind with fear and disgust.

Oh yes, Josie knew what her brother was, but she loved him even so, and listening to her parents now, screaming at each other like she wasn't even there she wondered just how she was going to get through till Christmas. It seemed like such a long way away. Today though, she just had to get out of there. She'd go and get dressed, she decided, and see if there was anybody knocking about on the estate who she could play with. She'd been allowed off school today because of Vinnie, so she didn't hold out much hope of seeing her friends, but anything was better than being stuck indoors with her warring parents.

Josie went up to her bedroom and dressed in the one pair of jeans that she owned; tatty flares passed on to her from an older cousin, which she was just about short and skinny enough still to fit. Though only just – she grimaced as she pulled them up and then, looking down, lowered them again, pushing them down on her hips so that the bottoms touched the floor. Grabbing her cowboy shirt and sniffing the armpits, she sighed. It hadn't been washed and she could smell it – though that was nothing new. Her mam had never been much of a housewife.

Josie sometimes envied her best mate, Carol; her mam always did the washing and Caz always smelled nice. As she pushed her arms into the sleeves anyway – there was nothing else to wear – she wondered what it would be like to live in a family where the kids had everything done for them. If Josie needed something clean, she usually had to wash it herself, more often than not in her own dirty bath water.

She made a final check of herself in the mirror on her window ledge. Her ginger hair, as ever, annoyed her. She kept it short. That way there was less of it for people to remark on. She spat on her hands and ran them through it, trying to tame it a little further, then checked her teeth – which were white as white; the thing she was most proud of – and headed back downstairs into the hall.

She slammed the door as she left, just to make a point. She felt angry. Defiant. Rebellious. Though she knew it was probably a waste of time as her parents probably wouldn't even notice she had gone. After walking around the streets for an hour, she realised that she had been right. Nobody was about. Nobody she wanted to see, anyway. She thought about calling at her sister's as a last resort. Though she didn't particularly want to. She couldn't stand Lyndsey – even though she loved her nieces and nephew – and knew all about her drugs and her thieving. She decided that she might as well go anyway – see if they were off school. Plus she was getting cold. It might be nice to go indoors for a while.

She started to walk the familiar route when she thought she heard someone call her name. She looked around but couldn't see anyone.

'Titch!' the voice called again. It was a man's voice. 'It's me, love.'

She looked across the road, finding it impossible to place it. It had seemed to come from there but there was no one on the street. Then something seemed to move at the edge of her vision and she looked up and realised she was across the road from Mucky Melvin's. He was waving at her out of his upstairs window.

Mucky Melvin was really old and really smelly; one of the people her mum and dad always told her to keep away from. She wasn't quite sure why – though the estate kids always speculated about it, if any of them ever asked a grown-up, they got the usual answer: 'Because I said so.' She knew he was disgusting though, because the council had to keep coming up to his house to fumigate it and get rid of all the rats. Hundreds of them, apparently. He lived like a tramp. He barely left his house, but when he did venture out, all the kids used to torment him and call him names. Noncey Melvin, they used to taunt him, and Smelly Melly. She didn't know what a nonce was, but she knew it was something bad. It was why they threw eggs at his house all the time too and, as Josie crossed the road, she could see the tell-tale streaks down the walls and the windows – only some of which still had panes of glass in.

'Alright, Melvin,' she said, stepping onto the opposite pavement. 'What's up?'

He was leaning out, one hand on the handle of the window, his shoulder-length hair, which was greying, hanging in stringy curtains either side of his filthy face. He was wearing the same thick brown cardigan he usually did – the cardigan someone had once pointed out was the same colour as his few remaining teeth. 'If I throw you some money down,' he asked her, 'will you get me some fags from the Paki shop?' He pulled his features into what might have been a smile. 'You can get yourself some sweets.'

Josie thought about it. She knew very well that she was meant to keep away from Melvin. Her mum was always telling her she had to ignore him. Given today, this was what made her mind up.

'Okay,' she said. 'Chuck us it down then. How much can I have for sweets?'

Melvin grinned. 'You can have a tanner, but don't be spending it on separates. I'll let you have one of my cigs when you come back.'

Result! Sweets *and* fags! Maybe this wasn't going to be such a bad day after all. Cheered up, for the moment anyway, Josie skipped back from her errand at the Paki shop, carrying the cigs – a packet of Woodbines – and the promised sweets. She'd chosen a quarter of Yorkshire mixture because of how long they lasted. A delicious mix of glassy sweets that you could suck for hours. She took her time though, to savour the first, which was pear shaped. So instead of walking the way she'd gone to the shop, she used the back-garden route. It made sense anyway – just in case her mam or dad were watching out for her.

She knocked at Mucky Melvin's back door and shouted through the hole in the smashed glass at the side, shuddering automatically as she took in her surroundings. She'd never been round here before and felt a little sick and scared. What about the rats? They'd all be in here somewhere, wouldn't they? There were certainly plenty of places for them to hide; the grass was massively overgrown, only flattened in small patches, where it had been used as a dumping ground for God knew what. There was currently an old, filthy armchair, what looked like a metal kitchen sink, and at least 20 overflowing bin bags strewn around. A playground, she decided, for all those filthy scary rats. She turned and banged harder on the rotting back door.

'Melvin, it's Titch,' she called. 'I'm back!'

Instead of coming to the door, Melvin opened another upstairs window.

'Good lass,' he said. 'You'll have to fetch 'em up for me though, Titch, I've hurt my back. Just come up – door's open!'

Josie watched as he closed the window and disappeared. She sighed. This hadn't been part of the plan and she stood on the doorstep undecided. Bleeding hell, his house stank, and now she had to go inside it. The other kids would take the mick if they even knew she had done his shopping, let alone actually gone in his house. Pulling a face, in advance of the stink that she knew would hit her nostrils, she took a deep breath as she turned the handle and stepped inside. And it was worse than she'd imagined. She felt immediately nauseous, seeing it and smelling it. What a bleeding pigsty it was. There was filth everywhere. Wallpaper was peeling from the walls, and some-one had written all over them in red paint. Words like 'nonce', 'Mucky Mel' and 'dirty bastard' were scrawled over the entire downstairs room.

'Hurry up, Titch!' Melvin called down. 'I'm dying for a fag. Don't take all fucking day!'

Josie had to swallow her nerves as she made her way up the stairs. The filthy, threadbare carpet stuck to the soles of her shoes, but she took her time, careful not to have to grab the handrail. She was beginning to feel a prickle of fear, and despite having her coat and scarf on she shivered as she realised that she could see her breath. God, this house was even colder than hers was. She wanted to hold her nose, so offensive was the putrid smell, but she was afraid that Melvin might catch her doing it.

Reaching the landing, she realised she didn't know where to go. There was one door to the left and two to the right, all of them closed. 'Where are you, Melvin?' she called.

The response was immediate and she almost jumped up in the air, dropping her bounty, as a door shot open just to her left.

'Boo!' Melvin said, chuckling at her startled expression. 'Come on in, kiddo. I have to sit back down. My back's buggered.'

Melvin's laugh was disgusting, Josie decided, as she followed him back in. Like he had a throat full of phlegm that he needed to spit out. His feet were bare, and he had on some filthy, striped pyjama bottoms over which the dirty brown cardigan hung open. His face was wrinkled and, close up, she could see how much his greasy hair was matted. It was easy to see why the other kids teased him so much. He *was* mucky. Filthy, dirty, mucky. Like he hadn't had a wash in a year. Josie didn't want to go anywhere near him and flinched from his touch as she handed him his fags and her hand brushed his long, yellow-brown fingernails.

'Hey,' she said as he took them. She was anxious to be gone now. 'Don't forget you promised me a couple.'

She waited impatiently, blinking to try and adjust her eyes to the dim room. It was the same room you could see from the street and as she glanced towards the window she saw that, instead of nets and curtains like most people had, there was what looked to be an old blanket blocking out the daylight. It appeared to be held in place by nails and had been cut up the centre so it could be moved apart, like proper curtains.

'I promised you one, Titch,' Melvin corrected her, as he passed her a Woodbine. 'Here you go.'

He set about lighting one for himself and immediately had a coughing fit. 'Oh fucking hell, this is fucking murder on my back,' he spluttered.

Josie regarded her single cigarette, which felt not quite enough. Despite her haste to be gone, the smoke wreathing between them gave her an idea. 'Can I smoke this one here, Melvin, and then take another one with me?'

'I'll think about it,' he said, passing a lit match towards her. 'I might. If you keep me company for a bit.'

She puffed her own fag into life and drew on it. She didn't feel quite so queasy now. 'All right,' she said. 'I'll stay for 10 minutes, but that's all. Me mam will be looking for me if I'm any later.'

'Saw 'em coming to take your brother off earlier. Is it true then, he's being locked up?'

Nosey bleeder, she thought. Trust him to already know that. Always peeking out of his bleeding window, minding everyone else's business. How did he know so much anyway? He lived a long way up the street from them. Yet he did. Somehow, Melvin seemed to see everything.

'Not locked up.' She corrected him. 'Just gone to like a boarding school, me mam said. He'll be back after Christmas.'

They both smoked in silence for just long enough for Josie to begin to feel uncomfortable. She'd finish up, she thought, and get out of there, back into the daylight. She was just looking for somewhere she could stub out the cigarette when she noticed that Melvin was now struggling to take off his dressing gown, his cigarette clamped between his lips, smoke blowing in his face. 'You'll freeze in here if you take that off,' she told him. 'Have you got an ashtray? I don't know what to do with this.'

'Just use the floor, kid,' Melvin told her, grinding his own out against the floorboards with his slipper. 'I'm back into bed, me,' he said. 'Can you give us a hand getting this off?'

Happy that he wasn't expecting her to hang around any longer, Josie started to pull the sleeve of his dressing gown in an attempt to help pull it from his shoulders.

Never in a million years did she see it coming.

* * *

Some time later, Josie let herself out of the smelly house. White-faced and sickened, she silently walked to her own house and, refusing her dad's offer of food – her mam was out – she went through the kitchen to where the bath was. After scrubbing herself till the water went cold, she went and told her dad, who was now parked in front of the telly, that she had a belly ache and was going to bed.

She counted out the steps up to her bedroom, numb with shock. No thoughts. Not yet. She couldn't think.

Chapter 4

Dear Mam (and say hello to the old man I suppose)

Well, it's been a week and I'm settling in okay. There's some right fucking divvies in here though, and they think I'm mental. I've made some friends; especially one called Billy and guess what? My other mate's called Vincent! Ha, and I always thought you was the only cow daft enough to give a son a name like that. (Only kidding.) Hope you're all well and thanks for the ciggies and chocolate. I could do with some more stuff though, Mam. I don't suppose you could nick me a radio from somewhere? (Only fucking joking, sir, I know you read my letters.) Can you send me some photos as well, for my room, and ask our Lyndsey if you see her, if you can have a Jimi Hendrix poster to send me. I'm not wasting a stamp on her, but I've put a letter in here for our Titch, hope she's okay. The other day, me and Vincent got caught pinching biscuits from the kitchen. It was a right laugh; you should have seen the fat cook woman chase us. She caught up with Vincent and pulled his hair, I nearly pissed myself laughing. We both got put on 'no privileges' for it, but it was worth it. It's too boring if you don't have a laugh. It's a massive place this, wait till you see it, it's like a big country manor. You'll feel as common as muck when you come down. It's fucking freezing though; even the fucking cockroaches are wearing overcoats. That reminds me; when you come see me, bring my big coat. You know, the one I would have worn to school if I had ever gone. Ha-ha. Right, Mam, I'm off now, it's nearly lights out and I

know I'm very clever, but I haven't learned how to see in the dark
yet. See you soon.

All my love, Vinnie xxxxxxxxxxx

Alright Titch

Thought I'd drop you a line seeing as how you'll be missing me
torturing you by now. Ha-ha, only kidding, I hope you're okay and
you better have cried for ages when I left. It's ace here, I might
even stay. (Joke.) I hope you're staying out of trouble. I've heard
that the girls' approved school is miles worse than here, can't have
you getting sent off as well. I've met some good lads here, but I've
had loads of fights as well. Tell the boys that I'm giving Bradford a
good reputation, and let Brendan know that I've started boxing so
I'll be able to knock him out when I come home. I've asked me
mam to send some photos, but don't let her send one of you, I
don't want fucking nightmares on top of everything else. Ha-ha,
just kidding, Titch. My mates were laughing the other day when I
was telling them about you. I told them that you always say you're
strawberry blonde and not a ginner. See, even they think you're a
funny little fucker. Well I'm getting off now, Titch, and I don't think
you'll be allowed to visit with me mam. Write me a letter back
though, with all that going to school like a little swot, I know you
can write.

All my love, Vinnie xxxxxxxxxxx

June read Vinnie's letter to anybody who would listen. She had
it with her, in her handbag, at the Bull.

He'd only been gone for two weeks and she had been working herself up into a right state waiting to hear from him. 'He's
punishing me, the little bleeder!' she'd moaned to Jock the
week before. 'Either that or he's narked at you.'

'Narked at *me*?' Jock had answered. 'What have I done?'

June looked at her hulk of a husband. Took in the baggy suit trousers, the greying shirt – with its familiar tramlines of braces – the equally greying hair, that had once been the same flaming red of his two younger children, the bulbous nose, the bulky middle … took it all in and considered where to start. 'Nothing,' she'd replied irritably. 'Exactly that. *Nothing*. You couldn't even be arsed to wave him off when he went!'

'Oh, that's right,' Jock had shouted then, 'blame me, you always do.' He'd shook his head dismissively. 'I can read the lad like a book, June. He's making you sweat for not putting up a fight for him, that's all. He'll write, don't you worry, and when he does, it'll be to whine at you for summat, just like it always is.'

Jock had been right. Not that she'd ever dream of giving him the satisfaction of hearing it from her. In fact when the long white envelope had plopped through the box that morning, she'd pounced. As soon as she saw the Brighton postmark across the top, she'd swiped it up from the mat and stuffed it down her nightie so that she didn't have to share it with the miserable git.

Still hadn't, in fact, and would only do so when she felt like it. After what he'd said about his own son, it was no less than he deserved. She had it now though, in her bag, just as she'd had since she'd got it. She'd been dying to get it out and parade it down the Bull.

Which she'd already done – they'd been in there an hour now – but the more pissed she became, the more often she would get it out to dissect.

Listen to this,' she said to Maureen now. 'Oh, he's such a funny little bleeder …'

Maureen was June's best friend – she had been since they were both in their teens. And also her relative, since she was

Jock's sister. She was like June in so many ways, but unlike her in the important ones; she was older and wrinklier, and, since she no longer bleached her hair like June did, a lot mousier, despite the amount of slap she optimistically trowelled on. She crushed out her fag, drained her glass of bitter and banged it down on the bar. 'June, I've heard it 20 fucking times. All right, *yes*, the lad's a comedian. Now put that bloody thing away and let's have another drink, okay?'

June stuffed the letter back into her bag. Maureen didn't understand. How could she? She was only Vinnie's auntie, after all. And probably jealous, June decided, because her own kids were thick as pig shit. She drained her own glass and flicked her hair and, turning her back on Maureen, smiled sweetly at the drunk propping the bar up next to her.

'Wanna buy a lady a drink, Bobby?'

He turned and snorted at her. 'You're no fucking lady.'

June rolled her eyes, but she was only mock-annoyed at him. No, she wasn't a lady – not that he'd know the difference – but she was still getting a drink out of him, one way or another. 'So,' she said, 'are you getting the drinks in or not? Cos if not, you can fuck off and fart next to somebody else.'

Maureen's laugh exploded out of her. 'June! You can't say that!'

June threw a withering glance at her sister-in-law. 'Can't I? I just did. If he thinks he's standing here, dropping 'em, without buying us a couple of drinks, he's got another think coming.'

Bobby grudgingly paid for two more halves of bitter, much to the amusement of Donald, the landlord.

'You've certainly got a way with words, June, I'll give you that,' he commented drily, as he scooped up the money that Bobby had scattered on the bar.

June winked at him. 'Flattery will get you everywhere, Don,' she told him. And though the comment was a throwaway one, she meant it.

Donald had run the Bull a good few years now, and she'd known him for all of them. As she would – it was her and all of her friends' local. It was the hub of the Canterbury Estate community, the Bull; the place where deals were clinched, plans were made and affairs started.

Donald was married, but he was also an incorrigible flirt, and June – having a soft spot for him – always enjoyed his attention. It would usually take the form of something more than just a wink or two, as well. Not tonight though. Maureen might be her best mate, but she had her loyalties – she'd grass her up to Jock in a flash. All it would take would be one little argument, and then she'd say anything to drop June in it with her brother. No, tonight she'd behave herself. No harm in trying to blag a few free drinks though.

'So,' said Maureen, who didn't seem finished with Vinnie after all. 'Did he write our Josie too? Bet she's been missing him like crazy.'

June nodded. 'Wrote us both.'

'Aww, I bet she was happy, the poor mite.'

June considered this. 'You know, come to think about it, she was a bit funny when I gave her it. A bit narky.'

'Narky? Why'd she be narky?'

June shrugged. 'I don't know. She's been miserable since he left – course she has; I know she's been missing him. They're two peas in a pod, those two – but when I gave her it, she didn't even seem to want to look at it. It was only cos I made her that she did read it out. And then the soppy little bleeder started crying halfway through.'

'Aw, bless her, June. You really think that's any wonder?'

June stared into her glass. No, it wasn't any wonder really. Of course she missed Vin – they both did – but, well, it just felt like she'd been hit by a ton of bricks. Hit by his leaving *way* more than she'd expected.

'I know,' she said to Maureen. 'I know it's hit her really hard, but, I don't know … she's really not herself – she's been walking round like a fart in a trance. Even Jock can't sort her out – and her being such a daddy's girl, as well. I don't know if she blames him, but it seems like it – she doesn't want to know him. Even gave him a slap the other day – cheeky little git that she is.'

'A slap? What on earth for?'

'For nothing. I swear I don't know what's got into her. All he did was try and get her to sit in his chair with him to watch the racing. Now that's not like her, is it? She loves her dad.'

'No,' Maureen agreed. 'That's not like her at all. But give her time; it's only been a couple of weeks, hasn't it? Have you written back to him yet?'

June sighed. 'Not yet.'

'Why ever not? I'd have thought you'd have done that the same day!'

'I know. And I want to. It's just so hard knowing what to *say*. I mean, he's all happy and that, talking about when I come down and visit. But I can't, can I? Old Saggy Tits made it quite clear – there won't *be* no visits. Bastards. Don't they realise? A lad needs his mother! And I mean, they might, mightn't they? She did say about weekends home at some point, so they might. But you know how these things work. There's no chance if he doesn't keep his nose clean, is there? And what're the chances of that happening, Mo? Zero. He's probably playing up already, if I know our Vin, the stupid little bleeder. Pound to a penny. Otherwise I would've had a call.'

They lapsed into silence then and June, her happy mood having drained away as quickly as her halves had, half-wished she'd not even brought the letter with her. The thought of the months ahead – no Vinnie, Titch with a face like a slapped arse, Jock being Jock – was just too depressing to think about. No, Mo was right. She needed to write back. He'd be bound to be waiting to hear from her, bless him. She was almost glad when the bell went for drinking up at 10.30. With Don off limits, and the letter still calling to her from her handbag, even the Bull couldn't work its charm tonight.

They left the pub, fur coats clasped to their throats to keep the bitter cold out. The rows of council houses opposite were now mostly in darkness and the leafless trees that lined the main road took on a sinister appearance. The estate looked a lot less friendly on a night time.

June felt the breeze stir her hair and shivered involuntarily. 'You walking back through the snicket, Mo, or coming down our street?'

Maureen shook her head. 'Too cold for the long way tonight. I'll cut through the snicket.'

June cast about to see who was around. Maybe someone else was headed that way as well. She didn't like to think of Maureen using the snicket on her own at night. It was always useful being able to use it in daylight, but nights were a different matter entirely. Without streetlights, the footpath served a whole other purpose; for robbings and fights or laying in wait, hidden, for someone with whom you had a grudge. Luckily there were a few others spilling from the pub as well now. 'Make sure someone walks through with you, then,' she said. 'It's dark up there.'

'Will you give over, June?' Maureen laughed, swaying slightly in her slingbacks, the night air catching the scent of her

Charlie perfume. Must have spritzed herself in the ladies before coming out. 'I should be so fucking lucky!' she said. 'Steven says I should wear a sign on my back saying "rape me" if I'm to be in with a chance.'

'He's a rotten bastard, that husband of yours – and you can tell him that from me. Right then, I'm off. I'll call round tomorrow when I get sick of looking at face ache.'

'Be as long as that, will it?' Maureen joked as she toddled off into the night.

For all that she worried about Maureen, June didn't mind walking home alone herself. She'd done it for years and its familiarity meant it held no fears. This was her patch – the Bull was only 10 minutes from home – and she'd have been shocked more than frightened if anyone jumped her. Not to mention giving as good as she got, she thought decisively, feeling a giggle form in her throat as the fresh air hit her. Must be more pissed than I thought, she decided, and even as she thought it she felt herself stagger. She giggled again when she heard the wolf whistle behind her, minutes later. Almost home, and automatically smiling to acknowledge her admirer, she was surprised to see that no one was there.

Then a gravelly voice. 'Over here, June!' Coming from above.

She didn't need to look up to know who it was now. Mucky-fucking-Melvin. She continued to walk without turning around.

'Give us a flash, June,' he shouted down. 'All them at the Bull will have had a good look.'

Now she did turn around. 'Why don't you just fuck off, you pervy bastard.'

She heard his dirty laugh and his window slamming shortly after. Fucking old pervert. Fancy him having the nerve to have a go at her! He'd know about it soon enough if she told Jock. Which she might do. He'd smash his stinking brains in, good and proper.

But for now she had more important business to attend to. Letting herself in the front door without waking the miserable old fucker up. She slid her key into the lock with as much care and deliberation as she could summon and, though it wasn't much, she was still pleased to note as the door opened that the downstairs of the house was dark and silent.

Good, she thought. She wouldn't be having an argument tonight, at least. Which in itself was a rare treat when both of them had been drinking, and as night followed day, knowing Jock, he would have been.

She tottered over to the sofa and sat down heavily, then pulled Vinnie's letter once again from her handbag, tears pricking behind her eyes as she did so. A picture formed in her mind, of a cold, hard prison bed. She tried to ignore it. It was just the drink – stupid mare – making her feel all weepy. Perhaps she should just put it away and go to bed. But then she thought of her poor boy, banged up, and how much he'd be missing his home comforts. No, she decided, she'd stay down here tonight.

She was comfy enough anyway, she thought, pushing the letter back into the black hole of her handbag. She'd just get her tights off – she hauled herself up again – just her tights, and then she'd be done for the night. But she'd barely got her thumbs under the waistband and started tugging when her balance went – oops! She really *must* be more tiddled than she'd realised – and fell back heavily. She was fast asleep in seconds.

When Josie came down in the morning, it was to find her mother sound asleep and dribbling, with her tights round her thighs. She stepped past her and, trying to be as quiet as she could, knelt down, laid and lit a fresh fire. That done, and with June still comatose and snoring behind her, she crossed the cold lino onto the square of old carpet that served as a rug, went into the kitchen and made a pot of tea.

It was only when she'd done that and poured herself a cup that she became aware of her mother stirring in the lounge.

'Have you shit the bed or something?' she wanted to know, seeing Josie standing there, mug in hand. 'What you doing up so early?'

June passed by her then, to go into the little toilet just off the kitchen, leaving the door open so she could continue the conversation from there.

'I've got school, Mam,' Josie answered, over the sound of June having her morning pee.

'And where's your dad?' June wanted to know.

'He's still in bed. Mam, it's only half seven.'

She turned then, grabbed a cup and poured her mum some tea as well. Then heard the flush.

'Ah, that's better,' June said emerging and taking the cup. 'Ta, love. What bleeding day is it, anyway?'

'Oh, Mother, it's Friday. Are you still pissed or something?'

'Hey, gobby,' June snapped at her. 'Shut it before you get a slap. I don't normally go out on a Thursday night, do I? I just forgot where I was for a minute.'

She stumbled back out, and Josie wasn't sure if she wasn't still pissed. What a state. Oh, her mates might think June was really funny, with her hair and her make-up and her holding court all the time. Thought she was lucky – some had said as much – to have a mum who was such a laugh; one who got all dressed up and went partying. Well, they wouldn't think that if they could see her like this, would they? All panda eyes and her 'gorgeous Marilyn Monroe hair', as she called it, looking like a heap of fairground candyfloss stuck on her head. Not to mention those tights, which she'd only half pulled back up, by the look of it. Not a pretty sight at half seven in the morning.

June called back to her, then. 'Josie, have *you* lit this fire?'

'Yes, I did. I thought you would be cold when you woke up.'

June looked impressed. 'Good lass!' she commented. I didn't think you knew how to do it.'

But Josie didn't bother answering because immediately she'd said that, she'd switched on the radio at her usual ridiculous volume, and drowned every other sound out.

Josie finished her tea and went to find her pumps to put in her bag. It was PE today, but she wouldn't be changing. She gave herself a pat down to reassure herself she had her shorts and T-shirt on under her uniform. Better that than have to undress in front of everyone.

'I'll see you later, Mam,' she called on her way out.

Josie first needed to walk up the street to get to the snicket – she'd usually cut through there to meet Carol and walk to school. It was something she'd done unthinkingly for almost all of her life. Years and years, now – up the road, into the snicket, out into the football field, and then on up the road to St Michael's. But now everything was different. Now, when she passed Mucky Melvin's, she held her breath. Fixed her eyes straight ahead and forced herself not to look – otherwise it felt like she might be struck down dead. It was like that game – at least, that's how she decided she'd have to think about it – that game where you dare not step on cracks in the pavement. You could die if you did that, as well.

Only when she'd hurried far enough up the street, did she start to properly breathe again. She then ran through the snicket fast enough to feel her breath coming in gasps, slowing only as she made the football field and stopped to wait for Carol, the sound of her pulse pounding in her ears.

Carol was Josie's best mate in the world. They had gone to St Michael's together since they were five, and had always stuck up for each other. Carol, who was plump and worldly-wise about most things, had dark hair, dark eyes and dark skin. A lot of the other kids called her 'Paki', but that wasn't true. Her dad had left when she was a baby, but he wasn't a Paki. He was an Egyptian and he was loaded, and some day he was going to come back again and give Carol and her mum loads of jewels and stuff from the pyramids. Then they'd be sorry, all them that called her nasty names.

Carol was also a fighter, just like she was, and if anyone ever called her a ginger nut, Carol would be right by her side help-ing dole out the sort of punishment that ensured it never happened again.

She was coming into view now and Josie waved. 'Hurry up,' she called, causing Carol to break into a run. 'Or we're going to be late again!'

'Me mum's hopeless, Titch,' Caz said as she fell into step alongside her. 'Didn't get me up in time. *Again*.'

It was the same every day, almost, and Josie found herself reflecting on why it was that she didn't need anyone to get *her* up just now. She'd only have to stir, and the pictures would flood into her brain, making her sweat and want to cry and cry and cry. She pushed the thoughts away, preferring to let Carol chatter on. About their school project, which was on the Vikings. About Jennifer Armitage, who had nits. About Mickey, a 12-year-old boy in their school who was totally in love with Carol. Or so she said.

'I swear, Titch – you should have seen how he looked at me when I was walking home yesterday. He wants to be my boyfriend, I just know it.'

Josie didn't know anything much about boyfriends, and didn't want to. Yes, she knew about *boys* – and about Vinnie and his friends, more than she perhaps ought to. But boyfriends … she shuddered. All that now felt like a very frightening place.

But Carol seemed older and not at all frightened. Should she tell her? *Dare* she?

'Don't you think?' Carol was saying, stopping for a moment on the grass.

Josie hauled her thoughts back to order. 'Do you want me to ask him for you?'

'Would you?' Carol's eyes widened. 'Would you really? Don't let on that I know though, will you?'

They continued walking, arm in arm. The field had a low, greyish mist still hanging over it. Josie liked the mist. And the space. And the sense that you could run through it. That you could run and run and maybe even disappear into it. 'Course I won't,' she said. 'I'll say I'm just wondering, that's all.'

'Ta,' Carol said. 'Today, then? And, you know – if you fancy someone, just let me know, yeah? And I'll ask them for you, okay?'

Josie couldn't think of anything she'd like less. 'You'll be waiting a long time then, Caz,' she said. 'Boys are shit bags.'

Carol giggled and squeezed Josie's arm tighter. 'My mum said I'm a bit more forward than you,' she told her. 'When you catch up, you'll fancy boys. You'll see.'

Josie thought this was a stupid thing to say. They were both 11 now – she'd just had her birthday. How on earth could she 'catch up' – even if she wanted to? She looked at her friend and wondered if the Devil really could hear everything she said and thought. It must be true because the nuns who taught them sometimes had even said so. She and Carol were blood sisters so they shouldn't have secrets. They'd made cuts on each other's wrists and rubbed them together, and that meant they were bound together for life. And now it was all going to be ruined, because Josie had a bad secret that she couldn't share.

Josie suddenly wished with all her heart that Vinnie was home. She thought of his letter and how badly she wanted to write back to him, but how scared she felt about actually doing so. He could read her like a book – he'd told her that once. What did that mean exactly? She wasn't sure, but she was frightened. That whatever she did or didn't say, somehow he'd just *know*. Her head was starting to hurt now. The pictures were beginning to flood her brain again. She decided not to think for a while, just go to school and get the day over with. Just like she had every day since.

Melvin stood in his window for some minutes after Titch had passed by, smiling to himself as he finally lowered the grimy makeshift curtain. It was something to get out of bed for, was the sight of her hurrying along the road, and he'd been up for a sneaky peek every school morning since.

Satisfied, he crossed the room again, and got back into bed, already sliding his hand down inside his filthy pyjama bottoms.

Chapter 5

Dear Vinnie

Nice to hear from you, son. I hope you're keeping well. Everybody keeps asking about you and I keep telling them how well you're doing. You need to knock the stealing off, Vin, or they'll bloody keep you there for ever. Saggy Sally came round the other day, she said you and your friends are getting into trouble all the time, fighting and that. If you want to be home after Christmas, love, you'll have to settle down. Your dad said hello. Miserable prat wouldn't give me any money to send you though. I've just sent enough for some baccy and papers. I will send you some more on Monday when I get my family allowance. I'm not talking to our Lyndsey yet, but the kids have been down so I asked our Robbie if he could bring me a poster for you. Our Josie is writing to you as well but she said she will post hers herself. Silly get said that she doesn't want me nosing at her letter. Well, for being clever, she will have to buy her own stamp now, won't she? I'm sorting something out with Sally to get down for a visit but she said it might not be for another week or two. She said you have to start being good first. So the way you're going, I might never bleeding get to see you. Hope you like the photos I've sent. All my mates say that I look like a film star on that one of me; I think they mean Marilyn Monroe, with my blonde hair. Ha-ha, just joking. Right Vinnie, I have to go now, but I'll write again next week.

All my love, Mam X

Dear Vinnie

Thank you for your letter. Very funny about my photo by the way.
Carol said to say hello. (I think she fancies you, so tell your new
mates that. An 11-year-old, ha-ha.) I told Brendan you were boxing
now and he said he is weightlifting, so he will be able to beat you
up when you get home. I told him he would have to take on both
of us. I always stay out of trouble unless I am with you. I hate it
when you're not here, Vinnie. I have no one to talk to. Can I ask
you something? Can the Devil really hear everything I say? One of
my mates told me that he could, even if I say it quietly. I was going
to ask Sister Josephine at school but I thought she might tell me
off for mentioning the Devil. I might ask Carol, she'll tell me truth,
she always does cos of us being blood sisters. It's not like having
my real brother there though, Vin, I wish you were home. Our
Robbie is going to nick one of Robbo's David Bowie pictures so I
will send it when I get some money out of my dad's pockets for
another stamp. I have to go now; Carol is calling for me to walk to
the post office, so I can send you this letter.

Lots of love, your loving sister, Josie Xxxx

Home. Home for Vinnie right now was a box. It was painted in
a mottled effect, with a white base and dark blue splatters, like
some alien had thrown up all over it. The floor – a continua-
tion of the walls, really – was covered in cold, hard vinyl, also
mottled like the walls, but with the pattern reversed, a look
that some idiot behind a desk must have dreamed up at some
point, following a brief to make it is as chilly looking as possible. It was around eight by six, maybe smaller, and was pretty
much identical to every other room on his corridor. A single
bed – lumpy mattress, lumpy pillow, shit-all springs – a 'desk'
that was actually just a strip of wood fixed along one wall, a

chair – also wooden – and a matching bedside cabinet and locker to keep his clothes and personal belongings in.

It did feel homey, though, sort of, now he'd made it his own. In reality, it was better than his room back at home, which had bare floorboards, and not much else bar a knackered set of drawers. Course, there was his bookcase, which he did miss, because it was his pride and joy, having been carefully crafted in woodwork lessons on those rare occasions he'd turned up at school. He'd brought some books with him, too, of course – his two Charles Dickens favourites – A *Tale of Two Cities* and *Great Expectations* – and his other favourite, *The Count of Monte Cristo*. He'd also personalised the expanse of wall above the desk with a bunch of posters, all carefully gathered from the magazines he'd stolen from the 'do not remove' pile in the library. They were pictures of models, mostly, plus a selection of pop stars: the Who, the Beatles, another of Jimi Hendrix, and the couple of photos of family he'd taken with him, plus some more June had sent in the post. It would do. It was something to look at, at any rate.

He lay back on his bed to read his letters through a second time, happy to hear at last from his family. But something niggled about Titch's one. He studied it again. There was definitely something wrong – what did she mean by all that crap about the Devil? Something was up, but he couldn't put his finger on what it was. He was just reading it for a third time, trying to fathom what Titch was getting at, when the door burst open, startling him. It was Vincent.

Such a small patch, the approved school, yet there were two Vincents in it. What were the chances? That he come in here and find there was already another him there? A hard lad, like he was and, having been there two months, well respected. As he would be; he was in for violence and using weapons. They'd soon been sorted out though, in the usual geographic way. Vinnie became Bradford Vinnie and his namesake Cockney Vinnie, him having come from the East End of London. That had been an eye-opener in itself, Vinnie having never been to London; he'd always thought of it as being very different from Bradford – the sort of place where only rich and famous people lived.

But Cockney Vinnie didn't like being called Vinnie anyway, so they'd now just become Vinnie and Vincent. And, perhaps partly because of the name-thing, good friends.

'Come on, mate,' he said now. 'You gotta get outside. There's only a fucking fight in the yard.'

Vinnie jumped up immediately. Fights were always worth seeing. 'Who between?' he asked, putting Titch's letter down.

'Bacon Neck Brian,' Vincent said. He looked excited. 'He's having a *right* old go at Mr Sullivan.'

Vinnie ran outside with Vincent, the letters now forgotten. This was too good to miss. It wasn't every day you saw a kid fighting with staff.

Bacon Neck Brian, who was in for persistent stealing and robbery, had earned his colourful nickname years ago, apparently, on account of being badly scalded when his mother had decided to throw a red-hot cup of tea at his head. The resulting skin grafts had left his neck looking like, well, streaky bacon, hence the name. He had a red-hot temper to match it, too.

As Vincent had said, it had all gone mad out in the yard. A circle of kids had formed around the fight, and they were all shouting and jeering. Mr Sullivan wasn't all that bad, as it happened, so Vinnie couldn't understand why Brian had kicked this off. Even so, Vinnie couldn't resist a swift kick to Sullivan's head when he ended up rolling around near his feet, Bacon

Neck Brian having got the upper hand and decked him. It made sense. All eyes had been in Vinnie's direction at that point, so it wouldn't harm his reputation to show a bit of unnecessary violence. That was how you made your name in a place like this. In any place – he'd worked that out long since. Letting everyone see you were a bit of a psycho.

Within minutes, whistles started to go off all around them and the yard began teeming with staff. And, on cue, all the lads suddenly stood to attention, wherever they were and whatever they'd been doing. They had all been taught this from the outset – it was one of the first things they'd learned. And for good reason, too; anyone found to be flouting this rule would lose privileges for a month. And that hurt. Nobody wanted to go a month without pocket money, fags, phone calls and writing paper. You would also lose your radio if you had one. Not that Vinnie did, as yet, but he already had plans to put that right. There were rich pickings to be had locally, or so some of the longer-term lads said, so he'd have it sorted soon as he had his first unsupervised trip into town.

After it had all settled down and Bacon Neck had been taken off to be disciplined, Vinnie went back to his room. As it was Saturday, there were no lessons, so he decided to have another read of Titch's letter before joining his mates in the recreation room. What the fuck was he missing here? He knew there was something; his sister's letter was plain weird. She would have normally cheered him up, he knew, because that was the sort of kid she was. She liked writing and he'd expected there to be pages and pages from her – telling him all about what was happening back on the estate, rambling on about what she'd been up to with Caz. But just this. This short, gloomy, sad thing she'd sent him. Weird. He folded the letter in two and decided that he would ask for a phone call. You couldn't usually make a call until you'd been there for a month – they'd already made that crystal clear – but he would go and ask anyway; say it was an emergency or something. Just in case he couldn't though, he decided to write back straight away, before joining the lads for a game of pool.

Alright Titch

How's it going? I just got your letter this morning. Fuckers hold 'em back from you for a few days in here, just for the fun of it. You don't sound too happy, sis, what's up? Nobody better be giving you any shit just cos I'm not on the scene. If they are, Titch, go see Pete or Brendan, or any of my mates, they'll get it sorted. I know you, and even though I can't hear your voice, I know what you're thinking. My old man says I'm the Devil incarnate, so ha-ha, yes, your friend is right. The Devil can hear you. Seriously though, Titch, I know there's something wrong. I am going to try to get a phone call this week, and if they let me I'll ring you one night straight after school. I don't know when though so don't wait by the phone every night. It might even be never and then you'd be like Miss Havisham, waiting for Pip. Ha-ha, do you remember when I used to read you that book? If the teachers in here only knew how much I liked books, I would get some right stick. I have to go now, mate, but keep yer chin up, okay? I won't be in here for ever, and I'll soon be home to make you laugh again.

Lots of love, your big brother Vinnie. Xxxxxxxxx

Vinnie called in at the office on his way to the rec room with his finished letter, pleased to see the eye candy that was Miss Maureen Biggs – a young, leggy blonde bird who smiled a lot and worked there at weekends, and an object of lust for almost all the boys.

'Afternoon, Miss,' he said politely. 'Can you make sure this gets posted today please?'

'Course I will, Vincent,' she said. 'Anything for you, young man.'

'Thanks, Miss,' he said, smiling shyly, 'and, actually, it's Vinnie.'

Miss Biggs returned the smile, revealing a row of almost impossibly perfect teeth. 'Sorry, Vinnie' she said. 'You boys and your nicknames! I don't know how I remember who's who, I really don't. Though I shouldn't really mix you up with anyone else, should I?' she added. 'Not with that lovely hair of yours.'

She smiled again and turned back to her desk then, but not before Vinnie could feel an intense heat flare in his cheeks. 'Um, yeah, thanks, Miss,' he mumbled, trying to untie his tongue before getting out of there as fast as he could, but with a definite spring in his step.

The main corridor of the approved school was quiet and echoey on the weekends, though on either side of it were classrooms in which teachers still lurked – coming in even though they didn't have pupils to teach, which made them swots and idiots, in Vinnie's opinion. And also fair game for being wound up, he'd decided, whistling loudly in an effort to annoy them.

But it was other prey, closer to his own age, that he was most keen on winding up this afternoon, if the chance arose.

Thoughts of Titch put to one side now, he wondered as he walked whether he'd be likely to get done for his small part in the Bacon Neck Brian fight. He didn't care that he might be disciplined for the sly kick at the screw. That was incidental. No, what bothered him – what really preoccupied him, and would do so till he'd done something about it – was the fact that Brian had now earned his stripes as far as the other lads were concerned. He would have the glory and the kudos that

Vinnie badly needed, if he was to secure a decent level of status in the pecking order.

He chewed his lip as he walked towards the rec room. It was on the weekends that the system at Swallow House was at its most vulnerable and, having quickly learned the way things worked in terms of routines and staffing, Vinnie knew that only a skeleton staff were employed on Saturdays and Sundays, which made right now a particularly good time to act. He'd also had quite enough of being fucked about by the older lads. He'd made his first mistake the very first week, having told a 16-year-old lad called Dennis to go and get fucked, when he'd tried to extort some of his precious tobacco from him. Next thing he knew, he'd been pinned up by three of them and warned that, as he was fresh meat, he'd just better do as he was told.

And he could tell they meant business. They were nasty, violent fuckers. And that definitely wasn't going to happen again. He needed them on side – something Bacon Neck Brian had now managed to achieve before him. He was a bit of a divvy, as far as Vinnie was concerned, but maybe not as much as he'd thought – because he'd been clever. The older lads would now show him respect and look out for him, and the younger ones would be breaking their necks to do anything for him. Vinnie wanted a bit of that. And he wanted it sooner rather than later.

He cracked his knuckles as he headed into the rec room and grinned at the memory of Miss Biggs's smile. Right now would be a good time, in fact.

Chapter 6

Saturdays were good days at the approved school. Or the 'community home', as the courts tended to call them these days, to try and make it sound less like the hell hole it still was. Conformity was all. Conformity was the word they had drummed into them constantly. Conforming at all times, in all things, was what mattered, but at the weekends it loosened up a little. The school had two kinds of pupils, the ones that lived in, like Vinnie, and the ones who went home. These daytime-only kids had been in shit but it was lesser shit than he had. They'd have been expelled from their schools, yes, but would still be allowed to live at home with their families – they merely 'attended' rather than being 'detained'. They made up at least half the pupils, so when they pissed off home to their families, there was a different, more relaxed feel to the place.

The staff were definitely more relaxed and even had a laugh with the lads sometimes. Not so much that you thought you could get one over many of them. Just enough to give you the impression that they were vaguely human. The best part of all, though, was that it was the day you got to spend your pocket money, along with any money your family had sent. The older lads – the ones allowed in town – brought back fags and baccy, which they would sell on to you at cost plus five roll-ups. Then there was the tuck shop. Here you could get sweets, chocolate and cans of pop. So although the regime was tough – all that bloody conformity – the weekends were for indulging in mischief.

This was Vinnie's third full weekend now, and he was beginning to get things sussed, and, on opening the rec room door, things looked promising. His friend Billy was laughing with another couple of boys Vinnie knew, over by the pool table. Vinnie liked Billy; he came from the same kind of background, and having the same sort of things to laugh about and relate to, they'd quickly formed an easy, uncomplicated friendship. More than that though, it was quickly clear that Billy idolised Vinnie and would, as a consequence, go along with whatever he wanted to do. Quite handy for what Vinnie had in mind.

'Now then, lads,' he said, joining the group, 'Who wants an arse whipping? An' I'm talking about pool, for those of you with dirty minds.'

Across the rec room, another group of lads – four of them – were playing cards, and were obviously having some kind of an argument. Voices were raised, one belonging to a big lad called Joe; a boy Vinnie hadn't had any sort of personal dealings with, but who he had still been busy keeping an eye on, because he had a reputation as someone not to be messed with. Joe would make a good target because he was a lad with some serious status. Vinnie studied him. If he took someone like him on – no small thing – he'd definitely get himself some status too, win *or* lose.

He carried on playing pool for a bit, but nodded over to them as he lined a shot up. 'Watch them fuckers, Billy,' he told his nervous-looking pool partner. 'That big one's a twat. There's gonna be a ruck in a minute.'

Billy took his shot and nodded to Vinnie in agreement. 'Best we keep out of it then, eh?'

Vinnie looked around for staff. There were none in the rec room currently, so this was particularly good timing; no staff meant no fucking interference. He grinned at Billy. 'Keep out of it? Fuck that, Billy lad, this might just liven up my weekend.'

Without taking his eyes off of the group, Vinnie propped his pool cue against the wall. He then leaned over, slipped his plimsoll off, and peeled his sock from his foot, before picking up the white ball and placing it inside. He laughed at Billy's now equally white face.

'You okay, mate?' he said quietly. 'You look like you're gonna throw up.'

'Vinnie, what the fuck? Shall I go get Vincent? They look about 16, and that big one's fucking massive!'

'Which is why he's the one we're gonna go for first, Billy boy. And no – fuck Vincent. We don't need him. We'll do this together.'

Vinnie shoved his plimsoll back onto his foot and picked up his cue. Holding the sock hidden in his palm, he grinned. His blood was still up from seeing Bacon Neck Brian giving Sullivan a pasting, and the lad's chatter about it, which was very much still ongoing, reminded him just how much he wanted to make a name for himself as well.

No fear. That was the thing. No fear. He could almost taste the blood, feel the thump of his heart in his chest, sense, rather than see, Billy quaking in fear beside him, feel his own features morph into a rictus that meant one thing – that he was going to give someone a proper pasting.

Billy had grabbed his cue now and was trying to psych himself up, hopping nervously from one foot to the other. Vinnie laughed.

'Follow me, Bill, just act natural like, okay?'

Billy licked dry lips. Not much chance of that happening.

Not that anyone had even noticed them; they were too busy slinging insults. Even from across the room, it was clear that the argument had got more heated, the group of four now split into two, with each pair making threats towards the other. Though as Vinnie and Billy approached, pool cues in hand, one of the smaller lads turned to look at them. 'D'ya want a fucking picture, like?' He snarled. He was a Scouser. Even better, Vinnie thought. He hated Scousers.

'Picture of you, cunt?' he said. 'Nah mate, you're too fucking ugly.'

Billy laughed at that. Which seemed to flick a switch. The whole group fell silent, looking at him, and Vinnie, in turn, assessed them. It was a shame the little Scouse fucker was one of the pair arguing with Joe, the big lad. Now he would have to fight both sides.

The little one decided to carry on, looking towards his previous tormentors for allegiance.

'Have you heard this, Joe?' he asked. 'Young ginger bollocks here fancies his chances.'

Vinnie felt the words like a slap. Fucking little cunt. He also noticed that Joe was now reaching into his back pocket. What for? A knife? Fuck. No time for small talk, then. He dived onto Joe immediately, aware of Billy's startled cry beside him, but with all his energies now focussed on whacking his loaded sock, which he held by the end to give weight and a bit of a swing to it, repeatedly into the big lad's spotty face.

He was soon aware that the little one had jumped onto his back now, to try and stop him, and then of Billy flailing around trying to get him off again. And with some success, too. After a short scuffle Billy managed to prise him right off and Vinnie could see he was now hitting him with his cue. Good lad.

The other lads, still apparently unsure what to do next, or who to go for, left him to get on with the job in hand – Joe's fucking face. Which didn't take long, a pool ball being such an effective weapon. In a matter of minutes, Joe – now pinioned safely underneath him – was covered in blood and minus several teeth.

Vinnie started laughing. It was an automatic thing – a kind of knee-jerk on seeing the pulpy mess he'd made now. He'd done a good job, but he wasn't done with Joe yet, even so. He dangled the sock, with its ominous bulge now equally bloody, half an inch from the now terrified lad's face.

'Tell me who's the hardest now, you fucking piece of shit,' he yelled. It had almost been *too* easy. 'Come on, tell me!' he screamed.

'Fucking get off me!' Joe answered brokenly. 'You're the winner!' He was crying. Crying and in very obvious pain.

'Come on, Vin,' Billy said. 'Leave him now before the staff come. He said you won, didn't he?'

Vinnie turned. Billy looked terrified. Good. He looked up at him, eyes blazing, still caught in the moment. 'That's not what I fucking asked, is it?'

Billy winced. '*Is* it?' Vinnie screamed again, at Joe. '*Is* it?'

Joe started to thrust his body frantically beneath him. '*Please* get off me! I forgot what you asked!'

Vinnie paused for a couple of heartbeats, while the rest seemed to hold their collective breath. There was a stillness in the room now, which he relished. 'Well, next time,' he snarled, 'you *won't* fucking forget.' Then he bent forward and bit down as hard as he could on Joe's cheek. He felt the blood hit his own cheek, a pungent warm spray of it. And as cries of shock erupted all around the room, Vinnie felt triumphant. *No one* would call him ginger bollocks now.

Someone must have run for staff, though, because no sooner had he thought that than he felt strong hands grip his shoulders and others round his ribs, as he was torn from his victim and dragged to his feet. Mr Bastion, it seemed, and Mr Henry.

Bastion was the head of the institute, and had a reputation for his no-nonsense approach, and Mr Henry was his side-kick. An English teacher, Henry had his own reputation – all the lads said he had a thing for young boys. It was a rare occasion that these two would both be here on a weekend, but, as he was hauled up bodily by the latter, he decided that, for his intentions, this was a bonus. Mouth still dripping with blood and spit, he grinned at them.

'All right, sir?' he said to Mr Henry.

Both teachers looked sickened at what they had just witnessed. Both looked at Vinnie with a new sense of – what was it? Shock? Respect? Fear? Any would do, Vinnie thought, as he let them drag him from the rec room. Yes. Any of those three would do.

He was not so much directed to as thrust into a chair in the office and immediately handed a roll of toilet tissue. He could still taste the metallic tang of blood in his mouth. His pulse was slowing now. He licked his lips. Raised his eyes.

'Clean your face up, you vicious little thug,' Bastion commanded. 'You're in serious trouble, young man.'

Vinnie tore off some of the bog roll and slowly wiped his face with it, holding Bastion's gaze as he did so. 'They started on us, sir.'

He noticed Mr Henry staring at him, disgusted. 'Oh, that's right,' he added. 'It's bound to be all *my* fault, innit?'

'It *was* all your fault, McKellan,' Henry confirmed. 'There's a room full of lads in there that will tell us it was.'

'Mr Henry, I *swear*. We were just playing pool, me an' Billy, and them other kids started shouting stuff at us. They were taking the piss cos I got ginger hair …'

'Did you see the *state* of that boy?' Mr Henry interrupted, upping the volume. He jabbed a finger twice in the direction of the rec room. 'He probably needs hospital treatment!'

Vinnie felt a surge of pride. Hospital treatment? That would mean notoriety, surely. 'It was a fair fight, sir, honest,' he said. 'He's *miles* bigger than I am. Was I supposed to just let him beat me up?'

Neither Bastion or Henry seemed interested in providing an answer. Instead of that, they exchanged a glance and shook their heads. 'We have to involve the police in this, Vincent,' said Bastion, giving him daggers. 'And we most certainly will do, come Monday. In the meantime, you will receive six of the best, right now. And will then be confined to your room for the remainder of the weekend.' He shook his head again. 'Until this whole sorry mess gets sorted out.'

And he would be sorry. He didn't doubt it. But that was fine; that was the price you had to pay, that sort of bother. That was the whole point they didn't get. The reason he *wasn't* that bothered; in the long term, it meant he'd get a whole lot *less* bother.

The six of the best – standard punishment in approved schools, if not all schools – was administered without any delay. It could be administered with a cane, or a ruler or a shoe – it didn't matter. Just as long as it was something that was good at inflicting pain. Mr Henry's weapon of choice was a leather shoe, an object he'd been acquainted with many times at his old school but never at the hands of this pervy fucker; the subject of many a rec room conversation.

'Come on, lad, drop 'em,' Henry told him, with a glint in his beady eye. He almost smiled at Vinnie. 'You know the drill.'

Vinnie stood up, placing the bloody bog roll on the desk just beside him, dropped his jeans to his ankles and positioned himself towards the seat of the chair he'd just been sitting on, gripping the backrest tightly with both hands. He then bit his lip in readiness for what was to come, and then as reaction, as the first part of his punishment began.

Old Henry started swinging away, the sound of the air-rush audible, and counted each strike out loud as Mr Bastion looked on. Vinnie refused to acknowledge the pain surging through him and turned to fashion the best grin he could manage at his observer. 'Come on, sir, is that all you've got?' he taunted Henry, causing the teacher to make strike six the hardest one yet. But not as hard as *he* was, Vinnie thought. Not by a long shot.

'Now get to your room, you little bastard, and stay there,' Henry said as he threw down the shoe.

Vinnie stood up, hitched up his flares and gave a mock salute. 'I'm knackered anyway, sir,' he said. 'Could do with a nice nap. Did you enjoy that, Bastion? Do you like watching boys get their arses smacked?'

'Get out of here!' Bastion snarled. 'Straight to your room and stay there. No tea or supper for you tonight, son.'

'Fuck you very much, sir,' he responded, beginning to enjoy himself despite the searing pain. 'Can't stand the shit you call food anyway.'

He was halfway out of the door when he felt the shoe hit his back.

Though he'd made a point of laughing as the shoe had been lobbed at him, Vinnie let his guard down just as soon as he was out of sight. His arse felt as if it had been thrust into a roaring fire, and he rubbed at it furiously as he limped back to his room. Nasty bastards, the pair of 'em. Bastion the bastard and Henry the arse bandit. Yeah, that's what he'd call them from now on, he decided. He felt lighter of heart than he had at any point, he realised, since he'd arrived at the shit-hole. Yes, he might have a swollen arse for a few days but it was worth it. It was *worth* it. Now he wouldn't have any more bother. Billy too, perhaps. He hoped he'd gotten away with it – respect to the lad. He'd torn straight in to help, even though he was plainly bricking it. As far as Vinnie was concerned that cemented their friendship for ever.

A successful Saturday, all things considered.

Monday arrived and Vinnie went to brick-laying for the first lesson of the week, as per usual. His group – a bunch of six lads he barely knew – were building a wall in the gardens at the back of the centre. The reason why eluded him, because it seemed pretty pointless, other than to give them something useful to do. Well, useful, that was, if building walls was your thing. And the one thing he knew he had no intention doing was spending the rest of his life slapping mortar onto fucking bricks.

The dimwits he was working with were like robots, too. All 'Yes sir, no sir, three bags full sir' morons. They never even questioned the futility in the exercise. Vinnie sighed and shook his head as he picked up a trowel and a bucket. He'd let these monkeys do the hard graft today, he thought. No point him killing himself when he had no intention of becoming anyone's labourer. No, Vinnie fancied himself becoming a carpenter. He'd really loved making his bookshelf and had taken real pride in carving intricate patterns into the sides. He had decided there and then that when he was ready to do some honest work, it would be something involving making things from wood.

And on his own – not as part of some brain-dead group of
wets. He preferred his own company much better.

He had only been there for 10 minutes when he was
summoned to the office. A tall lad of about 17 who he'd never
seen before, who looked like he could handle himself, had
come to escort him, and after washing his hands in the bucket
outside and wiping them on his T-shirt, Vinnie followed him
back into the building. The lad didn't speak so, taking his cue
from him, Vinnie kept his mouth shut as well. *Ignorant fucker*,
he thought. *Probably thinks I'm scared of him.*

They walked down the main corridor, their boots slapping
in time on the navy-blue lino, towards the office where Mr
Bastion was housed. Vinnie winced as he approached – it was
almost automatic. He hoped that he wasn't going to get the
shoe treatment again. His arse was still throbbing from
Saturday, the bastards. He glued a grin on his face and pulled
his shoulders back a little. He'd not been told what he had
been summonsed for, but it didn't take a brain surgeon to work
out that it would almost definitely be about Saturday. So he'd
go in smiling and just take what he had coming.

When they got to the door, the big lad knocked and glanced
at Vinnie. 'I don't know what you've done, man,' he said, 'but
good luck. I think you're gonna need it.' Then he smiled and
sauntered off, leaving Vinnie to wait to be called in.

Vinnie watched him go while he waited for the door to be
opened. Luck? He didn't need luck. He just needed bravado
right now. He was just thinking how much, when Mr Bastion
opened the door and, as Vinnie looked inside, all thoughts of
going in with a cocky attitude vanished, along with the half-
smile he'd stuck on his face.

There were two coppers – that was the first thing he saw, two
fucking coppers. Joe with his mum and dad, and … oh, fuck.

'All right, Mother?' he said, following Bastion in and trying to swagger, while at the same time trying to compute what the fuck she was doing there.

His mam looked as she always did: completely over the top. A big red coat, with what looked like Tarka the bloody Otter slung round her neck by way of a collar, lipstick the colour of freshly spilled blood and hair the sort of silvery blonde you saw on film stars. She actually looked like one herself, in this dour masculine company, and in any other circumstance he'd be pleased and proud to see her. As it was, the best he could manage was a nervous grin, and even that was forced. She was looking daggers at him.

'Lovely this, Vinnie, innit it?' she snapped. '*Innit?*'

She waited just a heartbeat, giving him scant time to answer, before adding, 'Sally's here as well. She's just parking the car up.'

So there was no chance of sweet-talking his way out of this one. Not now. Not now the Queen of fucking Sheba was here.

'Sit down, Vincent,' Bastion said, and then, pointing to the coppers, 'these policeman will be sitting in while we have a bit of a chat, but they will then need to talk to you alone.'

June bristled in her seat. 'I know the law, love,' she said, glaring at him. 'I'm his mother, okay? And I'll be sitting in any interview.'

One of the coppers nodded to Bastion. 'That's fine,' he said, glancing at Vinnie before smiling at June. 'We would expect Mrs McKellan to join us.'

There was a single empty chair in the room. Bastion nodded towards it and Vinnie sat down on it, wincing. The next 30 minutes were to shape the rest of his life.

Chapter 7

The social worker rushed into the room, puffing and panting, clutching her briefcase. There was a sheen of sweat across her forehead, which sat at odds with the chilly atmosphere in the room.

'So sorry I'm late,' Sally said, swivelling as she looked for somewhere to sit down.

'Up, McKellan!' Bastion barked. Vinnie duly stood up again and stepped aside for Saggy Tits, who smiled at him with something that looked suspiciously like warmth. Had she been missing him? Now, that would be a turn-up.

'Thanks, love,' she said, putting her case on the floor and shrugging off her coat. 'Sorry,' she said again. 'The traffic was murder on the way down.'

She sat down heavily on the wooden school chair that Bastion had brought in and parked next to June, before throwing a look at Vinnie that, if anything, topped his mother's. Vinnie tipped his chair back onto two legs and leaned it against the office wall behind him, his mind working overtime now. He eyed up the coppers. *These bastards look like they mean business*, he thought. He wondered if he was going to get formally charged or something.

'Sit up straight, boy!' Bastion barked, making him jump. 'And for God's sake, put that ruddy chair straight!'

The headmaster's face was reddening, Vinnie noticed, in anger and what looked like frustration. Well, it must be frustrating for him, Vinnie thought, having this shit to deal with. Having to have the coppers in his nice, well-behaved, goody-goody school. It was a slightly cheering thought. The police presence would really help Vinnie's reputation with the lads, even if it did potentially mean a spot of bother. 'Sorry, sir,' he said to Bastion, giving him a mocking salute for good measure.

If Bastion wasn't impressed, his mother was even less so. 'Stop acting the prat,' June snapped. 'You don't know how much trouble you're in, lad.' She glared at Vinnie and then turned to look at Bastion, 'Now. Are we going to start this meeting or what?'

A couple of minutes droned on and Vinnie found himself soon zoning out as Bastion started to read out some report he had put together – obviously had nothing better to do over the weekend. But as he read, Vinnie started zoning back in again, at first with a kind of pride, but then with an increasing sense that this was turning into a hatchet job. It was a report that was beginning to paint Vinnie out to be the Devil incarnate. A monster who'd viciously attacked poor Joe – poor Joe? *What* – without any 'provocation' or any 'regard for the consequences'? He read out about Vinnie's thieving, his poor attitude to learning and conforming, and finally, finally, he got to the point.

'So we feel that we have no choice,' he finished, with a tone of regret and exhaustion, 'but to ask that Vinnie be removed from this establishment, and placed instead somewhere more suitable for his needs.'

What? Thought Vinnie. *WHAT?* Be removed? What was he on about? There was no way he was going to swallow this shit. The whole point of assaulting Joe had been to give himself a bit of status here – not be shipped off somewhere else altogether. Christ – if they did that it would all have been for nothing! He leapt from his chair indignantly and almost

instinctively. 'Fuck you an' all, *sir*! My fuckin' *needs*!' He
pointed over to Joe, who was now actually cowering in between
his mum and dad, watching him. 'That fucking cunt started it!
Am I s'posed to do fuck all, eh? Just let him kick my fucking
head in? I don't think so!'

'McKellan, sit DOWN!' Bastion was off his seat now, as
well. As were the coppers. Vinnie grinned, seeing this, and
flexed his fingers automatically. If there was going to be a free
for all, best put on a bit of a show. 'What you gonna do, you fat
cunt?' he yelled at Bastion. June stood up herself, then, though
old Saggy Tits kept her fat arse in her chair. 'Go on,' June
snapped at him, getting herself in between him and Bastion.
'Go on, Vinnie. Just you fucking dare. I'm warning you,' she
said evenly, meeting his eye and skewering him with another
one of her looks. He withdrew immediately. He could have had
a right go with two coppers and Bastion – bring it on, son – but
his mother? Fuck that for a lark. He wasn't insane.

June remained standing till he'd sat back in his seat once
again, as did Bastion and eventually the still silent coppers, and
then everyone seemed to calm down. Well, outwardly, at any
rate; there was still a bit of an edge to the two coppers, and he
could see that one of them now had a set of cuffs in his hand.

What were they doing here anyway? It was a thought that
hit him belatedly. Did Bastion really think he was gonna kick
off that badly? Or – shit – was he about to be arrested? No, it
couldn't be that, surely? It was Monday now. So it couldn't be
happening. In his experience, if you were going to get nicked,
it happened as soon as you got caught. They wouldn't leave
him all weekend and then come for him, surely? He felt his
palms get clammy. No, it couldn't be that, could it? That wasn't
the way things worked. He *knew* that. They'd want as little fuss
as possible because it went on the school's record when the

cops got involved in shit. And then the school got extra hassle. So why *were* they here? If it was a case of him being shipped off to some other place, then they could do that themselves, couldn't they? Yet there were two coppers here. He wished he knew why.

He tried to fathom it as, after shuffling through a bunch of papers from her handbag, Sally began having her two penn'orth.

'Well,' she said, mostly to Bastion, while June continued to glare at him, 'since I only got the call on Saturday – which is not a lot of time, frankly – we've been unable to find Vinnie an alternative approved school.' She paused, then glanced at Vinnie, then looked at the two coppers. 'So am I right in understanding that you intend keeping him in custody until something suitable is offered?'

Vinnie almost choked, hearing that. What the fuck was she on about? Fucking *custody*? Was *that* why they were here? He looked at June, panic written all over his face. 'Mum?'

June could only shake her head sadly. 'It's out of my hands, son,' she said, shrugging. 'What do you expect? I warned you, didn't I? You just won't have it, will you?' She sighed. 'You never would.'

One of the coppers stood up then and walked over to Vinnie.

'Vincent McKellan,' he said, managing to sound bored as well as smug. 'I'm arresting you for an assault causing actual bodily harm. You have a right to remain silent ...' He produced the handcuffs as he spoke and reached for Vinnie's arms. 'Come on, son,' he said, softening slightly, perhaps seeing Vinnie's now stricken face. 'You know the drill.'

The copper was feeling sorry for him now, he could tell. He tried to adjust his expression by sheer force of will.

He stood up as directed, willing his legs not to give way beneath him, and forcing a grin, said, 'Yeah, man, I know the drill.' He looked back at June then and smiled. 'Get us a brief, Mam, okay? One that can sort these divvies out.'

To his horror, as he spoke he saw a tear slide down her cheek, forming a track through the powdery surface.

'Mother!' he barked, mortified. 'Sort yourself out! The nick's gotta be better than this shit-hole, I can tell you. Mother, *honest*. Get over yourself. I'll be alright, okay?'

She nodded at him, brushing at her cheek irritably, before spinning round to the social worker. 'How long, Sal? Before they find him a place? I don't want him locked up with …' She jabbed a finger in the direction of the hapless Joe, just so he could be in no doubt how she felt about him, '… with criminals and bloody animals!'

Sally smiled a sympathetic smile and put a hand on June's arm, and Vinnie recognised that she was anxious that his mother didn't really start kicking off, with old Saggy Tits the next focus of her anger. 'Soon, love,' she soothed. 'They don't keep kids in them places for long, I promise you.'

At that point Joe's dad let out an angry laugh and finally spoke. 'Criminals and animals?' he spluttered. 'You're having a laugh, aren't you? You've just described your son to a tee, love. They should lock him up and let him rot for what he's done, the bleeding toe-rag!'

June glared at the man as though she was going to start on him next, but, glancing at Vinnie again – now cuffed – she seemed to think better of it. Instead she turned back to him, reaching out to pat his forearm. 'Chin up then, mate, okay? You'll be alright, son. Go on.'

There was nothing she could do to help him and he could see that by the set of her shoulders as the coppers frogmarched him out of the office.

* * *

Outside, a small crowd had formed. Word had clearly spread quickly and, while he'd been busy packing his bag, it seemed that anyone who'd been able to had gathered in the drive to watch the proceedings. A chorus of cheers, whistles and shouts of encouragement formed a spirited vocal accompaniment as Vinnie was led out to a waiting police car by the copper he was cuffed to, who 'accidentally' bumped Vinnie's head on the roof as he shoved him into the back seat. Par for the course, Vinnie thought. There'd probably be more of it, too. He was more concerned about the haunted look on his mum's face as he waved from the back window as they drove off. He couldn't ever remember seeing her look so old. Maybe the old man was giving her some grief. He hoped not. It wasn't like his mum to take shit off him. But he wasn't there, was he? Had that changed things? Was she okay?

He also thought of Titch, suddenly. Shit. He didn't even ask his mam how she was, poor little bleeder. *I'll have to write to her*, he reminded himself, *and find out what the score is*. Mustn't forget. *Shit*. Mustn't forget.

The police station, they told him, would be a journey of about 15 miles, which he spent in silent contemplation of the passing fields, while the coppers talked quietly to each other. Vinnie wondered, for a weirdly exhilarating couple of seconds, whether to try the back door and make a jump for it. Wondered how he'd do it – how it would feel to experience his body thumping to the ground at speed, then rolling over and over, before halting the momentum, struggling upright again and sprinting towards the distant woods, the cops on his tail, like an Allied officer in a German prisoner-of-war camp. It was a compelling thought – fuck knew how long it would be before he felt fresh air again – but he wasn't stupid enough to try it. He knew they'd round him up in seconds.

It wasn't long before they reached the police station anyway, driving in via a back entrance halfway down the middle of a high street, where they were greeted by a desultory wave from a bloke in the car park and, when they entered the building, with a bored-looking nod from the desk sergeant. He was another fat bastard like Bastion, and had a 'seen it all, done it all, you're not such a hot shot' look about him. And he confirmed it while he booked Vinnie in.

'Little hard nut are we, eh?' he asked once he'd read out the charge sheet. 'Let's see how long you last in the holding cell, then, shall we?'

One of the coppers who had brought him in looked at the sergeant in confusion. 'Holding cell?' he asked. 'I thought he'd be given his own pad.'

'Not just yet, Gary, we're all out of superior rooms, I'm afraid.'

They all sniggered and, watching them, Vinnie scowled. Let the cunts laugh, he thought, pushing his chest out and flexing his fists again. He'd show them who'd have the last laugh.

But it wasn't his only thought; there was another one. One that he couldn't quite put his finger on. In fact, not so much a thought as a niggle of an emotion. One he didn't like the feel of, so he fought to keep it where it lay.

Which was in the pit of his stomach. 'Come on then, fellas,' he said, 'Show us me new pad, then. Only I'm a bit peckish, so I hope room service are still working.'

The other plod – the one he hadn't been cuffed to – suddenly grabbed Vinnie by the arm. 'Think you're clever, do you? You're nothing but a Yorkshire fucking tyke.' He grinned nastily. 'And guess what?' he added, glancing again at the desk sergeant. 'The lads in the holding cell have all had a few bevvies already and, trust me, they're gonna love *you*, lad.'

Without further comment to either of the others, he marched Vinnie through a door, and down a corridor, yanking him to a halt in front of the caged bars of a holding cell, the desk sergeant not very far behind.

Vinnie straightened himself right up and tried to look unimpressed by the inhabitants, three of whom were standing in a ragged row, presumably to greet him. They were a black bloke in his twenties, sporting a giant Afro hair-do, a couple of old geezers, filthy-looking (not to mention stinking) who were obviously tramps, and a fourth man who looked to be in his forties. He was covered in tattoos and obviously out of his tree on something, because he was sprawled out on a bench, a pool of recent-looking sick glistening on the floor beside him and contributing to the stench.

The copper unlocked the door and pushed Vinnie inside. 'Some entertainment, lads!' he quipped. 'You all be nice though, okay? He's just a little kid with a big gob.'

Vinnie slipped his hands into his jeans pockets and fashioned a grin for his bemused audience. He was shitting himself and he needed a strategy. Which of these fellow inmates was he most in with a shot at captivating? He needed to get someone on side, and quickly. The man who'd thrown up was beginning to stir now and pushed himself upright and, by some instinct – it wasn't rational, the man was stinking and covered in vomit – he stuck out a hand. 'Alright, mush?' he said. 'I'm Vinnie.'

The man laughed, but not unpleasantly, and immediately shook the outstretched hand. 'Now then, you little cunt, you're a bit young to be in here, aren't you? What the fuck did you *do*?'

The black guy laughed as well then and, having obviously risen at the sound of his approach – like dogs do when they hear the rattle of a tin – they all sat down again on the remaining benches that went around the three walls. Vinnie breathed a silent sigh of relief and joined in the laughter. 'Fucking GBH or ABH or something. Fuck knows. Whatever it was, I bit the big fucker's cheek off.'

The big bloke and the black man both laughed even louder, thumping each other on the arm. Maybe they were friends. The black man wiped his eyes then and said to Vinnie, 'Oh, for fuck's sake, that's livened us up a bit! I'm Maurice, man,' he said, holding his own hand out. Vinnie shook it. 'And this here's Grant. How long you here for?'

'I don't know,' admitted Vinnie, as the copper turned the key behind him. 'They're supposed to be putting me in a new approved school or something.'

'Approved school, eh?' The black guy scratched his head. 'Well, make yourself at home, Vin. And don't worry about these two,' he said, pointing to the tramps, who eyed him incuriously. 'They're only here till they sober up. Obviously.'

'Or fall down fuckin' dead,' Grant said. Upon which they both threw their heads back and burst out laughing again.

And as Grant laughed, Vinnie noticed the tattoo round his neck. It was a series of roughly inked blue lines – a dotted line, in fact – and underneath it, at the front, written in pretty shitty writing, was the faded and grubby instruction to 'cut here'.

Vinnie couldn't wait till he could get some tattoos. He'd remember that one, he decided. But for the moment – well, what now? They just sat here? That was what struck him most, the weirdness of the situation. That he was sat in a room with four men, two of them tramps. Nothing to do. Nothing to read. Nowhere to go.

Worst of all, they had started talking dirty. Not to him – now he was here he was no longer a novelty – but telling each other about birds they'd both shagged and what they'd done to them, which was a subject that, Miss Biggs aside, wasn't doing it for him. They weren't that young themselves, so chances were they'd be ropey old birds they were discussing, too. Yeuch.

He was bored stiff and began to wonder if he should ask for a pen and paper so he could write a letter or something to help pass the time. *Fuck!* he thought, remembering suddenly. *His letters!* They were still under his pillow in his bunk. He'd slipped them under there when he'd gone down to check out the ruck in the yard and hadn't given a thought to them since.

Fuck, he thought again, realising that was the last he'd probably see of them. At least for a while. How could he have forgotten them? What an idiot. And what were the chances – even if he asked the copper to call the home in Brighton for him – of him ever getting his hands on them again? Already been scooped up in the laundry no doubt, when they cleared the room to make way for the next poor sod.

He felt even worse when he realised that there was absolutely no chance of him being allowed to call home and speak to his sister now. He sat back and rested his head against the cold, unyeilding wall, feeling guilty. He felt bad about that bit. Poor Titch.

Still, he decided, it was probably something and nothing anyway. Whatever was eating his little sis at the moment was probably fuck all compared to the shit *he* was in.

Chapter 8

Josie lifted the nicotine-stained net curtains for what must have been the twentieth time and peered anxiously out into the blackness. Where *was* her mum? She should have been home hours ago. She'd left the house at about four in the morning, it had seemed like, and it was now after eight in the evening.

'Any sign of her, Titch?'

She jumped at the unexpected sound of her dad's voice. He'd been dozing, but clearly no longer. She shook her head.

'Bollocks to it, then!' he said with feeling, rising stiffly from his armchair, and reaching to grab his overcoat from the sofa arm. 'She's probably pissed off straight to the pub, Titch. You know what she's like. Telling all her fucking mates about what the boy wonder's been up to.'

Josie lowered the net. 'No she won't have, Dad,' she said. 'She knows better. I told her to come let me know as soon as she got back.'

She watched her dad shrug his coat on and slip his tobacco tin in the pocket, clearly bound for the pub now as well. It hurt her to think her mam might have gone straight to the Bull without popping home first to see her, because she knew how desperately she wanted some news about Vinnie. It had been on her mind since Saturday night, when her Auntie Mo had called round, saying the social worker had been on the phone wanting June. Something had happened – something bad

– because her mam had been in a mood all Sunday. Had he been causing trouble? If so, what kind of trouble? She'd asked, but her mam said she didn't actually know. All she'd say was that he'd been his usual stupid fucking self and 'gone off on one' with someone, which told her nothing she didn't already know.

She wouldn't have gone straight to the pub, would she? Surely not. But her dad clearly thought so, and maybe he was right. 'Yeah, love,' he said, 'and pigs might fly. I'm telling you, Titch, she won't give a fuck about what you said. Anyway, I'm off up to the Bull and I bet you a pound to a penny she'll already be up there.' He ruffled her hair. 'I'll see you later if you're still awake, okay?'

Josie nodded miserably and continued her vigil by the window, now following Jock's progress as he made his way up the street. It was the back end of November and the nights were dark and bitterly cold. Though hope was beginning to fade now, she still clung to it anyway, praying with all her heart that her mother, just this once, had remembered what she'd promised. She rubbed away the condensation that kept building up in front of her and squashed her nose once again against the window pane. There was nothing else to do, after all.

A couple of minutes later, Josie's patience was rewarded. She saw the lights of a car sweep round the corner and, even as she was prepared for it to drive past and disappoint her, she saw it slow and then come to a stop outside. It was a taxi, she realised, one that had been carrying her mum; even in the dark, June's platinum hair and that mad coat of hers were unmistakable, and, finally able to leave her post, Josie rushed into the kitchen to put the kettle on. She knew the drill. Knew how to put her mum in a good mood; June was hopeless without a cup of tea inside her, and a cuppa and the offer of a foot rub was the secret to cheering her up. And she would definitely need cheering up – Josie was pretty definite on that score. She knew how much her mam missed Vinnie and how hard it would have been for her to have to say goodbye to him all over again today.

She swilled out and rinsed the teapot, impatient now to hear all about Vinnie and, more importantly, if there was news of a release date. Since the 'thing' she couldn't bear to think about, she had been pining for her brother badly. Not that she intended telling him – she was clear on that – because that would cause murder, but merely his presence back in her life would be enough. That was all she needed. She'd feel safe again then.

'Kettle's on, Mam,' she called out, when she heard the front door slam. 'You have a sit down and take your shoes off, I'll be there now.'

'Don't bother!' came her mother's barked reply from the hall, causing her growing bubble of excitement to pop. 'I'm just changing these shoes and then I'm off.' There was a silence. 'Where is he? Where's your dad?'

Josie came out into the hall to see June wriggling her foot out of a shoe and looking at her enquiringly. 'Already up at the pub, I suppose?' Josie nodded. 'Typical! Well, he'd better keep out of my sight or I'll cause fucking hell up there, I swear!'

Josie's heart started to bang in her chest. What had happened? Why was her mum in such a mood still? How bad could it have been? She turned back into the kitchen and put down the tea-cup she'd been holding. 'What's up, Mam?' she asked, following her mum back into the living room. 'What's happened? How's our Vinnie? Is he okay?'

June was sitting on the couch struggling to remove her second shoe. She glanced up at Josie, looking livid and then, once she'd finally got the foot free, threw the offending sling-back across the floor.

'Our fucking *Vinnie*,' she ranted, 'is not okay, no.' She jabbed a finger against her temple. 'Not up here, he's not.'

Josie gasped. 'What's he done, Mam? What's happened to him?'

'*Happened* to him? I already told you – he has been his usual stupid fucking self.'

'Is he hurt?'

June leapt up and stalked past Josie into the hallway. 'Hurt? He'd have been hurt if they'd've let me get my hands on him, believe me. Now can you get out of the way so I can find my other slingbacks? Where the fuck did I – ah, there they are. Who put them there – *you*?' She stomped back into the living room and sat down heavily on the sofa to put them on.

'But, Mam, is –'

'But Mam nothing, girl!' she snapped. 'I'm really not in the mood for *you* giving me the third degree. I already told you. Your brother's been a bad boy. That's all you need to know – that he's been a fucking idiot, that he's not coming home, and probably not for a long time, okay? Now I suggest you piss off out of my sight and let me get ready before they call last fuck-ing orders!'

Josie stared at June, open-mouthed. What was she *saying*? Not coming home for a long time? *Why*? She watched in a daze as June stood up again to reapply her lipstick in the big mirror. 'But what happened, Mam?' she dared to asked again. '*Was* he fighting? Did he get into trouble? What?'

'I mean it, Josie,' she said, pressing her lips together and swivelling the lipstick back down. 'I'm really not in the mood for 20 questions right now.'

'But I've been waiting,' Josie said, feeling her own anger rising and her voice with it. 'Waiting all *day for you*! What's he *done*? And *when's* he coming home? That's all I want to know!'

June swivelled as she was popping the lippy back into her handbag. 'Don't you raise your voice to me, madam, you hear me? You best get out of my sight, cos I'm *this* close,' she squeezed her thumb and her forefinger together and glared at Josie, '*this* close to throwing a fit. I'm *fuming*, Titch, so don't push me any further, okay? Now, I say again, piss off out of my sight before you get a belt!'

Josie had no idea why her mum was in such a filthy mood but she also knew better than to push it when she was like this. She hesitated for a moment more – should she try, even so? But she knew it would be pointless; she'd get no answers, just a clip round the ear. But she wasn't staying home alone either. Grabbing her jacket from the back of the couch, and with tears springing in her eyes, she fled into the hall and yanked the front door open, shouting out 'Bleeding cow!' as she ran off down the street.

She was so upset with her mother that she forgot her most important new rule. She happened to glance across the street and her eyes were instantly drawn to a brightly illuminated upstairs window. Mucky Melvin! He had his grubby makeshift curtain held back and was watching her as she ran by.

Josie yelped and changed direction, feeling a wave of nausea rise in her stomach, running back past her own house and further down the street. She was almost blinded by her tears now but she didn't care who saw her. She ran for five full minutes, fast enough to make the air rasp in her throat, then, finally spent, she slowed first to a jog and then to a walk, sweat beading on her forehead and hair damp against her neck as she drew up outside the local youth club.

The lights were on. It was one of the club nights and there would be loads of kids in there. She didn't want to go in though. She never did. She didn't like a lot of the older kids who went to play pool, but she knew of somewhere else to go in any case.

There was a secret den just down from the back of the youthy; a den that her, Vinnie and a few others had made a couple of years back, deep inside a stand of overgrown shrubs and scraggy trees. They'd sometimes stash stolen stuff there and congregate for meetings. She'd go there, she decided. Yes, it was dark, but she felt safe inside. Hardly anyone knew about it and because there was only one way in and out, no one could sneak up on her there. It was as good a place as any, she decided, setting off towards the building, and definitely better than going back to her shitty home.

Having crossed the grass, Josie slipped through the gap in the perimeter fence and slid down the slippery, muddy grass bank to the bottom of the hill. She was at the back of the building now, and sat and waited for a few moments, but once satisfied that the only sounds were coming from inside the building above her, she began making her way across the area of wasteland in front of her.

Littered with old car tyres, cans, empty boxes and discarded chip wrappers, to anyone looking, it just seemed like a rubbish tip. But behind that, and known only to a very select few, there'd been a major excavation. The apparent wall of impenetrable brambles actually hid a sizeable retreat; space enough for half a dozen kids, at a pinch, to sit together, the scrubby ground buried under a damp and smelly carpet off-cut and light provided by stubs of candles in old jam jars.

Josie carefully parted the curtain of branches, fought her way through the scratchy bushes and pushed her way finally into the little space. Then almost jumped out of her skin when she first heard a sniffle and then, as her eyes gradually adjusted to the darkness, saw a figure crouched down in the corner.

Her fear was only momentary, though. The sniffle sounded female, and the figure tiny. 'Who's that?' she asked in a whisper.

'Oh it's you, Titch. Thank fuck for that, I almost shit myself then!'

'Caz?' Titch asked, peering at her. 'That you?' She shuffled a bit closer then sat back on her heels. 'What the fuck are you doing here?'

Carol sniffed again and Josie could see the white of a tissue or bit of bog roll. 'What's up, mate? You're crying. Has someone battered you?'

Carol wiped the tissue across her face and shook her head. 'No. No, it's not that. I'm fine. I'll be alright, mate. I just needed to get away from the house for a bit.'

Her as well, then. 'Why's that?'

'It's nothing. Just the usual. Mam, an' that. I'm much better now you're here.' Her eyes adjusted now, Josie could make out her friend's smile. 'What *are* you doing here anyway?' Carol asked her.

'Never mind that,' said Josie. 'What d'you mean – 'Mam, an' that'? What's happened? Has your mam started on you or something?'

For a few moments Carol said nothing. She just sat there, scrunching and unscrunching the tissue. Then she sobbed again, all at once, and reached her arms out to Josie, who pulled her in for a hug and held her tightly. 'Oh, Josie,' she said finally, 'it's not my mam. I wish it was. It's that bastard that she's with. Him. That black *bastard*!'

Crying out loud now, so much so that Josie felt compelled to try and shush her, she pressed her face into Josie's chest, her shoulders heaving. 'He's been doing stuff to me, Titch ...'

'Doing stuff? What stuff?'

'*That* kind of stuff. An' I'm sick of it …'

Josie pushed Carol away slightly and stared at her. 'Doing stuff like *what*? What do you mean, Caz? You mean Black Bobby has, right?'

Carol nodded and sobbed again and raked the tissue across her face again. 'Please swear down that you won't tell, Titch. You must swear, okay?'

'I will swear,' she said, understanding dawning. Carol *too*? 'I *do* swear – but what's he done to you?'

'Been coming into my bedroom,' Caz said haltingly. 'You know, when me mam's at the bingo and … touching me down there and stuff.' She paused to sniff. 'I mean he gives me cigs and sweets and that afterwards, an' I thought I could kind of cope with it, but it's horrible, Titch – horrible, and he's just getting worse and worse. Tonight he …' she paused and gulped. 'Tried to … you know … put his thing in me, and … and I managed to fight him off – and thank fuck for Blue – but …'

'Did Blue attack him?' Josie asked, wide-eyed. Blue was Caz's dog and she was a big alsation bitch. Josie knew she'd defend Caz with her life.

'Almost,' Caz said. 'Got between us. Scared the shit out of him at least … but …'

She stopped then, her face crumpling, and started wailing all over again. 'I don't know what to do, Titch,' she mumbled, burrowing her face into Josie's neck. 'I can't tell me mam, can I? She'll kill me. She'll say I led him on. An' he'll just lie, won't he? So you mustn't tell. You won't tell, will you? I've just gotta think what's the best thing to do. So just forget I told you, okay? Will you promise?'

Josie stared into the thicket, unseeing. Remembering. It had been four weeks now and her secret felt like a physical thing inside her. She was still cut and bruised, as well, down there. Where he'd forced his thing inside her. Raw. She shuddered.

'Caz, I'll never tell a living soul,' she said, stroking her friend's hair absently. 'I understand, and I'll never tell a living soul, I promise.'

Carol pulled back from her then and used the last twist of tissue to blow her nose. Then threw it into the blackness.

'I know you won't,' she said. 'An' I'll be fine. It's okay. It's just ...' She wrapped her arms across her chest and rocked slightly. 'It's just horrible in a way I can't tell you. It's just disgusting. It's ... You know, when men ... and they ...' She stopped and shook her head. 'Just be glad you *don't* know, Titch. *Really*. You don't *want* to know.'

The silence in the den lasted a full 20 seconds, and Josie knew Caz was struggling not to cry again. Black Bobby. Him as *well*. And he *lived* with them. The thought was shocking. The idea that he could just go into her bedroom any time he liked and do that stuff to her ... It was shocking and it was disgusting. No wonder Caz was so upset.

'I do know,' she said quietly, the words coming from her mouth without her even consciously deciding to say them. It was as if her secret had decided it was staying secret no longer, overruling her.

Carol looked puzzled for a moment. Then shook her head. 'No, Josie, you don't know. I'm talking about grown-up sex stuff. That's what I'm telling you.'

'I do know,' she said again.

Carol's eyes began to widen. 'What, you mean it's ... *God*, Titch, you mean your *dad*?' She clapped her hands to her mouth. 'Oh my *God*!'

Josie shook her head, stricken at the thought. 'God, not my dad! Mucky Melvin!'

Carol gasped. 'Mucky *Melvin*? *Fuck*!'

So Josie told her.

And in the telling, she felt alternately traumatised and better. Traumatised, remembering what she'd tried so hard to forget; his smell, his croaky breathing, his gnarly, stinky fingers, his greasy matted hair slipping and sliding against her cheek … But better – so much better – now it had all finally spilled out of her. Better that she didn't feel so alone any more, better that she'd been able to tell someone she trusted, someone she loved, someone who'd understand. It made her feel slightly less dirty.

'Shit!' Caz said, finally. 'The monster! The shitty, filthy monster!'

'You mustn't tell, Caz …'

'I won't tell. I promise, Titch. I'll *never* tell. But you should tell. This isn't like Bobby, Titch. If he's done that to you he needs to go to prison. You should tell. You should tell your mam and dad.'

Josie felt her heart thump at the thought Caz might tell on her after all. 'I can't do that!'

'Why not?'

'Because they'll kill me for being so stupid and going in there!'

'Course they wouldn't!'

'They would, Caz. You don't know my mam!'

In truth, Caz did. Josie knew that. And a part of her also knew her friend was probably right. But she just couldn't bring herself to even think about telling her parents. She just couldn't. She just *wouldn't*. Not *ever*.

'How about Vinnie, then?' Caz said. 'You should tell your Vinnie – he'll fucking kill him!'

Josie shook her head. 'That's exactly why I won't be telling Vinnie, Caz. He's already gotten himself in more bother and has to do more time. I can't tell him, Caz. He's in enough trouble as it is.'

'Well, you can't let him get away with it, Titch. Dirty old bastard! Why don't you tell your Lyndsey and Robbo, then? Robbo will know what to do.'

'I dunno.' She said. 'I did think about it but you never know with Lynds. She can't always be trusted to keep her gob shut, can she? I dunno. I just … well, I'm just so glad I've told *you*. It was killing me keeping it to myself. I feel so much better now I've told you. What you gonna do about Black Bobby?'

Carol looked sad again and shrugged. 'Same as you, I suppose. Nothing. Just keep it to myself and hope my mam decides to get shut of him. She's looking like she might do soon, at least.'

'You should sleep with a knife under your pillow,' Josie said. 'Threaten him with it next time.'

Carol smiled. 'You're a mental case. Can you imagine that? Me pulling out a knife threatening to cut off his dangly bits?' She giggled then, unexpectedly. 'Nice idea, though.'

Which made Josie giggle too. She realised she felt better than she had done since Vinnie went. It would be okay. They had each other and she knew it would all be better now. She wiped a dirty hand across her face and squeezed Carol's arm. 'That's settled then. We don't tell anyone. Not for now, at least. This is our secret.'

'Our secret,' agreed Carol. 'Blood sisters, okay?'

Josie nodded and the two girls made their way out of the den. She felt stronger now. Strong enough to cope with it on her own. Strong enough to cope with Vinnie not coming home yet. When you had a blood sister like Caz you could cope with *anything*, however horrible. She just hoped that neither of them was going to have to.

1973

Chapter 9

February

Jock reached behind the front-room door for his sheepskin coat. It was the back end of winter and was freezing outside, but that wasn't going to stop him going to work today.

Which wasn't like Jock. Normally even the mere utterance of the word 'work' was enough to send him scuttling back to bed. Jock had his own, much nicer, way of making money. And one that didn't mean grafting for some other undeserving fucker, either. Jock was a gambler. It was in his blood, same as it had been in his dad's before him. Coming from a family of bookies he'd had the horse-racing bug since he was a lad.

So Jock didn't really need to work – not all that often, anyway. Like most of the men on the Canterbury Estate the only regular work he did was his weekly trip to the dole office, to sign on for his unemployment benefit. If he fell short – perhaps needed extra money for Christmas or a party, then he'd do a bit here and there 'on the side'. The only other main spur to him making the effort to pull a few quid together was, as it had always been, June. New clothes, a night out – she was always on his case about something she wanted – and every so often, when the frequency of her nagging got too much, he'd do whatever was required to shut her up.

But not today. Today was different. Today he was actually looking forward to going to work. This particular job was a right little number and if he played his cards right, him and June would both be laughing. It was a gift, a proper gift, and he could hardly believe his luck.

He went into the hall, shrugging on his coat as he did so. 'Right, I'm off, then,' he called up the stairs. 'You coming along at dinner time again? Same place?'

'Hang on a minute,' June yelled back. 'I'm coming down.'

Jock went back into the warm front room to wait for her. He looked up at the clock and shook his head in irritation. Silly mare was going to have him late again.

It was a full couple of minutes before she appeared in the doorway – not dressed, as he'd expected, but still in her short flimsy nightie, her face still caked in the make-up she habitually went to bed in. She was sauntering across the room with a look that meant business. 'Come here, you,' she said, puckering her lips and making a grab for him. 'Give us a kiss before you go.'

'Piss off, you silly get!' he protested as he tried to dodge her. 'Fuckin' hell, June, a sniff of a few bob, and you're all over me like a cheap suit!'

Not that he minded, he decided, as she giggled at him coquettishly. 'It's not a few bob any more, you divvy,' she said. 'It's a few new pence, remember? Has been for two years now, in case you hadn't noticed.'

'Fuckin' decimalisation,' he growled. 'Never going to get the hang of it. They should have left well alone. Bleeding common market nonsense!' He extracted himself from his wife and waved as he left. 'Don't forget,' he called over his shoulder as he stepped out onto the pavement. 'Wimpy at 12. Don't be late, June, or you'll fuck it all up.'

June laughed as she waved him off. 'Don't worry, love,' she called after him. 'I'll be there with knobs on!'

He could still hear her laughing when he was halfway down the road, and when he looked back, she was still waving from the front-room window, the daft cow. Still, it gave him a warm feeling, made him puff up with pride. Despite their fall-outs, he still loved her to bits.

He quickened his step, his mind now back on the job at hand. Things to do, places to go, people to see. It was a good 20-minute walk into town, and a cold one, and he was anxious to get where he needed to be. He pulled the lapels of his coat a little tighter together, reflecting that there was perhaps one too many people involved in this thing. So he was nervous. He didn't mind admitting it.

Josie came downstairs, minutes later, to find her mother in the living room, admiring her reflection in the mirror.

'Not bad for an old bird,' she was saying (to herself, presumably, Josie decided) and arching her drawn-on eyebrows. Josie never understood why she did that – shaving them off and then painting them on again. Why? Why not just leave them as they were? 'And tomorrow you'll look even better,' June promised herself, grinning. 'Once you're wearing all your lovely new clobber!'

Josie stood just inside the doorway for a moment, watching her mother blow a kiss at her own reflection, clearly oblivious that her daughter was even in the room. It had always been a bit like that with her mum – and when Vinnie had been home, even more so. Put Vinnie in a room with them and it had always felt as if she became invisible. She was her dad's girl, always had been, and Vinnie was her mum's boy – that was just the way it was, just the way it would always be, probably. They

were poles apart, after all. Her mum was so unlike her. So glam-
orous and girly. So alien. Something Josie knew she'd never be.
Not any more, anyway.

'What *are* you going on about, you silly old mare?' she said
now.

June jumped, startled, and turned round to see Josie staring
at her.

'You daft cow!' she said. 'You scared me half to bleeding
death.' She flapped a hand at Josie irritably and stomped off in
the direction of the kitchen. 'Go on, get ready for school
instead of sneaking up on folk.'

Josie ignored that. It was still only eight, after all. Instead,
she followed her mother into the tiny kitchen, the same thing
on her mind as had been on it for ages now. It had been months
since they'd heard anything from Vinnie. Months and months.
And she'd written – what? – three unanswered letters? Four?
And still nothing back.

'D'ya think we'll have a letter today?' she asked as she
reached to put on the grill, though even as she did so she knew
it was more in hope than expectation.

'A letter?' asked June.

'You know, from our Vin.'

June sighed as Josie pushed past her to get a plate from the
shelf underneath the curtain-fronted worktop. 'Titch, you
know what he's like. Sending letters counts as a privilege and
pound to a penny he'll be all out of those. So fuck knows when
we'll hear from him, frankly!'

'Yeah, but he's got to send one *sometime*! It's been for
ever!'

June drained her tea mug and banged it down on the
Formica. Then, seeing Josie's expression, shook her head.
'Look, I'm just as upset as you, love. Honest I am. But you

never know – he might be allowed a phone call this week, mightn't he?'

Josie scowled as she stood on tiptoe to slide two slices of bread onto the grill pan. The business of the phone was a constant bugbear. 'Well, if you paid the bill, we'd be able to phone *him*, wouldn't we?'

'Shut it, gob shite,' June said mildly. Then she grinned at her daughter, which she'd been doing a fair bit just lately, her eyes lighting up, like she'd just been told she'd won the pools. She nudged Josie. 'If this job goes all right for your dad, *all* the bills will get paid this month,' she said. 'Every last one of them.'

Which wasn't what Josie wanted to hear. She'd heard enough about this 'job' of her Dad's already. Like a lot of what her parents and their neighbours on the estate got up to, it didn't sit okay with her. Why were they constantly trying to get things that didn't belong to them? It made no sense. Not to her. 'Goody two-shoes' they all called her. Well, let them. 'I don't wanna know, Mum,' she said. 'All I know is that it's dodgy. Half the fucking estate are on about it.'

June laughed, as she poured more tea and went back into the living room. 'No,' she called back. 'Half the fucking estate are *in* on it, you mean!'

Josie turned the toast over and watched the other side brown in silence, feeling the familiar rush of resentment that her mother didn't even seem to care that much about Vinnie any more. Stupid cow was too concerned with herself and her new 'clobber' to even give a fuck about him these days – and to think he was supposed to be her golden boy! Eighteen months he'd been in Redditch borstal – 18 whole *months*. Where had the time gone? It felt like he'd been gone for ever. It had been *so* long – there'd been the long spell before that, over in Manchester, at that St Augustine's reformatory place, as well.

Was he *ever* going to come home? She pulled her toast out and carefully unfolded the wrapper from the Adams best butter. And mother dearest, she thought as she scraped up slivers of glistening yellow, didn't even seem to give a shit.

'I'm off up to get ready for school,' she shouted as she went back through the living room, raising her voice above the din of T. Rex on the radio that June had just put on at her usual stupid volume. 'And maybe we could even go visit our Vinnie. When you've robbed me dad of all his wages.' She headed for the stairs then, toast balanced on her palm, remembering to duck as she did so, to avoid a slap from June on her way past.

Vinnie had been sentenced to three years the previous January. It should only have been six months in Redditch borstal, that was all. Just six flipping months. And then they'd finally have him home again. But, Vinnie being Vinnie, he just couldn't seem to keep his nose clean. According to June, who was the only one who'd seen or spoken to him – and only then because he was a minor so she had to be there when he was sentenced – he'd racked up four separate offences of violence and theft within the first month. And he was now paying the price, and it was a big one.

The only thing she could console herself with was that if he was good from that point on – well, according to what big tits Sally had said, anyway – that three years would be chopped by at least a third. Which, given that he'd already done 18 months there, meant he could be home by the end of the summer. Please, Vin, she thought to herself, *please* keep your nose clean. She missed him so much sometimes, it was almost like a physical hurt. Like someone had chopped off her left arm.

Having put her toast down on the window ledge that also served as her dressing table, she picked up her black, boy's-style school pants from the floor. She shook them out and dressed quickly. It was getting late now, so she'd have to eat the rest of her toast on the way if she wanted to catch up with Carol. Shivering in the bitter cold as she buttoned up her school shirt, she had a glance in the triangle of broken mirror that was propped on the sill. The sight that greeted her was as unlike her mother's as it was possible to be. Hair still cut short, boyishly, just the way she preferred it, her face – well, it was the same face that always gazed back at her. A mask behind which so much was always going on. A mask that said 'queer', that said 'boy', that got taunted. Not least, more and more, by her own mother.

'Why'd you want to look such a scruff-bag, instead of a girl?' June kept nagging, 'You're 13, Titch. You want to make more of yourself. You'll never cop off with a lad looking like *that*.'

Fuck her, Titch thought now. *Fuck the lot of them*. She looked exactly the way she wanted to. They could think what they wanted. She'd always been a tomboy. Had always much preferred being like her brother than like her waster of a sister, and since Melvin – she shivered again – that monster, that *bastard* – no one was *ever* going to mistake her for a girlie girl.

Dressed and ready, and with the toast gone all soggy in her hand, she ran down the stairs and slammed the front door as she left, anxious to draw a physical line and forget about her own worries and catch up with Caz, who had enough worries of her own. Well, one, actually. That bastard Black Bobby. Who her mum never got shut of after all. Perhaps Caz should've taken a leaf from *her* book.

June was excited. So excited that it was like something bubbling away inside her. She drew the curtains in the living room and piled coal on the fire, dancing round the room as she went. Warmth. It was like a drug, to have coal in such quantity.

It made such a change to be able to come out of the bathroom and get dressed without shivering her tits off.

It made *everything* better, she decided. She picked up her fancy new bra and twirled it around her head before putting it on. Then she smiled. She really loved Jock just lately. She must do, she decided, because since what had happened, she'd even been happy to put up with his fumblings under the sheets, which were happening pretty much every night. That was money for you, wasn't it? While he was giving her his spoils – and the wherewithal to have all that glorious, glorious black stuff – she could just about tolerate anything.

Though it was hardly the crime of the century. Titch might think otherwise, but in the big scheme of things, it was hardly the Great bloody Train Robbery. She finished dressing, and allowed herself another leisurely cup of tea, before grabbing her bag and heading next door to Moira's.

The 'job' had been a gift born out of real, regular work. Jock, Maureen's Steven and their next-door neighbour, Billy, had, along with a few other blokes from around the estate, been offered a couple of weeks' work from one of the lads down the pub who ran a demolition firm. He'd got the contract to knock down a large office premises, and needed a team to go in for two weeks to strip out all the unwanted office furniture the departing tenants – a loan company, an insurance firm and an accountants – had left behind. The better bits were getting sold on, the rest going into skips, and this was where the estate lads came in. Offered cash in hand for the fortnight and a bonus for finishing on time, there were no shortage of men keen to be included.

But, as it turned out, there was a much greater bonus up for grabs, as Jock and Billy found out the first day. They'd been at it a couple of hours, manhandling desks and chairs down from

the loan company's office, when they decided to tackle some of
the filing cabinets. The saleable ones already gone, these were
all destined for the skips, having broken locks or being otherwise in a state of disrepair.

Jock had just opened the top drawer to make the one they
were currently hefting more manoeuvrable when he saw a sight
that stopped him in his tracks. The drawer, which was otherwise empty, contained a huge bundle of club cheques – 50
books, it turned out, each containing £50 worth. The most
unlikely – not to mention astonishing – sight he had seen in a
very long time.

Club cheques were a well-known form of currency round the
estate; a way for the chronically cash-strapped to help make
ends meet. Unlike cash itself, they could only be used to shop
in certain places, and the local loan company agents would go
round giving them out, from house to house – up to the limit
any one particular person was allowed – then collecting the
cash back on a week-by-week basis. Charges were high; you
often paid back more than you originally borrowed just in
interest – sometimes double the loan value – but for the hard-
up residents of places like the Canterbury Estate, these loans
were often the only way they had available to them to pay off
big bills or buy Christmas presents for their children.

Jock was astounded. Here were 50 books, seemingly just
abandoned. A full £2,500 worth of cheques. And as he pointed
out to Billy as soon at they'd got them out and inspected them,
they were in cabinets that were destined not for another office
building, but for skips; undetected, they would just get thrown
away.

A meeting was called between the lads and a plan of action
formed – the first being that Jock (having been the finder, now
the self-appointed mastermind) would slip out to the nearest

phone box, call his sister Maureen – who had a working phone
– tell her to go and knock up June, and for the pair of them to
meet the lads at lunchtime, in the Boy and Barrel pub in the
town centre.

By the time lunchtime had come around, they had searched
all the remaining drawers and cabinets, and had a haul of three
bundles of club cheques in all – with a total value of £7,500. It
was the sort of money that none of them had ever seen in their
lives and, though not actual cash, it represented a means to
make cash, by buying goods with the cheques and then selling
them on. They could be minted in no time at all.

'But we need to hold our horses,' Jock cautioned at lunch-
time, once they'd all gathered at the pub – him and June,
Steven and Maureen, Billy and his wife Moira, plus the two
younger lads that were working on the job with them, and
who'd get a handsome cut just for keeping their traps shut.
'We've got to be careful,' he went on, 'because we don't know
if or when they'll miss them. There's a chance they might realise they've left them, and go back to get them, then see they're
gone, and start asking questions.'

'You're not going to put them back, are you?' asked June,
who had by now stashed the bundle Jock had given her safely
in her bag. 'Not now we've got 'em. That would be fucking
bonkers!'

Jock flapped a dismissive hand at her. 'No,' he said. 'I've
already been thinking about that. We'll hang on to one bundle
– that one you've got. Be senseless not to do that. You and
Maureen can take it now and stash it safe at home. But we'll
leave the other two where they are and leave those cabinets till
last. That way, if they do come sniffing round trying to find
them, they'll turn up two, think that's the lot, and hopefully
won't miss the other one.'

'But what about after?' said Steven. 'What if they don't realise till after? I mean after the stuff has all gone down the tip and they realise the cheques have gone missing?'

'We wait,' Jock said. 'Once the job's done – assuming they didn't realise they were missing and come and get them – we stash the other books and wait till we're sure the coast's clear.'

'How long's that gonna be?' asked Billy. 'It could take a long time for them to realise, couldn't it?'

'Why would they do something so fucking stupid anyway?' June wanted to know. 'I mean, how could you miss seven and a half's grand's worth of cheques?'

'I was thinking about that too,' Jock said. 'Might be decimalisation. Might be that they're old books and they're going to get new decimal ones printed –'

'That wouldn't make any difference, you silly sod,' June corrected him. 'A pound is still a pound and a fiver's still a fiver. More likely they just changed the look of them anyway. They do that now and again, don't they?'

'Yeah, but where does that leave us?' asked Steven. 'Does that mean we can even use them?'

'Sure it means we can use them,' Jock reassured him. 'If we get our skates on, that is. As of now, they're still in use – they must be; they're no different to the ones we've always had, are they? No, they're fine, I'm sure of it.' He scanned the group. 'Don't you think?'

Everyone agreed. 'But what about once we use them to buy gear?' Maureen asked. 'What then? When the shop trades them in won't they know straight away? They've got serial numbers on them, haven't they? Won't they see from the figures? They have lists, don't they, of dodgy ones? Won't they suss us straight away?'

But Jock was confident. If they didn't realise the cheques were missing straight away, chances were that by the time the loan company got to hear of it, it would be much too late for them to actually *do* anything about it. They'd be long spent, long gone, no real way of tracing them. And with the bundles having gone missing while still intact, it might even be that they didn't even have a record in the first place, because the serial numbers would be logged against a borrower's name only when the cheques were handed out to them. No, they all agreed, it was watertight in that respect, and a buzz of excitement began building. Chances were, they all agreed, that they were obsolete books anyway – forgotten precisely because they were soon to be replaced.

'And even if they realise and get two of the books back,' Jock finished, grinning. 'They're not having *that* one.' He nodded towards June's handbag. 'Two and a half fucking *grand*!' He raised his glass.

After blowing all the family allowance on cider and whiskey, June had held a planning meeting round at her house that evening. Maureen and Steven had come round, as had Billy and Moira from next door, Barbara and Joe from across the road and their neighbours, Doreen and John. It had turned out to be something of a party. But a party with a purpose, a plan of action having been decided. As the men had done the hard work – and having found the cheques in the first place, it would now be down to the women to convert the cheques into cash. And the best way to do this, everyone agreed, would be for the women to share the cheques out and shop with them individually, buying booze – bottles of spirits, vodka, whiskey, rum and so on – which they could then tout round the pubs at half price.

And even at half price, they'd soon make a fortune – even with just the one book of cheques. Then they'd pool it before splitting the proceeds. After that, the cash would be their own to do with as they pleased.

A brilliant plan, they all agreed, put together in a happy, drunken haze. What could possibly go wrong?

Chapter 10

'C'mon McKellan! Let's have you, you lazy little fucker!' shouted Mr Downey as he banged on Vinnie's bed posts with his keys.

Vinnie groaned. 'Aw, fuck off,' he mumbled, conscious of the light spilling in on him, of the biscuity morning smell of sweaty male teenage bodies, of the others – lucky buggers – still all snoring. He turned in his bed to face the wall and found himself nose to crotch with Suzi Quatro. A much nicer prospect all round.

'What was that?' Downey barked at him. 'What was that, ginger nut?'

'I meant fuck off, *sir*,' Vinnie corrected, pulling the rough grey borstal blanket over his head.

Like everything else about Redditch, the blanket was rough; rough as hell. Where approved school had been all about trying to educate lads like Vinnie, borstal had a different approach – the 'short sharp shock' method – the goal being to teach them a lesson they'd never forget, and so keep them away from adult prisons. In reality, though Vinnie'd not yet seen much of adult prisons, he'd certainly heard about them, and what he'd heard was that, in adult prison, you got to do what you wanted. Yeah, you were locked up, and yeah, you had to work to join privileges, but, outside of that you could do your own thing and chill – not have some tit banging on at you at all hours. No, to his mind, being here was *far* worse.

Downey, one of the officers – or screws, as the boys called them – was having none of his whining, much less his half-awake attempt at humour. He never did. Because he was a cunt. He ripped the blanket back, pulling off the sheet at the same time, exposing Vinnie, shivering in his vest and under-pants. 'It's 5.00 a.m., lad,' he pointed out. 'You know the drill. If you'd used your fucking tiny brain yesterday, you'd have had another hour in bed, wouldn't you? And then I wouldn't be here witnessing your equally tiny fucking cock shrivelling up in your filthy skidders, would I?'

With no other options open to him, Vinnie levered himself up and sprang from his bed, flexing and unflexing his fingers. He made a fist out of one of them and thought just how much he'd love to turn round and slam it right into Downey's hairy old-man knackers. He unballed it. 'Get out, then while I get dressed,' he said instead, feeling the draught snake round his ankles. 'Or do you wanna watch me take a piss as well?'

'Two minutes, you cheeky cunt,' Downey snorted as he left the room. 'Or I'll be back here to drag you out, got it?'

It was the hill and the medicine ball for Vinnie this morning, the legacy of yesterday's little 'incident' in the canteen. He groaned as he threw aside his grey prison garb and reached for PE shorts and T-shirt.

It was a far worse punishment, to his mind, than getting a good hiding. He would rather take a cricket bat across the arse any day rather than the pointless business of trudging up and down a bastard hill for an hour, carrying a fuck-off leather ball that weighed a ton.

Not only that, but he was still expected to do the usual two-mile run with the other lads straight afterwards. And all of it happened before breakfast. And if he or any of the others were late getting back from their run, they would miss their morning feast – (and it would bloody feel like one, after that lot) of porridge with jam and bread. No excuses. They were late back, they got nothing. They would simply have to wait till lunch-time, which meant the fat lads, the ones who loved their food the most, had the most to lose if they didn't make it.

And they often didn't. The regime at Redditch was tough as well as rough. Set in the middle of remote woodland, inside a huge, barbed-wire topped perimeter fence, it put Vinnie in mind of a concentration camp. You could run a long way – their daily two-mile run took place inside it – and know you were getting nowhere at all. It really was like you'd been snatched from the normal world. Designed to put off would-be serial offenders from going back into law breaking, it ran a programme that took no prisoners. It was do or – well, if not exactly 'die trying', spend half the time wishing you fucking *were* dead. After the run and breakfast, it was dorm cleaning, every single fucking day. Vinnie'd never seen anywhere as pointlessly pristine as the dorms at Redditch. Everything had to be spotless – everything.

He'd always thought his mam was bad enough; always on at him about being a sloth and leaving a trail of muck behind him, but in here it was ridiculous. It wasn't unheard of for a screw to insist that toilet floors got cleaned, inch by stinking inch, with a toothbrush. It was back-breaking work, and the only good thing about it was that it filled the day and stopped him thinking too much. He missed his mum, mad as she was, and he wasn't afraid to admit it – to himself if not to any other fucker.

When they weren't cleaning they were usually doing one of two things – either lessons, if they were school age, or trades, if they weren't. Bricklaying, very often, which didn't appeal to him any more than it had at the approved school. Pointless, to Vinnie's mind, not to mention brainless. Anyway, how many bricklayers did the world fucking need?

Yeah, a few got the benefit of going out with proper bricklayers, in the real world, but for most of them it was a case of practising in the school grounds, building walls and then dismantling them again till they learned to do it right. Vinnie preferred doing gardening. At least the gardening had a point to it. They had this area where they grew potatoes and carrots, which were actually used in the kitchen. Flowers and herbs too, so you felt you were making something useful at least.

Then, at last, if there had been no misdemeanours during the day, they were all allowed to take part in recreation in the evenings – usually TV and cards, playing table tennis or darts. Vinnie was good at darts, because his dad – who played for the pub team – had taught him, but more often than not he would leave the rec room early and go back to his bunk and get stuck into a book. You had to hide away to do that – to be seen reading was to get the piss taken out of you and, as Vinnie was trying to establish that he wasn't going to be one to mess with, things like that could put a dent in his plan. He loved to read though, and even if he only had a few books at his disposal, he didn't mind reading them over and over – especially the Dickens. He was just grateful for the chance to go somewhere else in his head.

Finally dressed, Vinnie went out to meet Downey, slamming the door as he did so. He grinned, knowing the three lads he currently shared the room with would wake up and not be able to get back to sleep. Good. Because he couldn't stick any of them. Henry with his 'groovy' this and 'groovy' that every

other fucking sentence, then Mick Hanley and Mickey
Timpson, both older than Vinnie, and both with the same
hobby – fucking pushing him about.

Though they might think again after yesterday, he told himself
as, Downey having given him the medicine ball, as promised,
he struggled up the steep and muddy hill, cradling it to his
stomach like it was a baby.

Knowing he'd caused such a ruckus was at least some sort of
consolation. Because, to his mind, the punishment wasn't fair.
He wasn't going to give the screws the satisfaction of knowing
he felt that, obviously, but what burned most right now – well,
after the pain in his throat from all the panting – was the injustice of being punished for doing right.

And he had done right – no one would ever be able to tell
him differently. It had been building up and up and enough had
been enough. So he'd stood up for the little guy and faced-
down the bully. Since when did that sort of thing deserve
punishment?

Not that he'd have done things any differently, *whatever* the
punishment. He'd done the right thing and he'd do the same
again – every time – because if there was one thing he fucking
hated it was bullies.

Kevin had come to Redditch only a month ago. He was the
same age as Vinnie, or thereabouts, just turned 17, but you'd
never have known it, because Kevin was tiny. He was scruffy,
too, and didn't seem to have come with any decent clothes.
Where the other lads, during their down time, wore flares and
tie-dyed T-shirts, Kevin seemed to live in nothing but old black
school trousers and once-white shirts.

He was a natural target, and all the other lads would duly
take the piss out of him, taunting him and trying to trip him up

on the gravel and stuff, but there was this one boy especially – a lad called Frank Pemberton.

Frank was also 17 but he was built like a brick shit-house, with a thick neck and short, wiry, black hair. He was inside for assault and aggravated burglary, and as soon as he was 18 he would be transferred to a mainstream prison to finish his sentence. So far Vinnie, being prudent and also wary, had kept away from him, but he didn't need to know him personally to know plenty enough about him; that he was mean and relentless and a persistent and cruel bully who, once he had found a target would never leave off tormenting him. Kevin was that target, it seemed, and Frank would regularly hunt him down, pin him to the ground and burn him with cigarettes for pleasure.

For some reason, Vinnie liked Kevin. He didn't know why, but he reminded him of a boy he knew a bit called Colin, back on the estate. Colin's family were dirt poor as well, the poor fucker, and he didn't own a single item of clothing that fitted. He was always starving, as well, as his mam never made him dinner, and he always had a snotty, runny nose. But none of that mattered. Not to Colin, or to Vinnie. He was a mate – funny as fuck and always up for a lark. A good kid. One worth defending.

And that was the thing with Kevin. Like Colin, he was a good lad. So Vinnie couldn't, for the life of him, understand what he was doing there. All it seemed he'd done was a bit of nicking. That was all. And it wasn't even as if he'd nicked anything that bad, either, by all accounts – just robbing food and clothes and that, and only because he didn't have a dad.

Vinnie had Frank's number from the first time he'd seen him in action, extorting cigarettes, like they always fucking did, from a smaller, weaker boy. And though he'd have to be careful

– not wanting to scupper his chances of an early release – he'd started plotting Frank's downfall straight away. He'd had to be patient, too, because it had taken a while for a perfect opportunity to present itself. But the day before, in the dinner queue, had proved to be the one.

He had timed his manoeuvre equally carefully. Making sure he was next to Frank in queue for serving, he accidentally bumped into him as he passed his plate forward for beans. It had the desired result, half a spoonful of beans ending up splattering onto Frank's tray, and provoking the predictable (and desired) response. He turned on Vinnie, furious. 'You fucking cunt, McKellan!' he snapped at him. 'You did that on purpose!'

'Did I fuck!' Vinnie argued, looking pleadingly at the screw who was serving. 'You saw that, didn't you, sir?' he said. 'I tripped!'

Predictably, the screw ignored him, even though he'd clearly heard him.

'Just keep out of my way, you ginger cunt, or you're dead,' Frank said to him, as the screw just carried on serving the next in line.

Vinnie grinned as Frank then headed off with his tray, making sure that he hung back now and kept his distance. He collected the rest of his food and a mug of tea and as he walked through the dining hall, made a note of where Frank had just sat down, and started making his way to the table opposite. This meant squeezing past Frank's table, which very much included Frank. Balancing his tray above his shoulder with one hand and with the mug of tea in the other, Vinnie leaned down to Frank's ear as he got to him and whispered, 'Touch young Kevin again, you scruffy bastard, and *you're* the one who's dead.' He then tipped the tea all down the shocked Frank's neck and back.

Frank leaped up, then, screaming, knocking the mug from Vinnie's hand, and within seconds the two boys were surrounded by screws.

'He tripped me up, sir,' Vinnie protested, as Mr Green grabbed him by the shoulders. 'And all cos I bumped into him in the queue!'

Frank himself was crying now. Spluttering and actually *crying*. Not so much the 'big I am' *now*, then, thought Vinnie. Good.

'Well?' Green wanted to know, his gaze seeking out all the lads in the vicinity. 'You saw that? Is what McKellan says true?'

There was the gratifying and immediate chorus of 'Yes, sir' that Vinnie had been counting on – bar his henchmen, they hated Frank, and they mostly loved Vinnie, so he'd have been seriously concerned if it *hadn't* happened. Know-it-all Downey though, watching from the sidelines with that assessing gaze of his – *he* hadn't been convinced, Vinnie could tell. He'd been watching Vinnie carefully throughout all the questions afterwards, and even though he couldn't prove anything (there was nothing to *be* proved – only Frank's version), he decided that he'd punish Vinnie anyway.

And that had been a learning curve in itself, Vinnie thought, as he toiled up the hill for what must surely be the last time. An hour? It already felt like half a day. He looked down at Downey, stationed at the bottom, checking his stop watch every minute or so. He'd had a lot to learn in the last pissing years of his life, and chief among the lessons had been one he hadn't even realised needed learning – that the screws seemed to be almost as sharp as he was. Not quite, but almost – certainly a good deal sharper than most ordinary run-of-the-mill adults who couldn't see they were being manipulated even if you went up and fucking told them – particularly his dozy mare of a mother. Almost, he thought, coming back down, breathing heavily, but feeling surprisingly fit and lithe now. Almost but not quite. Never that.

'No point in a shower, lad,' Downey said as Vinnie came down the hill for the last time. 'Go get a cup of water then it's straight back out here for your run.' His gaze met Vinnie's and he held it there, his eyes narrowing as he did so. 'Maybe you'll think twice about trying to pull the wool over my eyes in the future, eh, kid?'

'Piece of piss, sir,' Vinnie laughed as he trotted back to the front door, passing the lads that were amassing for their run just outside it. *The men who learn endurance*, he thought triumphantly, recalling one of his favourite Dickens quotes, *are they who call the whole world, brother*. Yeah, right, Downey, he thought. Something for *you* to bear in mind.

Fuck the burning in his thighs, fuck the run. Fuck Downey. He wasn't going to let the fat twat get one over on *him*.

Chapter II

By the time Josie came home from school on Friday afternoon, a couple of weekends later, June had already gone out. Noticing two roll-ups on the coffee table along with a note, Josie lit herself a fag as she tried to decipher her mother's letter.

Titch

Left you ten bob in the junk drawer. Get some chips and pop. If you need anything, go up to our Lyndsey's. Me and your dad will be late so don't be out all hours. Bed at 10.

Love, Mam

Josie snorted as she screwed up the note and threw it on the fire. That's that then, she thought, might as well go sit round at Carol's for a bit. It would be better than being in on her own all night; something she'd been having to do a lot just lately, now her mam and dad were swanning around the estate, flashing all their cash. She didn't bother getting changed out of her uniform. After all it was Friday, no school tomorrow, so it could stay. Grabbing her coat and the money, she flicked off the light and went back out onto the streets.

The atmosphere in the Bull was getting raucous. Jock, June and the rest of the 'club cheque gang', as they had recently named themselves, were crammed in together in one of the booths in the corner of the pub, where they'd been drinking steadily since the early afternoon.

There were two ashtrays in the centre of the table, one overflowing with cigarette ends, the other stuffed with £5 notes and coins. This was the 'kitty', the pool of money being rapidly depleted in the cause of getting them even more pissed than they already were.

'Hey, Jock,' June said, laughing as she watched her husband lurch sideways, while staggering to his feet to go to the bar. She passed him a couple of notes from the collection in the ashtray. 'Get some whiskey chasers while you're up there,' she ordered. 'I might feel like dancing later, and I can't do my Tina Turner without some of the hard stuff inside me.'

The others all laughed on cue as June also hauled herself upright, having to grasp the table edge to do so. She then made an attempt, only partly successfully, to twirl an increasingly unsteady Jock around.

'Sit down, you silly old get,' Jock slurred, pulling away from her. 'And let's have a bit less of the big fucking spender routine in here. You know what nosey bastards they all are.'

Jock was worried. And particularly about his mouthy wife. Despite the growing haze that was blurring the sharp edges of his thinking, he was aware that they'd been attracting suspicious looks. As they would – it wasn't like no one knew them, was it? Pretty much everyone knew where they came from and it didn't take a brain surgeon to work out that as they didn't normally have two pennies to scratch their arses with, they were acting a bit flash with their money.

In fact, looking at them now – as he tried to, steadying himself against the nearest chair – they looked like they'd come into millions. Which would of course make people wonder what the fuck they'd been up to – even Don the landlord must be wondering what the hell was going on. Because he didn't know either. And they weren't going to tell him. As Moira had said, it made no sense to shit on their own doorstep, so she and June had sold the cheap booze to town-centre pubs only. And they should maybe – least for the moment – be drinking in them too.

Jock blinked hard a couple of times to try and clear his vision. He was getting a bad feeling about the way things were going. Yeah, *he* knew that, all right. Knew how careful they had to be now. He must just make sure his bloody wife stopped forgetting. Stopped flashing the cash in front of the neighbours, stop behaving like a kid in a fucking sweet shop, because if she wasn't careful, she'd have the whole lot crashing down on the lot of them. And who'd be blamed when she shit hit the fan? *He* would.

Josie climbed over the fence of Carol's front garden, taking care not to land in any dog shit as she lowered herself down. The gate had been tied up with wire so that their stupid German Shepherd, Blue, didn't get out, which meant that if she was in the garden when Josie climbed over – having no choice – the stupid animal would start barking and jumping up at her, think-ing she was breaking in. And then, having sniffed her, try to lick her to death.

She wasn't around now, though, so she dropped to her feet unmolested and unlicked and, in the silence, could hear the sound of raised voices.

As she went down the path she could make out specific words, many of them swear words – it sounded like a loud argu-ment coming from inside. She banged at the door, hoping that this would be enough to stop it. She hated it when Carol's mam, Tina, was on one. She could be a right vicious bitch.

It took a while for the door to be opened and then only a crack, through which the tear-stained face of Caz peeped through. 'Oh, Titch, come in,' she whispered. 'They're at it again upstairs. I'm fucking sick of it. He's off his bleeding rocker, that black bastard.'

Josie squeezed through the gap in the door, pushing the stupid dog inside with her foot. 'Get in, you silly mare,' she said as she finally got inside. 'What's up with them two then?' she said, fussing over the dog long enough to satisfy her demand for attention.

'Fuck knows,' Carol replied, 'but he's just given me a slap for sticking up for me mum. He was calling her a slag and all sorts, and I'm not gonna sit there and say nowt about it, am I?'

Josie and Carol went to sit in the kitchen, trying to close off the noise coming from upstairs. They could hear what sounded like furniture being thrown around as well as the occasional angry scream from Tina, which made them start, but didn't seem to signify that he was getting the upper hand. In any case, already at the sharp end of Black Bobby's hand, Carol knew better than to interfere again.

'Do you want to come round to our house?' Josie suggested. 'There's no one in, and at least you wouldn't have to listen to it.'

Carol gave her a weak smile. 'I better not. That bastard might kill her if he knows I've gone out. No, better stay. I'll make us a cup of tea, eh. They'll stop soon – they always do.' She grimaced. 'Then I'll have to turn the record player on, so we don't have to listen to 'em doing you know what.'

Josie cringed, the horrible thing always lurking at the edges of her mind still. She thought of men, and what they did, and what they did it with, and she recoiled. She couldn't help it. Perhaps she'd never be able to. And Caz too, she knew, even though it had been a while since Black Bobby had tried it on with her. Caz didn't know why but she'd grown about a foot in the last year, it felt like. So maybe it was that. He didn't dare. They exchanged a look.

'Shush!' Carol said suddenly.

'What?'

'Silence,' she then mouthed, nodding her head towards the ceiling. She crept to the kitchen door and opened it an inch or two. 'Oh fuck, it's him. Coming down.'

Carol scuttled back towards the sink and turned on the tap to fill the kettle, just as Black Bobby walked in.

'What the fuck's she doing here?' he demanded, pointing at Josie.

Josie hung her head. She couldn't even bear to look at him. 'Her mam and dad are out, so she's come to see me,' Carol said mildly. 'Do you want a cuppa?'

Bobby reached Carol in three strides and belted her round the back of the head. 'No I fucking don't, and what've you been told about bringing people round here?'

Carol winced and put her hand up to guard against another whack. 'She's just come round for a bit, that's all. Where's me mam?'

'None of your business, you nosey little cunt.' Bobby reached round Carol and filled a glass with water. He then turned to Josie as he gulped it down, his Adam's apple bobbing. 'And you can fuck off an' all,' he said, having drained it in one. 'We're not fucking babysitters. Sling your hook.'

Carol stood behind Bobby, wildly shaking her head, but Josie stood up, even so. No way was she sitting around for more of this crap. It was worse than home, plus Black Bobby scared her. She couldn't understand why Caz's mum was still with him. But then she knew she didn't understand much about anything where men were concerned. Only that some of them – a few anyway – were just horrible.

'You want to come to mine, Caz?' she tried again, but Carol shook her head, as Josie expected. She wouldn't go anywhere without checking that her mum was okay.

'Okay,' she said. 'See you tomorrow then, okay?' Then she let herself out, slipping into the night quickly to stop Blue trying to follow. Maybe she'd pop round to Lyndsey's instead. It would be good to see her nephew and nieces, if not her stupid sister and revolting Robbo.

Josie and Lyndsey didn't really get along. Never had. With such an age gap, they'd never been close to one another, and since Lynds had moved in with and had kids by her last horrible boyfriend, there was little chance they ever would be either.

That her sister took drugs made Lyndsey a proper idiot in Josie's eyes, and she had abhorred Robbo since the first time she'd met him. She blamed him – for meeting her sister just when she'd been left by the last moron she'd shacked up with, for dragging her into their seedy druggy lifestyle, for keeping her poor when she could barely afford her kids. She was bleeding lucky social services hadn't taken them away.

And she wasn't the only one who found Lyndsey a waste of space. Her mam and dad hardly ever saw their elder daughter, even they only lived a few houses down on the same street. They never called up and Lynds never came down. They might pass and chat for a minute of two on the street, if one or the other was going to the shops or something, but it was only ever small talk because June had no time for drugs and druggies – and if she wanted to see her grandkids or them her, she'd always just send Josie or Vinnie up to fetch them back.

It was sad but it was the way it was. And would keep being, Josie reckoned, and much as she didn't want to be around

Lyndsey or Robbo, she loved her little nieces and nephew and she knew they'd be pleased to see her now.

She ran most of the way back from Caz's – and out on the street, since it was dark – hoping that when she got there the first thing she smelt wouldn't be the dreaded wacky baccy. She hated the smell of it – it made her retch – and she hated what it did; made everyone who smoked it turn into grinning idiots.

Walking around the back of the house, as she knew she'd never get an answer from the front door, Josie tapped on the window and tried to peer in.

'Auntie Titch!' a small voice called from the back door. Josie smiled as she saw Robbie coming outside. He was naked apart from a pair of grubby underpants.

'Ooh, get back inside, Robbie, you'll freeze out here!' she told him, ushering him back into the house.

'We have to be quiet, Titch,' he whispered now, putting a finger to his lips. 'Everyone else is asleep and I'm doing colouring in.'

Josie closed the back door as quietly she could and followed her nephew into the front room. It was a pigsty as usual, cushions scattered across the floor, with little Lou and Sammy fast asleep on top of them. Cans of Special Brew and ashtrays filled the entire surface of the coffee table, and an overturned tobacco tin and papers were strewn across the shaggy fireside rug. In the midst of all this, entirely as she'd expected, Lyndsey and Robbo were top-and-tailing, spark out, on the couch.

'You want me to make you a pipe up, Auntie Titch?' asked Robbie, climbing back up to his seat at the table. He was all of eight years old now, and the picture of perfect innocence. It was heartbreaking. He grinned and giggled at her. 'The idiot showed me how to do it properly.' He pointed to Robbo, and quickly put his finger to his lips again. 'But you're only allowed to call him that when he's sleeping.'

Josie pulled out the other chair and sat down on it. 'No, you're alright, kiddo,' she said. 'I don't smoke that stuff. It sends you loopy, just like the idiot. I can't stop long anyway. I just called in to say hello, that's all.'

Robbie frowned, then brightened as his eyes alighted on some of his artwork. He held up a picture. 'D'ya like my fire engine?' he asked. 'I did it to send to Uncle Vin. D'you think he'll like it?'

'He'll love it, kid. And I'll send it with my next letter. So you keep it safe and I'll call back for it, yeah?' He slipped it under his drawing pad, and as he did so, she noticed he was goose-pimpled. 'You warm enough, Robbie?'

He shrugged and looked up at her. 'I'm okay,' he said. 'We got no gas till Monday, I don't think, so we can't have the fire on. I can always get mum's dressing-gown though.'

Fuming that her sister had once again put beer and fags before heating for the kids, she felt in her pocket for the coins June had left her for chips, marched into the kitchen and put a couple of shillings in the gas meter. She would make do with toast once she got home. She might even have some beans with it, she thought. She wasn't in the mood for walking down to the chippy anyway, she decided, as, stepping over her sleeping nieces, she went to put the fire back on.

She then gathered up Sammy and Lou, one by one, and took them both up to bed, while Robbie got back to his colouring, though this time in the armchair, nearer to the fire. And throughout all of this, her stupid sister and her equally stupid boyfriend never even stirred. Not even once. They really were beyond belief.

'Here,' she said to Robbie finally, having found him a stray chocolate biscuit in the tin at the back of the kitchen cupboard, 'got a treat for you. Make sure you don't touch that fire, okay? I've got to go now. And off to bed with you when you're tired – and that's an order, mush.'

Robbie grinned. 'I'll do you a picture next, if you like, Auntie Titch. So's you can put it on your bedroom wall and make it pretty. What shall I do? You want a pony?'

'I'd like a unicorn,' she answered immediately. 'That's like a horse but with a horn. Like a rhino has, only prettier. They have flowing manes, and they're white and they're magical creatures.'

Robbie frowned. 'But I don't have a white colouring pencil. An' the paper's white, too, so –'

'Make mine a rainbow one, then,' she said. 'Any colours you like. Make it a colour-changing one, one that's magic.'

Just like it would be a magic trick if her sister shaped up and looked after her kiddies properly, she thought sadly as she made the short journey home.

It was just coming up to ten by the time Josie'd eaten and gone to bed, having had her beans on toast in front of the telly. Still only early, but she wanted to be sure she was asleep before June and Jock got in. They were bad enough sober, but she definitely didn't want to have to lie there and listen while they crashed about, pissed as farts, downstairs.

Not that she could sleep. She hating being in the house on her own all the time while her mam and dad got pissed down the pub. At least Caz had a dog to keep her company. She missed Vinnie so much, particularly on evenings like this when, alone in the empty house, she felt so lonely.

She was also kept awake by a simmering sense of anger – was she the only one who cared anything about her family? Her mam and dad were up to God knew what – she didn't even want to think about it – and her sister didn't seem to give a shit about anyone or anything – least of all her three poor little kids. And as for Vinnie … well, Vinnie was locked away somewhere, wasn't he? Did *he* care? Did he think about her? Worry about her the way she worried about him? She hoped so, but what could he do about anything in any case? Even Caz – Caz had loads of her own shit going on, didn't she? Why was life so complicated? So bloody miserable? She turned over to face the wall, feeling suddenly tearful. Why couldn't her brother just come home and make things better?

She was still tossing and turning an hour later, when she heard the door go. Which was odd – it was still too early for her mum and dad to be home, surely? So who could it be? She never locked the door as June never took a key and besides they only had one. She sat up and listened, scared.

She always kept her door shut – she could never get to sleep with it open – and watching it creak open now, spilling light from the landing into a block across the floorboards, she clutched her bedspread to her chest, hardly daring to breathe. Was she going to die now? Was she about to be murdered in her bed, just like the old lady in one of the books Vinnie had told her about?

'Alright, Titch?' It was Robbo. She'd know that voice anywhere. And that silhouette, all scraggy limbs, in the doorway. She exhaled, relieved. Much as she couldn't stand the sight of him, he was a much more welcome sight than the one her imagination had suggested might be standing there.

He looked pissed, of course, and she already knew he was stoned. 'God!' she said. 'Thanks for that! You really scared me, Robbo!'

'Sorr' bout that,' he said, stumbling into the room unsteadily, blocking the light out. 'You haven' got any more money, have you? There's fuck all in and our Rob said you'd been round an' that, and I'm starving. I'd kill for a bag of chips.'

'So would I,' she said angrily. 'Only I had to put it in your sodding meter. Because it looked like you'd spent your gas money on beer and dope! *You're* starving. What about poor Robbie?'

Robbo blinked at her, then shuffled a little further towards the bed. Then over-balanced, and landed heavily, half sitting, half lying across her legs. He smelt rancid. Of stale beer and old fag smoke. He disgusted her.

'You cheeky little fucker,' he said mildly. 'We get money tomorrow, okay? It's just tonight, that's all. Go on, Titch. Please?'

Josie recoiled, pulling her legs up and hugging her knees to her chest. 'I told you. I don't have any. Now get off my bed, Robbo, and go back home. I want to get to sleep. And me mam and dad'll be back in a minute.' She clutched the blanket to her chin again, all too easily imagining a scenario where he passed out again – out cold, on her bed.

But it seemed she had misread his mental state.

'Oooh!' he said, trying to rise again, unsteadily. 'Look at you, all prim –' he mimed her hands clutching at the bedspread. 'You gone all shy with me tonight, Titch? Gone all scaredy?'

He laughed then, and made a lunge for the bedspread, grabbing a handful of material. 'What you hiding under there, eh?' he said, yanking on it. 'What you got in there, you little fucker? Something for the lads? Go on, Titch. Don't be a spoilsport. Show us your tits!'

This couldn't be happening, not again. This simply couldn't be happening. 'Fuck off! Fuck off, you dirty bastard!' she screamed. 'I swear I'll tell, I will! I'll tell right now, soon as me mam's home! Get OUT!'

Robbo jumped back as if she'd slapped her, then as soon as he was out of kicking range, put his hands on his skinny hips and stared at her. 'Fucking hell, Titch,' he said. 'Calm *down*! I was only messing about! I'm not going to touch you.' He threw his hands up, the palms gleaming palely at her. 'No *way* was I going to touch you! No fucking *way*. You should be so lucky, kid,' he finished, stumbling back out the same unsteady way he'd come in, then clattering noisily back down the stairs.

Josie ran across and shut the door again, wishing he'd fallen down them and died at the bottom, then pulled her chest of drawers across to block it as best she could. Then she got back into bed and curled into a tight trembling ball.

Lucky? Luck could leave her well alone, then.

'Stop shivering!' Downey screamed, 'you soft little bastards! Get yourselves in fucking line, quick sharp!'

Having been dragged from their beds at 6 a.m., the lads from C Block had woken to two barked-out bits of news from Mr Downey, and neither of them were good. One was that they were to form three orderly lines out in the yard – while still clad only in their underpants – and the other was that they were going to be punished.

Vinnie groaned wearily as they made their way outside. What now? Frank again? He hoped so. Hoped the fucker got shit raining down on him on a daily basis. Though the balance had now shifted, which brought him great pleasure. He had a loyal fan in Kevin, now he knew Vinnie had his back, and Frank knew to keep his distance. Job done.

Lining up, Vinnie turned to the boy next to him, Blond Barry, a lad from further down his wing. He was standing there shivering so much that his teeth were actually chattering. 'Wonder what's gone off?' Vinnie whispered, rubbing his hands vigorously up and down his upper arms. 'What do you think? Bet that spaz Pemberton's done something again. Pound to a penny, isn't it? God, I'm fucking *freezing*. Whatever it is, this cunt had better hurry up – I'm not missing my scoff for no fucker.'

Barry pulled a face. 'Dream on, Vinnie,' he said. 'If they say we miss brekkie we miss brekkie and that's that.'

That was Barry all over, that was. Defeatist. One of those lads that always said they just wanted to do their time and keep their heads down – which meant they would take any fucking thing that came their way.

Not that Downey seemed to want to drag things out in any case. 'Right,' he boomed, his breath forming a small cloud in front of him. 'Father Duffy has informed me that one of you little fucking heathens has been nicking his communion breads.' He paused to scowl at them, scanning the boys' expressions. 'They were there before your block went to Mass this week,' he continued, 'and gone immediately after. So your rooms are being searched as we speak and woe betide the robbing little bastard when we find him. Mr Conlan is conducting the search and you'll remain out here till he's done. Anyone got any fucking objections?'

A collective low groan was the only response. Everyone knew what this meant. Conlan was an even bigger bastard than Downey, and anyone who had given him reason to be annoyed with them this week would now get their rooms completely trashed. Which, in turn, would mean a minimum of five days in the block, three of them spent on basic rations of bread and water. Most of the lads didn't actually mind the five days but, depending on who it was handing out the punishment, that word 'minimum' was key. You could get 10 days, if they felt like it – and Conlan often felt like it – or even 15, and that was a killer.

They stood for 10 minutes – time enough to get frostbite, Vinnie reckoned, or, at the very least, your nuts shrunk to raisins – before Conlan and Duffy came outside. And to a collective lowering of anxious shoulders as they saw what Conlan carried, which was a small plastic bag which looked like it held the communion wafers, or, more correctly, the 'body of Christ'. Well, 'correctly' if you believed that shit, anyway.

They walked straight to Downey, and Conlan whispered something in his ear, which immediately elicited a grin. A sadistic grin, too, the kind he was best at. He walked towards the lads then, and then along the rows, stepping on bare feet as he did so, being careful not to miss anyone out.

Vinnie clamped his teeth together and clenched his stomach as Downey passed through his own row, feeling the hot gust of his breath as he paused momentarily, leaning his weight to maximum effect.

That was what Downey did – liked to shit them up, make them wonder if it was their turn, pausing here and there, sometimes backing up and taking a second pass on some hapless quaking fucker. But today it wasn't Vinnie's turn – he had better things to do with his time than nick fucking communion wafers, frankly – and Downey eventually fetched up at, and stayed in front of, a half-caste lad in the middle of the second row.

'So, Francis,' he said softly, but still loud enough that everyone could hear him, 'you thieving black bastard. Fancied a bit of Father Duffy's communion, did you? What's up, didn't he have no fucking bananas?'

The lad's name was Kenny Francis, and he'd been in borstal nine months, for nicking cars. Even with Vinnie's side-on view, it was clear by his expression that it hadn't been him who'd committed this particular crime, but if Downey had him singled out it was odds-on that didn't matter – he must have pissed someone off at some point and was now going to pay for it. Vinnie wondered who the someone was who'd planted it – some full-on cocky sod; must be. Because Kenny Francis wasn't a lad to be messed with – not if you had any sense. He definitely wouldn't take this lying down.

Or from Downey either. 'Fuck off!' he responded. 'That's not come from my room and you know it. Fucking risk the block for a few wafers? Do I look like a spaz?'

'No, Francis,' Downey said, leaning in towards his face, 'you look like a wog.'

Just as everyone knew would happen, the moment the words were spoken, Kenny immediately took a swing for Downey. And just as everyone knew would also happen, Conlan was there in an instant, and both screws started battering him with batons.

He put up a mammoth fight, but he was pinned down within minutes. Vinnie and the rest of the block could only stand there and watch in disgust as the screws dragged him, bloodied and beaten, towards the shower blocks.

'Let's hope Father Duffy had a wank this morning,' Vinnie whispered, to no one in particular, 'or Francis will get another arse-whipping in the showers.'

Some of the lads around him giggled nervously, but no one answered. They'd all heard the rumours about the priest – and knew they were more than rumours, too; they'd all at one time or another seen the state of the lads who had been summoned to 'meetings' with him. If that was what Kenny Francis had coming, no one wanted to even think about it, let alone talk about it.

'Go on, then!' Father Duffy shouted now, as he hurried along to join the others in the showers. 'Get off back to your block, boys, or you'll miss breakfast!'

'Well, the rest of us should be safe then,' Vinnie quipped as he and the others jogged back. 'You know what they say – once you've had black, you never turn back.'

He felt a clip across his head as Mick Hanley cuffed him. 'Shurrup, you fucking queen, and get a shift on, will you? It's Friday. Jam duff day. Come *on*.'

Mick sprinted ahead and Vinnie followed him, the tension dissipated. It was always like that when someone else had it coming, the poor bastard. A pity, but also a relief: it wasn't *him*. All his thoughts were now focussed on breakfast.

The atmosphere in the dining hall was predictably subdued. Everyone knew about the room searches and they all knew that somebody from C Block would – right this very minute – be taking some kind of brutal punishment for something they hadn't done, because of something they *had* done to annoy another lad higher up the pecking order.

The lads from Vinnie's block were especially quiet. Each of them knew their rooms would have been well and truly trashed now, and that any precious, tucked-away bits of baccy, sweets or chocolate would have been stolen for the benefit of the fat bastard screws. A shake-down wasn't pleasant any time and, coupled with the probable fate of Francis at the hands of Duffy, it would, Vinnie knew, set the mood for the rest of the day.

The screws weren't gone long. The lads were still only half-way through their breakfast when Downey and Conlan returned, expressions set, either side of a now broken-looking Kenny Francis. They escorted him up to the counter to get a tray of food and then quickly guided him back out, through the now silent dining hall. He would be going down to the block for at least five days, everyone knew, and Vinnie wondered what he had *really* done for them to be so keen to get him off the main landings.

'He'll have done fuck all,' Mick answered when Vinnie asked him. 'Them cunts are just a bunch of racist bastards. They're just trying to break him down, that's all. Just doing it because they fucking can. Scum, the lot of them.' He shook his head and pushed the remainder of his breakfast away. 'Poor cunt will have had Father Duffy up his fucking arse, just because his face don't fit. That's how it works, Vin.'

Vinnie gave an involuntary shudder. The thought of it was putting him off his jam duff as well. And with the grim image came a sudden and intense sense of claustrophobia. A kind of nausea. He needed to be out of this sick, depraved hell. 'I've got to get out of this fucking hole, Mick,' he said. 'If that fucker comes near me, I'll kill the cunt, I know I will.'

Mick laughed. 'You'll be alright, McKellan,' he said. 'Duffy's not into ginger snaps.' He clapped Vinnie on the back as he scraped back his chair. 'Must dash, got a fun-packed day building walls ahead. So have you. Or are you doing your Percy Thrower bit? Either way, don't work too hard, mush, okay?'

Vinnie smiled as Mick left, his mood lifted slightly. He wasn't that bad, as far as roommates went. He could be quite entertaining when he wasn't slapping Vinnie about, and today Vinnie needed a laugh. He downed the rest of his chocolate and then went to check the damage in his room in the half hour he had to kill before he was due to meet his team down in the visitors' grounds.

Once in there, his mood plummeted again. Surveying the chaos in the one place he felt he could let his guard down, he felt a bad feeling mushroom in the pit of his stomach. It was the same feeling that assaulted him regularly these days; a mishmash of loneliness because he so missed his mum and his little sister, and anger and frustration and weariness. It was exhausting living with constant threat, having to maintain that constant vigilance; of knowing you existed in a dog-eat-dog environment and if you weren't top, at best you got shit happen to you, and in the worst case scenario, serious shit happen to you – you got fucked, both literally and figuratively. Those *fucking* nonces – it sickened him just how everyday a thing it was that the screws used the boys there for their own perverted ends. And you could do fuck-all about it – *he* could do fuck all about it. Just count the days, count the days, count the days. And hope against hope that nothing happened – nothing that would require him to do something that would see his sentence extended again.

He thought about writing to Titch, then thought better of it. He'd eased off on the letters now – hadn't written home in ages. Was grateful whenever he lost the privilege of writing home. Because he just couldn't do it. He'd try but he'd always end up giving up, because he didn't have a single fucking lighthearted thing to say.

He did some desultory tidying then sat down on the bed, his photo of Titch looking down at him accusingly. Sod it – he had to do it. No excuses. *Sit and write to your fucking mother, at least!* He ordered himself. Then, rummaging for a pen and his refill pad, he began.

Dear Mam

Bet you thought I'd done myself in or something didn't you? Ha-ha …

But his mind wouldn't deliver up a single next sentence. He stared for a couple of minutes, willing himself to just get on and write *something*. But nothing came. And it was almost time to go now anyway.

He closed the pad and set off to start another mind-numbing day.

Chapter 12

June was getting irritated. It had all seemed like such fun at first, raking in all the lovely money. It had been so good to have it – to feel it and smell it – that she hadn't minded Jock banging on about them not arousing suspicion, hadn't minded not being able to spend most of it. She wasn't stupid – she knew just how fast curtains could start twitching if they started doing up their houses and going out in fancy clothes, so, initially, at least, she'd been happy to play it safe, and restrict herself to bags of food and extra coal.

But being so careful had gone on long enough now, surely? It had been almost a month now and she was sick of having money but not being allowed to spend it. Yes, she'd sent a few fivers off to Vinnie – though, given the strike, fuck knew where they'd ended up – and she'd also been able to sneak the odd miniskirt but, to her mind, Jock and the others were being way too cautious. Most of the cheques had been cashed now and nothing bad had happened, so wasn't it about time they all started letting their hair down? She had a wish list and she was itching to start ticking things off it, principal among them being a much longed-for holiday in Blackpool.

'Oh I don't know, June,' Maureen said, when she popped round to run the idea by her. 'We do something like that and the rest of 'em'll go fucking apeshit. And you know what the nosey bastards round here are like. Someone'll grass. Just you watch.'

'But what's to bleeding grass *about*, Mo?' June persisted. 'No one knows where it's come from, do they? And how can anyone grass about us taking a bleeding holiday?'

Maureen shook her head. 'I don't know, June. We really don't want to blow this. What does Jock say?'

'Jock?' June said. 'Nothing! He doesn't know anything, does he? You know what he's like. Which is why I thought we should just go ahead and *do* it. Once it's done and paid for he won't be able to bring himself *not* to go. Be like burning tenners. No, we just have to get on and *book* it.'

Maureen laughed. 'Tell you what then, I'll agree to it, but we can't all go together – we'll need to do it in turns. How about me and Steve go this weekend –'

'Why should *you* go this weekend?'

'Because that's the deal, June. People'll take much more notice if you and Jock go.'

'Why?'

'Because you've been so flashy! And you know what Jock's said – you've got to be a bit more savvy and a *lot* less all about with it. Which means it'll be much more sensible – and much less likely to annoy your husband – if me and Steve go first.'

June scowled. Maureen was right, of course, which really annoyed her. 'Anyway,' her sister-in-law rattled on, 'I've thought what's best to do. If anyone asks you can tell them we've gone to me mam's, and you and our Jock can go next week. Yes, that'll work. I can say you've gone to visit our Vinnie, can't I? And our Titch can stop with us while you're away.'

June thought for a minute, still a bit narked that Maureen was going to get to go before them, despite knowing it was probably the right thing to do. It had been her idea after all.

And it had been her idea to sell the remaining cheques around Buttershaw – the women there would snatch their hands off for a cigarette butt, let alone club cheques at a couple of quid a go. They'd keep their traps shut as well, as long as June went along personally. No one in the area – unless they were really stupid – would want to get on the wrong side of either Jock or June's families.

So, really, June thought irritably, it was her *right* to go first, and having to let Maureen and Steve do it annoyed her. She'd already planned it in her mind – her and Jock relaxing with knickerbocker glorys, having their photos taken wearing 'Kiss Me Quick' hats, strolling along the prom, followed by a piss-up at one of those posh pubs by the central pier.

'Alright then,' she relented, feeling the excitement dampen the irritation, 'you go first, but not a word to Jock or anyone. Especially our Titch. If she finds out we're off on hols without her, she'll go bleeding mental, the maungy little mare.'

'So why don't you take her?'

'Take her with us? You have got to be joking! I spend more than enough time looking at that miserable face of hers as it is.'

'Well, she *is* a teenager, Ju,' Maureen pointed out.

'Yeah, but our Vinnie was never like this. It's like she's had a fucking personality transplant, honestly it is.'

'Well, she's probably missing him, isn't she? They were always very close, Ju.' She sighed. 'But you're right. I was thinking only the other day. Where's that lovely little niece of mine gone?'

June shook her head. 'Been possessed by a moody mare, is what, Maureen. Even Jock can't seem to make her smile, and he *always* could, couldn't he? Perhaps you're right. Perhaps she's just missing Vin – God, *I* fucking am, bless the little bleeder – well, the not so little bleeder these days. Though that won't stop me cuffing him round the ear when he *does* get home, believe me.' She frowned then. 'No, we'll go on our own this time. Then – well, next time, we'll see about Titch coming along. In the meantime, let's get on and get this lovely lolly, eh?'

It didn't take long to raise sufficient to pay for the holidays. It was only a matter of a couple of days of going round the Boulevard on the neighbouring Buttershaw Estate, and they'd finally got the last of the club cheques off their hands, and a tidy pile of cash to divvy up between them.

And Maureen hadn't wasted any time booking her holiday – had gone into town on the bus and straight down to Wallace Arnold's to book a coach.

She was round at June's that very Friday afternoon, ready to go, standing on the doorstep dangling her door keys and giggling like a school girl. *So much for being against the whole idea*, June thought, taking the bunch of keys irritably.

'So you'll keep an eye on the house for us an' that?' Maureen wanted to know. 'Water the cactus? And, um … June?'

June looked hard at her sister-in-law, knowing that something else was coming, and that it wasn't going to be something she wanted to hear. She felt as prickly as her sister-in-law's ridiculous spiky plant.

Maureen blushed the colour of her lippy. 'Look, don't go mad but I've got a confession. It was so cheap that I booked for five days.'

'*What?*' June demanded. 'We're supposed to be keeping this fucking quiet!'

Maureen flapped her hands to try and shush her. 'I know, June, but –'

'But nothing, you greedy cow! They'll all be asking questions if you're gone that long – you *cannot go* for that long! You're just a greedy bleeder and you're going to fuck this right up!'

Maureen's expression hardened then. She clearly wasn't going to take that. 'I've booked for five days, June, and I'm going for five days, and that's the end of it. Wasn't it you who called it a gift horse? Well, I'm having my fucking gift! We've never had a proper holiday before and we're going, so stop your mithering. It's booked now, so that's that. Like it or lump it.'

There was nothing June could do apart from swallow her sister-in-law's attitude, but she was seething as she finally waved her off. Why should Maureen go swanning off on holiday before her, anyway? It wasn't fair – it was she and Jock who'd masterminded everything – well, mostly – so it should be her who had first dibs at reaping the rewards. Blackpool really rankled. Blackpool made her furious; now she'd have to listen to Maureen droning on about it endlessly, when it should have been her and Jock doing it first and droning at *her*.

Selfish cow, she thought, firing up a cigarette and puffing the smoke out angrily. Mo had spoilt her day now. Put her in a thoroughly bad mood.

Right, she decided, looking at the clock. Still plenty of daytime left. She needed cheering up now and she had some time to kill before she had to meet Jock and their mates in the Bull, and she intended to spend every bit of it shopping. Why shouldn't she, after all? If that bleeding Maureen could just piss off for five days, then she was going to have a right old spending spree herself. And everyone else could just shove it up their arses.

* * *

Titch had been sitting reading her dad's morning newspaper when she heard the sound of the car pulling up. After quickly throwing away the cig she was puffing on, she ran to look out of the window. Wafting away the smoke clouds, so her mam didn't know she'd been smoking in the house, she almost choked on her fag-smoke as she saw her, laden down with carrier bags, waving a taxi off. *What the fuck has she come as?* Titch thought.

June was wearing a fur coat – a real beast of a coat, big and spotty. The sort of coat you only saw on the TV or at the cinema. The sort of coat she was pretty sure she'd never seen in Bradford. Bloody March too! Only a show-off like her bleeding mother would think it apt to wear a fur coat in the spring. She must be roasting alive, Josie thought. And what was in all those bags? She ran into the hall and pulled the front door open.

June looked up. 'Ah, you're in. Go on, give us a hand then, simpleton. Don't just stand there looking gormless – grab some of this lot!'

Titch untwizzled some of the plastic bag handles that had become tangled around her mother's fingers, aghast at the weight of them once she'd finally got them free. She took them into the lounge and plonked them down on the sofa, where they slithered and spread out, all white and pink and yellow, like glossy butterflies' wings.

It was like Christmas. No, more that that, better than that. She'd obviously been to Kirkgate market, and – Josie gasped, realising – even Busby's. Was that where she'd got the coat from? Fucking hell, she never even got to go to Busby's at *Christmas*, to see Santa, like all the other kids seemed to, no matter how hard she pleaded and begged.

'I bet you haven't got me owt, have you?' she asked her mother hopefully. Though at the same time, she wasn't sure if she wanted anything anyway – where had the money come from? There must be so much of it to get all this lot. Which frightened her. What exactly had they done?

'Titch, gimme a fucking minute, will you?' June said, adding the rest of the bags to the pile. She grinned and ruffled her daughter's hair. 'I have got you summat as it happens, but go make us a quick cuppa while I stash all this lot from your dad.'

'You'd better,' Titch agreed. 'If he sees that coat on you he'll go mental.'

'Oh, not this,' June said. 'Sod him. I'm keeping this on. I want to see the look on everyone's faces, don't I? Anyway, what you doing standing there gawping? I said to go and make the tea while I get this lot out of sight!'

Titch shook her head as she went to the kitchen, her day suddenly feeling much brighter all round. Who cared where they got it anyway – she was getting a present! 'Yeah, mam,' she shouted back as she lit the gas under the greasy kettle. 'Like he's not going to notice anything when you walk in the pub dressed like a bleeding leopard!'

'Fair point,' June conceded, amid much exciting-sounding rustling. 'Anyway, come on back in here, love. I found your present.'

It was in a small bag, and straight away Josie could see what it was. Well, what she hoped it would be – a record. And it was. It was Lou Reed's 'Walk on the Wild Side', which was currently in the charts and was her most favourite song, *ever*. For a moment or two she simply stood there and gazed at it, unable to believe she actually held it in her hands.

June chuckled. 'Pleased? See, I'm not such a miserable old fart, am I? Knew you'd like it.'

Josie felt a glow of affection for her mum, hearing that. She had a record. A record of her very own. She couldn't believe it. 'Mam, I *love* it. How did you –'

'Know? Because I'm your mam and I know what you like. Nah, to be fair, it was just a lucky guess. The man in the shop said all the kids were raving about it. So I went for it. He said it's going to go to number one, that one, you know.'

The glow dimmed, to be replaced by something much more familiar. That nagging sense, which was ever present, that if she'd been Vinnie, her mam *would've* known what she liked. She pushed the thought away. It didn't matter. It just was what it was, and she wasn't about to change it. Specially with Vin so far away and her mam missing him so much.

God, she couldn't wait for him to get home so she could show him, she thought, carefully pulling the record from its sleeve and being careful not to touch the grooves and scratch them. She slipped it back again – she needed to get round to Caz's house to play it. Her parents' record player was rubbish – it played everything too slow. And as this was her first ever record she didn't want to risk damaging it with their ancient stylus. And Caz would love it, too. She still couldn't quite believe she had it.

'Thanks, Mum,' she told June, who was by now inspecting the contents of her other bags, and piling some of the smaller ones into the bigger ones. 'Kettle's nearly boiled, and I got the cups out, so can I go to Carol's, so I can play it?'

'Go on then,' June said. 'But you just make sure you're home at a decent hour. Your dad an' I'll be down the Bull and I don't want to have to worry about you walking home late. No going down the backs, okay? And if it gets late, you're to go and stop up our Lyndsey's, okay?'

Josie gave her mum a hug before she left, clearly startling her. She smelt of some sort of powerful, exotic perfume. Stop at Lyndsey's? There wouldn't be much chance of that. She'd rather sleep in the street than spend a night under that pervy git Robbo's roof.

Chapter 13

On the way, Titch inspected the record again more closely. She wanted to read every single tiny bit of writing on it so that she knew what was what in case anyone asked. Even the bits that were scratched on the vinyl itself, round the hole in the middle, so no one could call her a liar when she told them she had it. It puffed her up with pleasure, the thought of going into school on Monday, the owner of her first single – and what a single, too! She couldn't wait. It would be so good at last to have something to impress people. It had been so hard, moving up to secondary school and having to try and fit in. Back in primary, it was almost all kids from the estate, who were as hard up for material things as she was. But now it was different, and trying to fit in with the kids from the more affluent estates was almost impossible. In fact, she'd mostly given up. But this would show them. They were all going to be so jealous.

She sniffed the cardboard sleeve, remembering how Vinnie had once told her that he loved sniffing the pages of a new book in the same way, and how he'd shoved his copy of *Murder on the Orient Express* under her nose to prove it. And he'd been right. The paper in books just smelled different from other paper. Enticing, somehow. As if the words themselves were reaching out to pull you in. God, she missed him. He should be here now, sharing this.

A loud whistle interrupted her thoughts. She looked up then and in doing so she realised where she was – just across the street from Mucky Melvin's. She looked around her. The street was silent again, and there was no one about. It was dusk and the air carried a mild whiff of grease: people cooking chips, sitting down, eating tea. She carried on, careful not to look up towards the window across the road from her, shoving the record up under her jumper as she went. She was just crossing the road diagonally when she thought she heard something again, and as soon as she turned around, nearly shot a foot into the air – Mucky Melvin himself was stood there, right behind her.

She turned to run, instinctively, but even before her legs could begin moving, she felt a rough yank on her arm, and almost lost her balance. And in a matter of seconds, felt a stinking hand being clamped across her mouth, and the violence of being bodily hoicked back down the street, clamped by a strong unyielding arm across her chest.

Unable to make any sound other than a muffled grunt, and all too aware that the street was still empty, she squirmed and struggled like a wild animal against his terrifyingly strong grip. He'd pulled her only a matter of yards; not as far as his house – just into the alley that separated the row of houses and gave access to the backs, where a tall evergreen hedge scraped and shifted as they passed, emitting a pungent, piney scent.

'You'll only make it worse, Titch,' Melvin whispered, almost conversationally, as he huffed his way along the alley between the neighbouring houses, his stinking hand under her nose making her retch. His grip was starting to crush her chest now, in his effort to keep her from escaping, and she was only now aware that the record must be gone. *Please, please, please let someone be out in their yards*, she prayed desperately, kicking her legs out to try and crack his shin or trip him up, and trying not to let her mind take her to the place where she knew Mucky

Melvin's was right now. She could tell by his breathing; the same raggedy rasp she remembered so well and that he was emitting from disgustingly close to her ear.

But there would be no one. It was cold, it was getting dark and it was tea-time. If she could only open her mouth wide enough to be able to try and bite him –

'Shit!' his voice took on a sudden explosive quality and in the same instant she was propelled from his grasp. She didn't know how or why, only that she was aware of him falling – the force of his weight against her shunting her a good foot in front of him, before he crashed down onto the ground like a felled tree. She wasted no time in stopping to find out, either. He must have tripped in the gloom; stood on something, tripped on something. She didn't know and didn't care, just made her legs work like pistons, propelling her down and along and out of the end of the alley, her lungs almost bursting and her throat catching fire. She didn't stop running till she fetched up at Carol's house, where she began thumping furiously on the door.

'Where's the bleeding fire?' Carol was already asking before Josie could even see her. Then, the door fully open and their eyes meeting, added, 'Christ, Titch – you look like you've seen a ghost!'

Josie's lungs seemed to still have a life of their own, rising and falling and stopping her getting her words out.

'What?' Carol said, pulling her inside and shutting the door with her foot. 'What's happened, Titch? What's up? What've you done?'

Josie shook her head. 'Not me,' she managed to get out. 'Wasn't me. It was Melvin!'

'Melvin?' Carol said, herding her into the kitchen. 'Mucky Melvin?'

Josie nodded. 'He grabbed me –'

'He *grabbed* you? What – *where?*' she asked, pulling out one of the mismatched vinyl chairs and pushing Josie down on it. 'You mean you went in his *house* again?'

'No,' Josie said. Her hands had begun to shake violently. She could still *smell* him. 'No, no, never. He just grabbed me – right in the street!'

'Bloody hell – in your *street?* In broad *daylight?*' Carol glanced out of the kitchen window. 'Well, broad-ish. The filthy bastard!' She sat down too. 'And then what happened?'

'He just grabbed me and tried to pull me down the alley, and he had his hand over my mouth so I couldn't even scream, and he was –' She shuddered. 'Oh, God, Caz, s'pose I hadn't got away from him …'

'The shitty fucking bastard,' Caz said again. 'So how did you get away from him?'

'I don't know. I think he tripped on something, or maybe slipped. No, probably tripped. One minute he was behind me – he was holding me against him, like, at the front –' She drew her arms into a circle in front of her to demonstrate. 'And the next he went down like a ton of bricks, and I just legged it. Christ, Caz, what am I going to *do?*'

Carol stood up again and put her hands on her hips. 'You want some pop? The man's been and I told him me mam wanted some leaving. She'll go apeshit, like, but I'm not bothered. Dandelion and burdock. In the fridge. You want some?'

Josie nodded, biting her lip to stop herself from crying, and trying to still her trembling hands by smoothing Blue, who, perhaps having sensed that she needed her in some way had climbed out of her basket and trotted across to Josie, plopping her velvety head into her lap.

Carol got the pop bottle out of the fridge and carefully opened it to stop it spurting, then poured two glasses and placed them down on the little kitchen table.

Josie reached out for one, then thought better of it, and lifting the dog's head from her lap, went over to the sink and washed her hands as thoroughly as she could first, using a squirt of washing up liquid.

'I can't tell my mam,' she said, sitting down again and stroking Blue. 'I just can't.'

'Why not?'

'Because I just can't, that's all.'

'I think you should – s'pose he tries it again and this time he doesn't trip over?'

Josie sipped at the drink, the bubbles still dancing on the surface and tickling her top lip. 'Because what if I do and then they go for him an' it comes out that he – well, what he did to me before?'

Caz shook her head. 'It won't. He's not going to admit that, is he? He'd have to be mad as well as mucky!'

'But he might. S'pose he tells them I was asking for it or something?'

'Asking for it? That's just mad. Come on, Titch – you really think he'd ever do that?'

'Yeah, but –' Josie sighed. She wished she *could* believe he wouldn't. But she never told before, and she was happy that she hadn't. And she just knew telling now would make things bad for her. That somehow it would come out – she might blurt it out herself, even. That the not telling had made *her* seem bad, all by itself. Like she mustn't have even *cared* much.

How badly she wished Vinnie was home – she was counting the weeks till his release date in September now. How badly she wanted the summer to be done with. How badly she wished he could just go round and punch Melvin's lights out. She should have told Vin when it happened in the first place, she realised. He might not have been home but he'd have sorted it out for her. One way or another, he would've. He'd have sorted it so that bastard never thought, in a million billion *years*, that he'd got away with it. That he could try it on again with her now.

Her friend must have been reading her thoughts, she decided. 'How about you tell Vin?' Carol suggested. 'You've got to tell *someone*. I mean, it's not like Black Bobby used to do to me, this, is it? This is different, Titch. I mean, this is him trying to kidnap you, almost, isn't it? So's he could *rape* you.'

The word hung there between them, stark and singular. He'd raped her before and might have raped her again. Titch felt her chin begin to wobble at the thought of what might have been, and for the record she'd now lost, and the peace of mind that had been destroyed, and she fought to hold back a fresh bout of tears. She wasn't going to give him the satisfaction, the bastard.

'Hey,' said Carol, obviously seeing her face going. 'Count yourself lucky anyway, mate. Least you haven't got tits to grope, like I have.' Then she mimed it, squeezing both of hers and grinning, at which Josie, sniffing back the torrent, at least managed a wan smile.

'I can't tell Vinnie,' she said. 'For one thing mam's *still* not paid the bloody phone bill, and for another thing, he'd go completely mental – *completely* mental – and he'd end up being banged up for another God knows how many months, just when he's about to come home. No, Caz, I want him back and I'm not going to do anything that might make him do something that'll stop that happening.'

Carol shrugged. 'Fair enough. Got to tell someone though, haven't you? Hey, there's a thought,' she said. 'What about your

Lyndsey? Maybe she'd know best what to do. Maybe she could send her Robbo round to put the frighteners on him even. Or maybe tell your mam *for* you? Something, anyway.' She drained her pop and banged her empty glass down on the kitchen table then, startling Josie. 'Men, eh?' she said, rolling her eyes.

Chapter 14

The record, it turned out, was unbroken. Josie had told Caz all about it and how she knew she'd never see it again, but when she walked round to meet her down behind the youthy on the Saturday, it was to see her friend brandishing something in the air; something that resolved itself into something recognisably slim and square, Caz's expression confirming it was what she hoped it was.

'I don't believe it!' Josie exclaimed, as Caz passed the record to her.

'It's not broke or owt, either,' she confirmed.

'But how d'you –'

'I walked that way and saw it,' Caz said as they headed round the front to see who was hanging out. 'After you'd gone, Black Bobby and my mam started up all over again, so I decided I'd get out of there and take Blue out for a walk.'

Josie pulled the record out of the sleeve. Caz was right. It didn't look like it had come to any harm. It felt like a miracle. 'Where was it?'

'Just on the pavement, down from yours – it was just lying there. No sign of Melvin. His lights were all off. And *he* obviously hadn't seen it. Well, no one must have, must they? I thought about dropping it round then but I didn't like to come and knock. Not with Blue with me and with your mam and dad maybe home from the Bull. I didn't play it,' she added. 'Promise.'

'Oh, Caz, you should've!'

Carol shook her head. 'No I shouldn't. Not before you. But you could come round to mine and play it now, if you want to. And Titch,' she said looking at Josie hard. 'have you told your Lyndsey yet?'

Josie looked at the record. She was glad she had it back, but she suddenly wasn't sure she *did* want to play it now. It felt tainted; like she'd never be able to look at it without remembering. And that made her angry. Angry with that bastard Melvin. But most of all with herself. No, this time she *was* telling. For definite.

'No,' she said. 'But I'm going to. Swear on my life, Caz. That sicko's not going to get away with it a second time.'

Josie spent the rest of the day brooding on it. On the one hand, she desperately wanted to tell someone who might be able to do something; on the other, the same feelings of fear and shame kept ambushing her as last time. She hated trouble and knew that this had trouble written all over it.

She needed to wait though. To time things so she'd get her sister on her own, because the one thing she didn't want was for that idiot Robbo to start poking his nose in. He was an idiot druggy and you never knew what he might do if he found out. Most of all though, he had a big mouth and the one thing she felt sure of was that if he knew, the whole estate would too.

So she'd wait. She'd wait till she knew he wasn't going to be in, or come barging in on them and start asking questions. And though she'd been up twice – once to get little Robbie down to see his nan, and once to take him back again – it wasn't till the following Monday evening that the opportunity to get Lyndsey on her own finally presented itself.

It was tea-time and she was sitting in the lounge watching *Crossroads*, when she heard her mum call out something from the kitchen.

'Did you want me, Mam?' she called, and, when June didn't answer, she got off the sofa and went in to see.

June was at the sink, with her back to her, scrubbing away at the collar on Jock's one good white shirt. 'Did you call me, Mam?' Josie asked again.

June turned around, bar of Palmolive soap in hand, clearly surprised to see her standing there. 'What? Oh – oh, no, love. I was just shouting at that gormless pillock out there.' She nodded her head in the direction of the back yard.

'What gormless pillock?' Josie asked, joining her at the window and peering out. There was nothing and no one out there as far as she could see.

'The gormless pillock who lives with your stupid sister,' June told her. 'He's gone now. I just clocked him scampering over the backs like a bleeding ten-year-old. Pound to a penny he'll be on the trot for some drugs or that bloody wacky baccy. *Idiot* …'

She turned back to the sink.

'What d'you want him for?' Josie asked, realising she might have found her moment.

'Want him for? Nothing! Just wanted to let him know I'd seen him. He's good for nothing, that one, and shifty with it.' She turned around again. 'Anyway, why'd *you* want to know?'

'Oh, nothing. I just thought I'd pop up to our Lyndsey's and see the kids while he's out, that's all.'

Her mother lifted her carefully painted brows and observed her. 'What, *now*, you mean? In the middle of your precious *Crossroads*?'

Josie felt a guilty blush start. She didn't miss a thing, her mam, that was for sure. 'Yes,' she said, trying to think on her feet. 'I promised Robbie yesterday. He's been doing me a painting and I told him I'd go round and pick it up. You know, and have a play, and that.'

'What about your tea?' June wanted to know. 'I'm dishing up soon as I've done this. I thought taties, mince and cabbage was your favourite?'

'It is, Mam,' Josie said, once again feeling guilty, 'but I won't be long. Just leave mine in the oven, it'll stay warm enough for me.'

'Well, okay,' said June. 'But me and your dad are off up to the Bull for a couple as soon as he's out of the bath and we've eaten, so we won't be in when you get back. Don't forget your tea, mind, or you'll be getting it dished up tomorrow, okay?'

Josie grabbed her jacket from the back of the couch and slung it over her shoulder. 'I won't, Mam!' she promised as she slammed the front door.

Josie ran the length of the few houses with her eyes fixed ahead of her, the horrible memories she'd worked so hard to bury over the years now fresh and sharp and ugly in her head. Bastard. *Bastard.* He was *not* going to get away with it again.

She went in via the front door to find her sister in the living room, sitting on the couch smoking, as per usual. She had *Crossroads* on too, though Josie could see she wasn't really watching it. Just staring in the general direction of the telly. What was she thinking? What the fuck did drugs do to the contents of a person's head?

The girls were on the floor playing with an old catalogue and some pencils. But there was no sign of her nephew.

'Hi Lynds,' she said. 'Where's Robbie?'

'Auntie Titch!' the girls cried, pleased as usual to have some-one round who might actually play with them. 'Auntie Titch!'

Her sister looked up at her. And she didn't look *that* stoned, thank goodness. Just tired. Which perhaps anyone would be with three nippers running around.

'Off round at some kid's from school,' Lyndsey said, then looked at Josie more carefully. 'You alright, mate?' she asked. 'You look like shit.'

'Oh, Lynds,' she said, glancing at her nieces, who were now headed towards her, arms outstretched. 'I've got something I have to tell you. Something bad.'

'Bad? In what way bad?' Lyndsey asked, as Josie dropped down to give the girls a cuddle. 'Upstairs, you two,' she told them. 'Go and play in your bedroom. Your Auntie Titch and I have things we've got to talk about. Go on – scoot.'

She scooped a couple of magazines onto the floor to clear a space, than patted the space next to her on the sofa she'd created. Josie duly sat down.

'It's Mucky Melvin,' she began.

'That old fucker?' Lyndsey said mildly. 'What about him?'

Josie swallowed. Where did she start? But almost as soon as she opened her mouth to answer, she found she didn't need to think – it was as if her brain had long ago written the script, ready for the telling. She told Lyndsey everything, even though she hadn't meant to. She was only going to tell about him grabbing her the previous Friday; about him pulling her into the alley, about losing the record, about telling Caz and what she'd said about Lyndsey being the one who'd know what to do. But once she started, it was as if she had no control over her own mouth. It seemed to come out like a torrent, with a mind of its own, and before she knew it she was telling Lyndsey how he'd lured her into his house with the promise of a ciggie, how he'd made her go upstairs to give him them and have a fag and then overpowered her, how he'd ripped down her pants and how he'd forced himself inside her – and all the while Lyndsey, probably a bit stoned because she generally was, sat and listened, her eyes widening to saucers as she drew on a tiny roll-up.

'The filthy old cunt!' she said finally, batting smoke from in front of her. At least it wasn't that horrible sweet wacky baccy smoke, Josie thought. And at least she didn't seem *that* stoned. Not yet. Her hands were shaking again, she realised, and she balled them into little fists. Would they shake every time she thought about it, always?

'So you're saying he *raped* you?' Lyndsey went on. 'That *fucking* pervert! You really mean that? That he stuck his fucking prick in you three *years* back?'

Josie nodded miserably. 'It was just after our Vinnie left. Right after.'

Jesus!' said Lyndsey. 'That makes you – what – 11? God, that's disgusting that is. *Jesus!* No, no – it's more 'n that, actually. It's *child* abuse, Titch. That's what that is. That's *molesting* you! *Jesus!*' she said again, stabbing the end of the fag into the overflowing glass ashtray on the sofa arm. 'Why the fuck did you never tell anyone about this?'

'Because I *couldn't*,' Josie said plaintively. 'Mam would've killed me!'

'She fucking *would*, Titch – what were you thinking even going *in* there? How many times have you been told? Were you *mad*?'

'Exactly! I just … I just …'

Just *what*? She wasn't even sure she knew. She could hardly articulate it, even though the memory was still pin-sharp in her head. Would that it wasn't, but it would always be. She was beginning to understand that. How she'd stomped off, feeling angry, feeling like everything was about Vinnie, feeling, some-how, like 'sod it', like she'd do what she liked. Was there even a part of her that wanted something bad to happen to her? Just so her mam would notice she was *there*?

Well she'd certainly got her wish. No doubt about it.

'I know,' she said now. 'I know that *now*, Lynds.'

'And now he's back for seconds, is he? God, just you wait till I tell Robbo. He'll kill the old fucking tramp.'

'No!' Josie cried out, '*No*, Lynds!' Then, remembering the girls upstairs, she lowered her voice again. 'No, Lynds, *no*. What'd you have to tell *him* for? I didn't tell you because I wanted Robbo to know. That's the *last* thing I want! I'm only telling you because you're my sister, and I thought you might know what to do!'

Lyndsey shook her head and, in a rare gesture of physical warmth, grabbed one of Josie's hands between her own. 'Titch,' she said, 'that's just it. I *do* know what to do. Have Rob go round there with me and help me punch his fucking lights out!'

'No!' Josie said again. 'You mustn't tell him, Lynds. You mustn't! If you do that, then it'll be all round the estate and I can't bear that. And s'pose our Vinnie gets to hear of it once he's home? He'd go apeshit! No, Lynds, you mustn't tell Robbo!'

Lyndsey let Josie's hand go and reached for her baccy tin. 'Okay, okay!' she said. 'But what *do* you want to do then?'

Which was the problem. Had *always* been the problem, right from the first time. What *did* she want to happen now? She didn't even know. She hadn't thought past the business of unburdening herself – of just telling. Of not having to carry it all around any more.

'I just thought – oh, I don't know, Lynds – couldn't you speak to the police or something? Have them go round there? You know – warn him off and that? Threaten him?'

Lyndsey snorted disgustedly. 'The fucking bizzies? That's the *last* thing we'd do, divvy! No, mate – trust me, if anyone's going to threaten him it's going to be me and Robbo.'

'But I don't want you to tell Robbo. You promised you wouldn't tell Robbo!'

'Titch, you're not being sensible. Don't you see, I've *got* to tell Robbo. Yeah, I could warn him off, but Robbo can *properly* warn him off, can't he? No, that's the way. We'll put the frighteners on. We'll sort everything out for you.'

'But you won't tell mam and dad?'

'No, I won't, Titch.' She shook her head slowly. 'No, let me think this through for a bit … No,' she said at last. 'No, you're right. No point in telling them, is there?'

'Promise?'

Lyndsey reached out and patted Josie's forearm with her cold fingers. 'I promise. Don't you worry, kid, leave it with us. We'll sort the bastard out for you. And don't *you* be telling anyone else either, alright? You got that?'

Josie nodded. As if *she* was going to tell anyone anything about it! Why would her sister even *think* that?

'I won't,' she said. 'Not anyone. Only Caz knows, that's all. And she'll never, ever tell because we're blood sisters.'

'Good,' Lyndsey said comfortingly, patting her for a second time. 'Just forget about it now, okay? Don't you worry. Mucky Melvin won't be touching *you* again.'

'But what are you gonna do?' Josie wanted to know, still fearful about involving Robbo. He was so off his fucking head most of the time he might do anything.

'We're gonna make that bastard wish he'd never been born, mate,' Lyndsey told her. '*I'm* going to make him wish that *so* much. It'll be my pleasure. So don't you worry about it. And if he ever tries to touch you – or even *speak* to you again – you just tell him to fuck off and that you'll be speaking to *me*, okay?'

Josie refused Lyndsey's offer to make her supper and walked home feeling thoroughly miserable. She'd thought she'd feel better now – and maybe she did – but it was completely overshadowed by another worrying feeling. What was that story she remembered hearing in school? That was it – *Pandora's Box*. She remembered going home and asking Vinnie if he'd heard of it; how she opened the box and all the bad things flew out, and she couldn't get them back inside again, except for one – hope. And Vinnie had told her that it was something called an 'allegory', about how humans should know when to leave well alone. Should she have done that? She knew she shouldn't but she felt that all the same. That a lot of bad things would come flying out. Having hope didn't seem much of a consolation, either. Nothing she ever hoped for worked out.

She was glad to get home to a quiet empty house, and went straight to her bedroom without bothering with her tea. It was way too early for bed yet, so she spent some time trying to read but failing, so just lay in the gathering darkness, silently saying an 'Our Father' and hoping that tonight she would sleep without dreaming. She wasn't a holy person but the nuns always said that you could pray to God for anything. She mused for a moment about why the nuns always looked so miserable and then threw in a 'Hail Mary' for good measure.

She thought of Robbo and what the nuns might think of someone like him, and how he might react when Lyndsey told him what she'd told her. How weird it was that it was *him*, of all people, who was going to put the frighteners on Mucky Melvin – when he'd tried doing almost the exact same thing himself. Well, kind of, in his pathetic, stoned, ineffectual way.

Looking back, she decided she could have fought him off easily. He just thought he'd try it on and when he realised he wasn't wanted ... She wasn't scared of Robbo. Not really. He was just what he was – a stupid idiot. And what *he'd* done was something she'd definitely *not* be telling Lyndsey – not at any time, ever. Which depressed her to think about – why did *she* have all this horrible shit to deal with? What was it about her that made these things happen?

It was because she never told. That's what she kept coming back to – what the nuns would say. Because she didn't tell in the first place. If she'd told then maybe someone would've got rid of Mucky Melvin. Maybe Saggy Tits Sally would have had him arrested. That was the sort of thing she was good at. And if she *had* told, Robbo would've *known* to keep his filthy druggy hands off her, and Melvin himself would be history. She so wished he was history right now.

She stared at the David Cassidy poster pinned to the back of her bedroom door, and tried to tell herself she'd done the right thing telling Lyndsey. That Carol was right – that it *had* made her feel a bit better, and that she could trust her sister to put him straight and scare him off. But though she could just about persuade herself that telling Lynds was better than having not told, she couldn't see anything good coming out of that idiot Robbo being involved.

But she *had* told. So there was nothing she could do now either way.

The banging on the door had started as a distant, muted drumming. In a jungle somewhere, deadened by miles of dense and dripping foliage; a jungle in which June was currently hacking her way, in order to get to ... now, where exactly *was* she headed? All she knew was that the sound was getting louder and louder, and that soon she'd be ... Bang, bang, bang, bang, bang, bang!

Consciousness came all at once, hammering against her eardrums, and she yanked the eiderdown up round her ears. Where was Jock? Was it him? What the fuck was going on?

Bang, bang, bang! Finally it hit her. It was the front door.

'All fucking *right*!' she screamed down, at the top of her lungs. 'Shut the fuck up! I'm coming, okay?'

She threw the covers back, shivering as the cold air hit her bare legs, and rose unsteadily to her feet, feeling groggy. Unable to locate anything warmer, she reached for the negligee that matched her new baby-doll black nightie, then padded downstairs, popping her head round the living-room door when she reached the bottom, to check the time on the guitar clock on the wall. Eleven thirty in the morning – Christ! She'd slept that late? How had *that* happened? And where was Jock?

'Okay, okay, leave the fucking knocker on!' she yelled as she approached the front door, only stopping in bewilderment as she pulled it open to reveal two uniformed policemen on the step.

'Morning, June,' said the tallest of the two – who appeared to be a sergeant. He grinned at his colleague before taking his time looking her appreciatively up and down. 'Good,' he said brightly. 'I see you were expecting us.'

June scowled at him, in no mood for grinning cops on any morning, let alone one after the night she decided she must have had last night. Eleven thirty? What fucking time did she make it to bed?

'In yer bleedin' dreams, plod,' she snapped. 'What do you want anyway? Only I'm freezing me tits off stood here.'

'Mind if we come in, June?' the other copper said, equally

brightly. What the fuck did these two have to be so cheerful about?

'I do mind, as it goes,' she said. 'Our Vinnie's still locked up, so we've got – let me see – about three more months before you start harassing us again. Now, what do you want?'

The tallest copper cleared his throat. 'Well, June,' he said, 'it's about these stolen club cheques – the ones that were taken from the site your Jock was working at a while back. We've been following a bit of a chain and it all seems to lead back to you, June. So again, shall we come in or do you want to conduct this on the doorstep?'

June managed to curl her lip into what she hoped was an innocent-looking smile. 'Club cheques?' she asked. '*Club* cheques? Are you right in the fucking head? I've no idea what you're on about, mate. Now, is that it? Because from where I'm standing, you couldn't conduct a fucking church choir, let alone an investigation.'

June glanced at the shorter of the two, who seemed to be staring at something on the floor. She followed his eyes to see her morning post scattered on the lino in the hallway. Just as her mind registered what it was he was staring at, the copper bent down and picked up a postcard. A postcard that might have meant nothing whatsoever, were it not for the 'Greetings from Blackpool' written in swirly writing diagonally across the front.

He was way too quick for her. Before she could reach out and snatch it up, he'd already done so and was now holding it out of arm's reach to read. Typical Maureen, she thought, staring at the back of it, or rather the front of it: a cartoon couple, fat and sunburned, eating ice-creams on the beach. Brilliant. Fucking brilliant. He started reading aloud now.

'*Dear Jock and June*,' he read, addressing his words mostly to his sniggering colleague, and adopting a high-pitched posh lady's voice, '*cash the rest of our paper money in – wink, wink, nudge, nudge – because me and Steven might come back here with you and Jock. Wish you were here, love Mo.*'

June made a second attempt to grab the postcard, but once again the copper was too quick for her. 'Give it here, you lousy bastard. I'm sure that's a fucking offence, that is – tampering with the Royal Mail!'

He held it above his head now, seeming amused to see her jumping up to try and get it. How dare he fucking laugh at her, he and his dumb fucking mate.

'Sorry, June,' he said pleasantly, 'not when it's evidence, it isn't. Shouldn't have been so greedy, love, should you?'

He slipped it into a pocket then, and patted it for good measure. 'And just so you know, there's no point in you putting on that "butter wouldn't melt" face, either. This –' he patted the pocket again '– just sort of seals it. We already knew most of the picture already. Them fuckers up Buttershaw are not as scared of you as you and your little gang like to think. Anyway, Jock around?'

'No,' said June, her mood growing as black as her expensive nightie. 'He's gone to Torre-fucking-molinos. What do you think?'

And how she wished that they really could. Ideally *now*.

Two months later, June was carefully cutting an article out of the *Telegraph & Argus* newspaper. 'Oh What a Tangled Web We Weave' read the headline, and beneath it was a black-and-white picture of June, Jock and eight others, all in their Sunday best, outside Bradford Courts, smiling for the camera.

Our Vinnie's gonna love this, thought June as she folded the cutting and placed it on the fireplace. She grinned as she remembered the day in court. The judge had shaken his head in disbelief as they all, one after the other, had been called up. They had all pleaded guilty of course. No getting out of it, but the fine and the warning had been worth it. All that money they'd spent and enjoyed, and then the look on that judge's face. Priceless.

Chapter 15

September

June couldn't remember that last time she'd felt so happy and yet so anxious all at once. So much as if everything was slightly shifted off kilter. In some ways it had felt as if the time had passed so quickly, yet in others it felt like a lifetime had passed. Vinnie was almost 17. It didn't seem possible.

She squealed when she saw him – her boy! Home at last! And then again as, when she ran to him to try and give him a squeeze, he lifted her up – right off her feet, too; she couldn't believe he was tall enough to do that – and planted a kiss on the top of her head.

'Alright, Mother?' he said. 'Well, I'm back.'

'Oh, put me down, you daft bleeder,' she said, hoping he wouldn't. Not just yet – he was home and she wished the whole world could see.

He did put her down then, and grinned at her, cupping a hand to his ear – God, his hair was so *long* now! – and saying, 'What's that? Nope – I can't hear that kettle whistling!'

She followed him inside then, marvelling at him. He looked so different. She'd clocked that the minute she'd clapped eyes on him, studying him minutely from the first second she'd seen him, strolling up the road carrying his case with such a swagger. She hadn't seen him since last Christmas, so it had been a while now. And that had been a rare treat in itself. He saved his visiting orders for Brendan so he could keep in touch with his mates. Which wasn't surprising, she supposed. Why would he want to waste them on his mum? She'd reminded herself of that so many times over the last couple of years, so that Christmas visit had been a real shock. He'd grown so much. Become so manly.

And now he'd changed again. There was something. Something tangible.

He was taller still. That was a definite. He'd grown a good couple of inches. And he was leaner; not so much thinner – he'd always been a stringy little bleeder – as less soft, less boyish. He had proper man's muscles now, as well – no doubt all that manual labour the screws made them do – and his jaw seemed to be set in a firm, angular line. He'd grown a moustache, too – a proper bushy one. It was red like his hair was, only flecked with brown and blond too. It was odd seeing him with it, but it suited him. June couldn't wait to take him down the Bull and show him off.

She hurried into the kitchen to fill the kettle. He'd had a long journey: the train from Redditch, and then bus journey from the city centre, then the walk – it must have taken him a good five hours or so and, if she knew him, she didn't doubt he'd have stopped along the way, too, to catch up with a couple of his mates.

It had been a bit of a shock opening the door to him after so long away; watching him carefully set his case down, take off his immaculate new Crombie coat, smooth that silky-looking shoulder-length hair. She'd have liked to touch it, but didn't reckon that would go down too well.

Tea, that was the thing, she'd thought. Make him a cuppa. Let him settle. Josie'd be home soon – home like a bleedin' whippet, June knew – she was that desperate to see him. Jock too, she thought, even though his only comment before he headed off to the bookies earlier was to say that he hoped his idiot son would keep his fucking nose clean from now on.

Which was a bit rich, coming from him, given how they'd spent *their* summer. She smiled to herself then; she couldn't wait to show Vinnie the piece from the *Telegraph & Argus*. See where all those fivers came from – see where that smart coat had come from, for that matter.

'Tea won't be long, love!' she called through to the living room, her face wreathed in steam as she poured.

Vinnie was watching TV when she went in with the cups, sitting in his dad's chair, elbows on knees, leaning forward, intent on it, ignoring her.

'What you watching?' she wanted to know. 'Here you are love –'

He took the proffered cup without speaking.

June sat down on the sofa, feeling ignored. 'Turn that off, will you? I want to talk to you!' There was a silence. He was really glued to it. '*Vin!*' she said more insistently. She didn't do being ignored. 'You've only just got home, for fuck's sake!'

Now he did turn towards her. 'Shush, Mother!' he said. Then he stood up and went over to turn the volume up a bit. 'Look!' he said, pointing. 'Bombs! Bombs've been going off in London!' He shook his head. 'I fucking knew it. I knew they weren't lying, the little fuckers. I *knew* it!' He grinned at June as he sat down again, this time next to her on the couch.

'Bombs?'

'The IRA, Mother. They haven't declared it yet, or owt, but they will do. Just you wait.'

June studied the screen. It was a station. King's Cross. It looked bad. She turned to Vinnie. 'How would you know about that, then?'

'I was locked up with a couple of them, wasn't I? Mad fuckers, the pair of them. Call themselves 'political prisoners' apparently. Looked just like any other fucking mad Irish to me.'

'And they did *that*?' June nodded her head towards the TV.

Vinnie shook his head. 'Not them, Mam. Their "brothers" – that's what they call their mates – they were the ones planning it. We weren't supposed to know, or owt, but one of them got stoned one night and blabbed.' He shook his head again and laughed. 'And they fucking have!'

June felt her stomach clench, seeing Vinnie so excited. There they were, watching folk being led out of the station, bleeding and terrified, and her son was laughing – her son seemed to actually find it funny. There was blood and glass everywhere, loads of injuries, people shaking, people crying. She might not be perfect, she thought, but laugh at *that*? At all those innocent people hurt and – yes, they were already saying so – being killed? There was nothing funny about that. Nothing at all.

'Vin, mate,' she said. 'It's nothing to laugh at. This is fucking terrible. Fucking IRA. Why'd you want to hang around with the likes of them?'

Vinnie laughed again, and it sounded strange. It was a man's laugh. No longer a boy's laugh. 'Mother, you have no fucking idea, do you? It's fuck all to do with me anyway. I was just saying – they said they'd do it and they did do it. You've got to think of it differently anyway. You've got to think of them as like soldiers. That's what they are – soldiers. Fighting for their cause.'

'They don't look like soldiers to me,' June said. 'I've known plenty of soldiers, your own uncles included. Let me tell you, they don't go around killing ordinary people going about their business.'

Vinnie got up again and switched the telly off, then slurped his tea. 'Anyway, enough of that. What's been happening around here, then? What have I missed?'

That was better. A change of subject. Maybe she'd feel a bit less on edge then. She leapt up and grabbed the cutting from its home on the mantelpiece. 'Have a read,' she ordered, passing it to him. 'You'll piss yourself laughing.'

And he duly did. 'You mental bastards!' he chuckled, shaking his head. 'And you wonder where I get it from! And only a fine – how d'you manage to pull that off? You're lucky you didn't end up banged up yourselves!'

'Not that lucky, really,' June said. 'I almost had a coronary when the bloody judge or whatever it was sentenced us. Right twat, he was. He read it out as though we were all going down for six months, then, right at the end, after a pause to make us sweat, the evil bleeder, he finally tells us that it's "suspended".' She shook her head. She still blanched at the memory. 'My life was flashing before me eyes, son, I can tell you.'

Vinnie laughed. 'Oh, mother – how I wish I'd been there to see your silly face! But what about Titch? She wasn't in on this, surely?' The idea seemed to concern him.

'You're kidding,' June reassured him. 'She's no different, son – still a goody two-shoes. Fuck knows where she gets it from – must be your dad's side.' She giggled. 'Shivering bleeders, the lot of them.'

'She's alright, Mam,' Vinnie said. 'We've just all babied her, that's all. And maybe that's a good thing. When's she home anyway? I've got to get on. People to see, places to go.'

June's face fell. 'You're not out already are you? I was thinking we'd nip down and get some take-outs from the pub. I can pay him on Friday, and we'll have a bit of a party to celebrate, eh?'

Vinnie shook his head. 'Sorry, Mam, but I've got things I need to do. I've got to earn some money and I've got a couple of people I need to catch up with. Brendan and Pete, you know? They've been in touch and they promised me they'd sort me out when I got home. I'm meeting them in the Bull in a bit.'

'Tonight?' June tried again. 'Can't it wait till tomorrow? Little Robbie can't wait to see you – been rabbiting on about you non-stop, he has. He even did you a picture. *Another* picture,' she added, looking at him pointedly. She hadn't intended to bring it up, but where letters and gifts were concerned it had all been a bit one-way fucking traffic these last months.

Vinnie gave her a look that seemed about to be accompanied by a rebuke, but he obviously thought better of it. *Good,* thought June. She wasn't having him trying to throw his weight around. She was still his mam and her say-so was her say-so.

'You just reminded me,' he said instead, leaping up again and putting his tea down on the mantelpiece. 'I've got something for you.'

He went out into the hall then and returned with the suitcase, which was brown and battered. June had never seen it before.

'Where'd you get that?' she asked him. 'They give 'em out at borstal now, do they?'

Vinnie placed the suitcase down on the sofa and shook his head. 'One of the screws gave it me,' he said. 'Said he didn't need it any more. So I had something to put my stuff in …' He opened up the lid.

There were two packages inside, all carefully wrapped in brown paper, and nestled between his few bits of clothing. He lifted one out and passed it to her. 'Careful, mind,' he said. 'It's delicate.'

June immediately felt bad for feeling cross with him. He might not have written but she obviously *had* been in his thoughts, after all. She placed the package on her knees and opened it carefully, as directed, peeling back the layers of paper, wanting to savour it, having absolutely no idea what it might be.

'Oh, you shouldn't have, Vin,' she said. 'It's not even like you've got any money. Oh, Vin, you *shouldn't* have!' she said again, unwrapping the final layer to reveal a china shire horse. And a big one too – almost a foot high, it was, complete with yoke and saddle and even little leather reins. 'Oh, Vin!' she said, pulling it free and holding it up so she could properly inspect it. 'It's beautiful.'

'Isn't it?' he agreed. 'But give it here a minute, cos there's more.'

'More?' June looked up at him wide-eyed as he took it from her and placed it on the floor.

'Yes, to *go* with it. Here,' he said, passing her another carefully wrapped parcel. 'Now this one's *really* delicate, so just be careful opening it, okay?'

June held the parcel on her lap like it was the Crown Jewels. She didn't know what it was but it couldn't have been more precious. She could feel tears pricking in her eyes and if she'd been their Mo looking at her, she'd have given her a slap and told her not to be so daft.

But how could you not? She thought, turning back the paper, *how could you not, when* ... 'Oh, Vin!' she gasped, seeing what now sat on her lap. 'Oh, Vin, this is *amazing* – it's fucking gorgeous!'

It was, too. By anyone's standards. It was a gypsy caravan, just the right size to sit behind the shire horse, made out of what looked like, no, definitely were, matchsticks. The detail was amazing, right down to the tiny curtains that hung in both the windows and the matching seat pads for the tiny table and chairs inside. It was all finished off with a gleaming golden varnish and a tasselled trim running around the arched entrance. It was the nicest thing she had ever seen or owned in her whole life and if a tear slipped down her cheek she no longer cared.

She stood up carefully and took it to the window-sill, clearing a space for it, then fetched the horse to hitch up to the front.

Vinnie looked on all the while. He didn't say anything but she could see just how proud he was. As he should be, she thought. He was so clever with his hands.

'I'm going to leave that right there,' she said turning to hug him. He let her. 'So all the neighbours can see it and see how talented you are.'

She sniffed and Vinnie laughed. 'Mam, if you look around you'll see plenty of them, honest. And the shire horses. Everyone makes the gypsy caravans in borstal and the shops in the town sell the horses to go with them. It's a right racket.'

'A racket?'

'Well, not that kind of racket. But I didn't just make mine. I made a few of them, actually. Some other things as well. You know, for the other lads, like, so they could take them home to *their* mams. Kept me in chocs and baccy, that did. And it passed the time.'

'Well, I don't know about that,' June said, clearing the rest of the clutter so her present could be properly centre-stage. '*I've* never seen one. Not round here, anyway. Oh, Vin,' she said, moving the net aside and hooking it round one of the handles. 'It's just lovely.'

'Well, I'm glad you like it, Mam. Cost me a fortune in matches, that did! Anyway, I'd better get on. Like I said –'

'Things to do, people to see. You already told me. Oh, Vin, can't you stop at home just for one bleeding night? And what about little Robbie?'

He re-clasped the suitcase clips and lifted it off the sofa. 'Tell our Titch to nip up and tell him I'll try to stop by and see him later. Right now I'm off to unpack, okay?'

He crossed the room then and patted her shoulder. He really *had* grown. 'Mam, calm *down*,' he said. 'I'm home now, aren't I? And I'm stopping home. For good. Which means I'll be here the next day and the next day and the next day. I'm not going anywhere, okay?'

June crossed her fingers behind her back when he said that, hoping against hope that would turn out to be true, and that the stirring of anxiety in her stomach was just indigestion.

She'd take some Milk of Magnesia, she decided. That should sort it.

Chapter 16

Vinnie's room hadn't changed. Not one bit. It was exactly the same as when he'd left it three years earlier, as if locked in a time warp, or sealed up because the contents were radioactive.

The door creaked as he opened it wider and stepped in. Literally nothing seemed to be different. Not a clean lick of paint, no different blanket top, nothing. Even his old drawers were still drooping out of their casings just the same the day he'd gathered his few things from them and filled the bag he was to take to approved school.

He sighed as he ran a finger along the dust that had gathered on his beloved bookcase and wondered, not for the first time, if all mothers were as lacking as June when it came to making an effort. He felt strangely disgruntled at the prospect of living again amid so much mess and squalor. Whatever else Redditch had been, it had been clean. But at least all his books were still there. He checked the titles that he'd left behind – a few Agatha Christie novels, a book about James Dean and his second favourite book, *Nicholas Nickleby*. He'd loved that one, because Nicholas was a bit like him really. Yes, his own dad was still alive and kicking, whereas Nicholas's wasn't, but Vinnie still felt it was him who had to look out for his mam and sister, and he certainly had an uncle who never thought he'd amount to anything. Actually, scrub that – he had two or three of them.

He touched the spine. He'd left that one for Josie to read while he was gone and she must have put it back again, bless her.

'*Que sera, sera,*' he said out loud, flinging the case onto the bed. It was now a bit lighter – and, without his mam's gifts, a lot less fragile – but it still caused a mushroom-cloud of dust.

There wasn't much in the case bar his books and his clothes, but at least the latter were clean. Putting the novels to one side, he pulled out a T-shirt and some jeans from the few items of clothing he possessed. He changed into them quickly, feeling the chill on his bare skin. Even though it was only September, it was an unwelcome reminder of things to come. There would be no more warm pad to return to on winter evenings; he was back to a place with only one source of heat – the fireplace in the living room downstairs.

Dressed and warm again, he hurriedly placed the books back in the bookcase, smiling wryly as he slid each into the space it had created; time really had stood still in here. His few photos went on top, his remaining clothes into the creaking drawers – another wry smile then; he'd have to go back to relying on his mum to wash his laundry. Fat chance! It more likely meant a weekly visit to the bag wash, if he was to have any chance of keeping his things half-decent.

Once changed, he hurried down again, grabbing his Crombie from the newel post, and shrugging it back onto his shoulders. It was as precious to him as his matchstick-modelled caravan was to his mam, and the most expensive piece of clothing he'd ever owned. Camel, rather than the usual black, it hung remarkably well on him, given that his mum had no choice but to guess which size to get. He felt a familiar flicker of guilt for not having written in so long, because he couldn't have been more excited when the parcel had arrived for him at Redditch. It was the envy of everyone, the coolest thing ever – particularly worn with his ox-blood dealer boots, too. He smoothed it down appreciatively – *not bad for a Canterbury lad, eh?* – then smiled, realising where the cash had probably come from. Odds on it was the proceeds of a few of those stolen club cheques. Well, he could do worse than get a bit of that kind of action himself. 'Don't wait up!' he called to June as he left.

He wondered about Pete and Brendan as he walked. Would they look different? Would they still have room for him in their lives? He also wondered if they'd got themselves birds while he'd been away. That whole business had been worrying him a bit when he was locked up. They'd both written him letters, quite regularly, too – and now and again had mentioned some girl or other. Vinnie hadn't had the pleasure of such encounters and it bothered him – he didn't want to look stupid if his mates decided to talk about shagging and stuff. He decided he'd lie if he had to. Say he'd pulled loads of birds when he'd had weekend leave or something. And if they didn't believe him? Well, he'd just threaten them with a slap.

Vinnie was looking for lots of things – sex being one of them – but he definitely wasn't looking for trouble. It might come and find him – probably would, in fact. And if it did, so be it. He would deal with it. But he wasn't on the hunt for it right now. He was much more interested in settling back into estate life, re-establishing his order in the hierarchy (and in that regard his 'just-out' status would definitely be a major asset) and getting a piece of whatever was currently going down. Yes, one day, he'd get a proper job – something with woodworking, perhaps. He really fancied that. But real work – proper grown-up work – that could wait for a while. Right now he had some living to do.

Living and re-connecting, Vinnie thought, particularly with
his little sister. He didn't need reminding how much she had
missed him, and as he drew up outside the pub he felt a slight
pang of guilt about not hanging around to see her. But only a
small one – after so long away, the thought of being looked at
and scrutinised and (in his aunties' case) patted was reason
enough to make the Bull his first stop and to first celebrate his
return with his mates.

Pete laughed at loud as soon as he saw him. 'Fucking hell, Vin,'
he said, slapping him across the shoulder. 'You look like fucking
McCloud with that 'tache, mate!'

Vinnie laughed. It was good to see his mates after so
long. 'And you two still look like the ugly cunts I remember,'
he answered. 'Alright, Brendan? You getting the beers in,
kiddo?'

'Kiddo?' Brendan snorted. 'I'll get the first one for your
cheek, but you can't con me. I know you jail wallahs get a bit
of spends to come home with.'

You're on,' said Vinnie as they headed up to the bar. It was
almost like he'd never been away.

Though there was still a fair bit of catching up to do. No talk
of birds, thankfully, but lots of gossip about who'd been up to
what and, more importantly, who was on the up and who
wasn't. He'd returned at a pretty low time, what with the
miners working to rule and everyone fearful of losing their jobs
– that three-day week he'd been hearing about and everything
– not that either concept meant much; none of his mates had
regular jobs not to go to. It just meant less money around and
less stuff to rob.

'So, what's going on?' Vinnie asked his mates as soon as
they'd got their second pints in.

'Not a lot, mate, If I'm honest,' Brendan told him. 'Things aren't great. There's a scrap yard we've been keeping our eye on, but nothing's concrete yet.'

'What about your Robbo?' asked Pete. 'You're not already knee deep into his little scam, then?'

'Gimme a chance,' Vinnie said. 'I've only been back five fucking minutes! Anyway, what scam? We're talking the same idiot Robbo? I'm surprised he's still standing, let alone running a scam. It's all he can do to tie his own fucking shoelaces, isn't it? Well, that was the case last I heard.'

'Same one,' Pete confirmed. 'So I'm told. Something to do with Melvin, up by yours.'

'Melvin? What, Mucky Melvin? You being serious?'

Pete nodded. 'Yep. And he's on a right little earner by all accounts.'

Vinnie laughed scornfully. 'Robbo? Teaming up with old fucking Mucky Mel? Well I knew he was a chancer but getting involved with him? That's low, even for that prick!' Vinnie laughed and ordered another pint, while his friends exchanged what looked like an anxious glance.

'What?' he said. He didn't miss much these days. And what he didn't miss he wanted to know about.

Brendan finished his pint and slid the glass across the bar next to Vinnie's empty. 'You got the wrong end of the stick, mate,' he said. 'He's not doing a scam *with* Mucky Melvin. He's doing one on him.'

'Now that makes much more sense,' he agreed. 'What's he got on him?'

Again, he sensed an anxious pause. 'What?' he demanded.

'Listen, mate,' Brendan said. 'It's not for me to say, is it? People talk an' that, but no one really knows, and that's the truth. You maybe want to ask your Lyndsey.'

'So she's in on it, too, is she?'

'I dunno, mate,' Brendan said again. 'Look, you need to ask her.'

It had been a long time since Vinnie had tasted alcohol and he'd intended to savour it. And he had been, but there was something in Brendan's tone that took his appetite for beer away suddenly. What was his idiot sister up to now? Prostituting herself for drug money? He wouldn't put it past her, and he wouldn't put anything past that moron of a boyfriend of hers either. Perhaps he'd better go see, though, because there was something in Brendan's tone that wasn't sitting easily with him. His sister was 26 now. She could do what the fuck she liked. So why the looks?

'You know what, mate?' he said to Brendan. 'I might just do that right now. I promised little Robbie that I'd look in on him anyway.' He drained his second pint and clapped his hand against his mates' backs. 'Maybe catch up with you in here later?'

'Yeah, maybe,' Brendan agreed, though he didn't look hopeful.

Odd, Vinnie decided. Very odd. But then this was his sister and that idiot they were talking about. Nothing that pair got up to would surprise him.

Walking back up through the snicket to his sister's in the gathering dusk, Vinnie wondered how well his nephew and nieces would remember him. Three years was a long time when you were just a nipper – would Sammy and Lou even know who he was? By now, their memories of him would be pretty hazy.

Little Robbie, though – perhaps he would, because Titch would have reminded him. He knew the lad still thought about him at least because Josie had sent a fire-engine picture he'd done for him in with one of her letters. It even had Vinnie's name emblazoned on the side of the truck. He'd displayed it proudly on the wall of his room along with his family photos and posters. Bless the little tyke. He wondered how he was. Was it a bit better than it used to be? He hoped so.

But the evidence outside told a different story. As he walked up their path it was like going back in time. Had anything changed here? He doubted it. The front was certainly no different – a mess of broken toys, overgrown weeds and random bits of wood – and when he knocked on the same peeling paint on the same filthy door, it felt like he'd never been away.

It was no different inside. Getting no response from his knocking he tried the front door and finding it unlocked, pushed it open and stepped into the hall. A couple more steps took him to the living room and, pushing that door open too, he was greeted with the scene he half expected. The TV was on, the fire was lit, the room was a sea of the usual mess and, in the midst of it, his older sister and his nephew.

'Now then!' he boomed.

'Uncle Vin!'

Robbie leapt up on seeing him. 'Yay! Uncle Vin!' He ran across the room then and cannoned into Vinnie, arms as wide as his grin. 'Nan said you were coming home! Have you come to watch the telly with us?'

'Fucking hell, mate!' he said, casting his eyes over his nephew. 'Whoah there! You'll have me over! And look at you! You're so big – how old are you now?'

'I'm ten!' Robbie told him proudly. 'An' I'll be 11 in January! Mam! Mam, look who's here! Auntie Titch, come downstairs! Uncle Vin's here!'

Robbie ran into the hall to shout for Josie to come down and Vinnie smiled at his enthusiasm. It felt good to be looked up to, which he knew he was. Young Robbie thought of him as some kind of hero, always had. Hardly surprising given the idiot of a man he currently lived with.

Robbie had certainly grown up a bit, and from the size of him, he was going to be a big lad. He already had impressive muscles and looked a lot older than his years. He'd be okay, Vinnie decided. Able to look after himself. Well, as long as he didn't take after his excuse for a mother.

Vinnie looked across at his elder sister, who barely stirred at the sound of her son's voice. She was sitting in exactly the same place on exactly the same couch, the same lazy-lidded half-smile frozen on her face. So, here too, absolutely nothing had changed. No, it was worse – she couldn't even wait till the fucking kids were in bed before chasing the fucking dragon, by the looks of things.

'Vinnie!' he turned around to see his younger sister enter the room. Christ, he thought – now she *had* changed. Where'd she get those lanky legs from?

Just like Robbie had, she crossed the room in an instant and threw her arms round him. 'You might have fucking waited for me to get home!' she told him, her voice muffled by his coat as she clung to him.

'And you,' he countered, 'might have made the fucking effort to bunk off school so you could *be* home!'

She was still in her uniform. In fact, if Vinnie wasn't mistaken, she was wearing one of his old school jumpers. He recognised the frayed cuffs and a splat of green paint that had never washed off. He chuckled to himself and did a quick mental calculation. What was she – 14? Fuck. When he'd left she'd still been in primary school. He pulled her off him and held her away from him, grinning, trying to get his head around how much she'd changed. And she was obviously doing the same, because she laughed at him. 'You growing that bum-fluff on your face for a joke?'

He glanced across at his older sister. Thank fuck for his younger one, all things considered. She'd got sharper since he'd left, but in a good way. 'Where's the girls?'

'In bed,' Titch said. 'I just got them off.' She frowned. '*Again*. They were already off – and then *you* come banging on the door.'

He became aware of a tugging on his coat. Robbie. 'Uncle Vin! Uncle Vin! Can we go out and play footy?'

'With me in this?' Vinnie joked, smoothing the lapels of his Crombie. 'You'll be lucky, mate! Tomorrow, maybe. After school. I gotta speak to your mum now, okay?'

'And it's time for bed,' Titch said. 'Because I have to get off now too.'

'You're off?' Vinnie asked, feigning disappointment. Much as he was pleased to see his little sis, he didn't want her earwigging while he was talking business with Lynds. 'Charming!' he pretended to huff. 'Thought you'd be desperate to see me! I walk in the door and you walk out of it!'

'I told you,' she said. 'I rushed home *specially*. But mam said you were off to the Bull for the night, didn't she? And there was no way I was sitting in on my own, was there?' Her expression softened then. 'And I've got to meet up with Caz anyway. We've got some homework to get finished.'

Vinnie grinned again. 'Mam said you were still a goody goody. She was right, then? Right, young fella,' he added, sweeping Robbie up onto his hip. 'Time for bed, then, mate, I think.'

'Yay!' said Robbie, throwing his arms around Vinnie's neck. 'You going to tuck me in, Uncle Vin?'

'Tuck you *in*, mate? *How* old d'you say you are now?' He smiled at his nephew and glanced across at his feckless older sister. 'Oh, go on, then, you big sissy,' he said. The poor little bleeder. What kid deserved *that* for a mother?

He said goodnight to Titch, promising to catch up with her properly the next day, and by the time he came down again, the kitchen strip light was switched off and she'd gone. Lyndsey, however, seemed not to have stirred since he'd left her, and there was still no sign of Robbo. There was just the smell of him – the stale greasy stink the whole place had, and which he remembered as if it was yesterday.

Jesus, he thought crossing the room and roughly shaking his older sister, what a way to live a life. If there was one thing he was never getting into, ever, it was fucking heroin – it fucked you up like nothing else.

'Christ, sis,' he said, as she spluttered and cleared her throat. 'I can't believe you're on the gear already. Can't you wait till they're in fucking bed at least?'

She roused herself a little and pulled herself up into a semi-sitting position. She looked a state; even worse than he'd remembered her. Her long hair – once dark and glossy – was as lank and dirty as his was clean, she had dirt under her nails and spots on her face.

'Fuck off, Vin,' she said. 'You come to see us or just fucking moan?'

'Let me see,' he said, casting his gaze around. 'Bit of both. State you fucking live in. Those poor fucking kids. Don't you have *any* shame?'

'Yeah, yeah, save your sermon for someone who cares,' she said, flapping a dismissive arm and reaching for her baccy tin. Anyway, you alright? How was your holiday?'

'Educational,' he told her, feeling suddenly twice the age that was written on his birth certificate; as if he'd lived more life in three years than she had in ten. 'Anyway, it's Robbo I'm after. I hear he's got something going on that I might be able to get a piece of. Where is he?'

He could see Lyndsey struggling to focus as she tried to roll a joint, squinting as she crumbled a warmed lump of Lebanese black onto the tobacco. He watched her with distaste. Fucking drugs were for morons. She was out of it on heroin almost as soon as she got up in the mornings. And now she was topping up with this shit as well.

'Out and about,' she said.

'Collecting off Melvin?'

She looked up then. 'You know about that?'

'I know about lots,' he said, sensing that there *was* something he ought to know here. 'So. What's he into him for?'

Lyndsey blinked at him, then stared at him, then eventually lifted a finger and tapped it clumsily against the side of her nose. 'None of your sodding business, little brother,' she told him, enunciating the words carefully.

'Course it's my business,' he said, expecting that. They wouldn't want to cut him in, would they? 'Look, we're family, aren't we? Anyway,' he said, thinking on his feet, the bit between his teeth now,' I know *why* he's into him because *everyone* knows why anyone would be into him – because he's a fucking *nonce*, Lynds – I just wondered how much he was into him *for*.'

Lyndsey's expression changed then. 'You do?' She looked shocked. 'Well, for fuck's sake don't tell her anything about it, okay?' She shook her head. 'Because what she doesn't know can't hurt her, can it? We said we'd sort it and we sorted it ...' Her slurring was getting worse now. 'An' maybe, now you're back –' he watched her lips curl into a half-smile. 'We could even put the price up a bit, couldn't we?'

Vinnie tried to make sense of this. Who was the *her* she was talking about? What was Lyndsey on about? Now *he* was back? 'Lynds!' he snapped as she lit up and drew deeply on the roll-up. 'Wake the fuck up, will you? *Why* not tell her anything? What d'you mean?'

Lyndsey sat back against the greasy dirt-coloured cloth that had once been an embroidered head rest for their battered sofa. 'You need to even *ask*, Vin? You know what our Titch is like … goody two-shoes –'

'*Titch*?' His mind was whirring now. 'What's Titch got to do with anything?'

Lyndsey's mouth opened and closed then opened again as if she was about to speak. He waited, but she couldn't seem to get any words out. None at all. *Why*?

'I said,' Vinnie said again, 'What has Titch got to do with anything?'

'Nothing. I –'

'Don't lie to me, Lynds.' He crouched down now, feeling the hairs on the back of his neck prickle. What the *fuck* had been going on? 'I mean it. What the fuck has been going down here?'

It seemed a real effort of will for his sister to formulate the next sentence. 'Look, he pays us, okay?'

'Pays you for what? What's he done?'

'For keeping quiet –'

'About?'

'Vin, I just *told* you.' She looked at him as if he was the stupid one. 'About Titch.'

'What *about* Titch?'

'About what he's done.'

Vinnie felt an icy calm begin to descend on him. 'And what *has* he done?'

'Well, she says rape, but –'

'*Rape!*' The icy calm deserted him. Had he just heard what he heard? He stood up again, stiff-legged, mouth agape.

'Rape?' he said again. 'You're telling me he's fucking *raped my little sister?*'

Lyndsey waved the joint in front of her. 'Well, she says rape, like I say but, Vin, honest, I just think he groped her. How would she have known, *really*? You know what she's like – she –'

Lyndsey didn't manage to finish the rest of what she was saying as Vinnie had grabbed her by her cardigan and hauled her to her feet. '*Raped* her? When? Where? When the *fuck* did all this happen?'

'Ages ago – Vin, will you fucking put me down please! Back when you went –'

'When I went?'

'Just after you got sent down. I think it was –'

'You mean three fucking *years* back, he did this?' What the *fuck* – that would have made her *11!*'

'Vin, please,' his sister whined. 'You'll wake the kids up!'

'I'll wake more than the kids in a fucking minute, Lynds. You mean you're telling me you shits have been blackmailing that bastard for three fucking *years?*'

She shook her head wildly, still clinging on to the last of the smouldering roll-up. 'God, no!' she said. 'We didn't know anything about it, honest! This has only been in the last three or four months, since when he tried it on again –'

'Tried it on *again?* What the fuck!' He let go of her and she flopped back down on the sofa and started to snivel.

Vinnie clasped one fist in the other, fighting a powerful urge to punch her. 'Yeah,' he said, 'and you know why? Because he *got away with it the first fucking time*, that's *why!*'

'I told you, Vin – we didn't *know*. She didn't tell *anyone!*'

'You fucking *liar*!' he said, opening his fist and slapping her hard across the face.

His hand stung. His head hurt. He couldn't believe what he was hearing. His little sister raped. His Josie – fucking *raped*! An image sprang to his mind that he couldn't shake away. The shower block. Broken boys. That fucking twisted cleric. And then Josie. That monster, Melvin. *And him not there for her.*

He stepped away from Lyndsey for fear of slapping her a second time. It was like a physical impulse he was struggling to control. Thank fuck Robbo wasn't there right now. Thank fuck for that at least. 'And what you've done,' he said slowly, 'You messed-up piece of shit – what you and that *cunt* of a boyfriend of yours have done is tap him for cash. Not do the right thing – the pervert *raped your fucking little sister*, Lynds! – not killed him or maimed him but tapped him for fucking *money*!' He stood over her breathing heavily. 'You make me sick.'

Lyndsey looked up at him miserably. 'Shit, Vin – what the fuck difference does it make now? It's done, isn't it? And this, like, this *stops* him at least, doesn't it?'

Vinnie shook his head, disgusted, not wanting to hear her, not wanting to even look at her. His mind was reeling. He needed to think.

'You don't say a word, okay?' he told her. 'Not to Titch. Not a *word*. I mean it, Lynds – and if I find you've been over to him for more money, I'll do fucking life for you, I mean it.'

'I won't, Vin. *We* won't. I promise.' She stood up unsteadily then, and for a moment Vinnie thought she was going to try and put her arms around him. Fuck that, he thought, stepping back, revolted by her.

She didn't though. She staggered far enough to grab the back of the armchair by the doorway, and then she threw up.

He didn't stay to help her clear it up.

Chapter 17

Josie lay in her bed and wondered what the time was. She remembered that it was Wednesday, but since school had broken up last Friday she'd lost track of the days. All she knew was that she was bored out of her brains. There seemed to be nothing doing anywhere. And no money to do it, even if there was. Their spell of wealth certainly hadn't lasted long.

It had all been a bit of an anticlimax, Vinnie coming home, as well. Everyone was either busy, or in a mood, or – most of the time, it seemed – both. God, she couldn't wait to grow up and *do* something with her life. As it was, she didn't even have anything to get up for. Frustrated and irritable, she tugged the blanket tightly up under her chin, trying to keep warm that little bit longer, before the moment came when she'd have to get out and put her feet on the freezing lino on the bedroom floor.

How she wished she'd been born into a different family. How she wished she could be one of those posh kids off *Crossroads*. They even had tellies in their bedrooms, they did! She tried to imagine the luxury of being able to lie in your bed and watch telly at the same time; you wouldn't have to get out of bed at all then, not for the whole of the school holidays.

But she wasn't a posh kid and she knew she'd have to get up eventually – if for nothing else than to light the fire. The house was freezing and without the fire lit, it would only get colder. So it might as well be now. She was wide awake, and in a mood that wasn't going to improve. She flung the covers off and leapt in the direction of the wash pile, grabbing her woolly cardi and wriggling into it in a matter of seconds. One thing she was an expert at, she thought to herself ruefully.

With no sound in the house, she was surprised when she came down the stairs, both to feel an unexpected hint of warmth coming up to meet her, and to see her mother.

June was in her usual position, facing the mantelpiece mirror, above a fire that, to Josie's surprise, had already been long lit. She was dressed and applying lipstick – her usual violent shade of red.

'You shit the bed or something, Mam?' Josie asked.

'Cheeky mare!' her mother retorted. 'It's bloody 11 o'clock, madam. Half the day gone already. Anyway, go on back upstairs and get dressed. I've just been up the post office and our Lyndsey needs you up there.'

'Up the post office?'

'No, you dozy cow. I've just seen Lyndsey *in* the post office. She needs you round hers, and quick smart, please.'

Josie frowned. Why? What'd she have to go round Lyndsey's for? She'd been up her sister's twice this week already, and on both occasions, though she'd come specifically to help out with the little ones – *as a favour* – she'd had this weird sensation they didn't want her round there. Probably got some new scam on the go. That was her reading of it, anyway. Or some other dodgy goings-on, with one of Robbo's divvy mates or other. So she'd been only too happy to take the hint.

'What for?' she asked her mother. 'Only I've got stuff on already. And since she's been such a narky cow with me, I don't see why I should anyway. Why should I jump to attention just because *she* says so? I'm not her *slave*. I'm not just put on the earth to be at her beck and call!'

June shot across to the chair in which Josie had now plonked herself down and flicked her across the head with the tea towel she'd been dabbing her lips with. 'You'll do as you're bleeding told!' she said as Josie ducked. 'And like it, too. You've got to go round, anyway. She's gone and got herself knocked up again by that div. So she's got to go and get rid of it, hasn't she?'

Yeah, Josie thought, *just like that last one.*

'What, again?' she said sarcastically.

'Yes, *again*,' her mother conceded, sighing. 'He's fucking simple, he is, that one. Anyway she's got to get to hospital –' she glanced up at the clock – 'inside the hour, and she needs you to stop there for a couple of nights to see to the kids for her.'

'Stop over?' Josie protested. She did *not* want to do that.

'Yes, stop over. But not for long so stop your moaning. She'll sign herself out day after tomorrow. So you won't have much to do.' June flapped a hand towards her. 'Now go and get dressed, will you?'

Josie hadn't thought her mood could get any worse, but now it had – God, two nights alone with that perv Robbo? It wasn't fair. She glared at June. 'Why me? Why not Vinnie? He's missed the kids. He told me. He'll do it, Mam, I'll bet you.'

June started gathering bits of make-up and throwing them in her handbag. 'For Christ's sake will you stop arguing with me for once and do as you're told? Of course Vin can't do it. He's a *bloke*, Josie. Blokes don't know the first bloody thing about kids. You should know that! Now get up those fucking stairs before I take my hand to you!'

Josie stormed up the stairs and slammed her bedroom door for good measure, expelling what scant heat had managed to venture up there. *Bastards*, she thought, rummaging for yesterday's jeans and a blouse and tank top. They treated her like dirt, the lot of them. She yanked a drawer out for socks and slammed it back in as loudly as she could. If she was lucky she'd wake her brother and her father up as well. Serve them right – both in their pits. Both snoring. Both nursing hangovers from last night, probably.

Bastards. Everyone had a life except her.

There was a taxi pulling up at Lyndsey's as Josie approached ten minutes later, which her sister, carrying a small suitcase, was hurrying out to. She looked drawn and pale and stooped and Josie felt an unexpected pang of guilt about her earlier rant. No wonder Lynds had been so moody. It all made sense now. It must be pretty shitty to be her, Josie decided, having to go and have another abortion, but the last thing Lynds needed was another baby to take care off – specially living with that low-life of a boyfriend of hers. If she had a decent bloke she wouldn't have to scrabble around so much just to live, would she? Mind you, Josie reasoned, if she had a decent bloke she wouldn't be in this mess in the first place. Certainly wouldn't be wasting what little money she did have on bloody drugs. She trotted the rest of the distance, making a pact with herself that she would never ever let any of that happen to her, *ever.*

'Thanks, mate,' her sister said as she drew level. 'Thanks for doing this. They're up and dressed. They just need something to eat, that's all.'

Josie could see the three of them, lined up in the front window, already waving. Poor mites, she thought, feeling guilty all over again. How could she not want to take care of them?

'They'll be fine,' she reassured her sister as she climbed stiffly into the back of the taxi. It wasn't all bad, Josie thought – least she'd be off that shit she smoked for a couple of days.

'Just keep an eye on them for me,' Lyndsey said. 'You know what that divvy's like – he'd let them run wild. He's still in bed, by the way. Just shout if you need him for owt, won't you? I'll try to sign myself out tomorrow, if I can. If not, the next day, promise.'

Josie shut the car door and waved her off. That would be the last thing she'd do, she thought, as she walked up the path to her waiting nieces and nephew. Shout for Robbo? Not in a million years. He could stay in bed for the whole two days as far as she was concerned. And he'd just better watch himself around her, that was all. She felt her shoulders stiffen, and her fingers curl into knuckles. She wasn't scared of him, she told herself. Why would she be? He was an idiot. Any crap from him, and he'd fucking know about it.

The children, predictably, were going off like bottles of pop. 'Auntie Titch, Auntie Titch, Auntie Titch!' they all chorused. 'We're so excited you're coming to stay!'

'Might be,' she corrected little Sammy, as she swung her around. 'If I have any nonsense off any of you, I'm going straight back to Nan's. Okay?'

They all promised they'd be angels – which they were with her most of the time anyway – and with no sign of life from the idiot upstairs, she made them lunch with what she could find in the cupboards – eggs, beans and toast. Then, hearing suspicious sounds of activity overhead, told them to get down and go and find their coats.

'Are we going to the park, Auntie Titch?' Robbie wanted to know.

'Yes, we are,' she said, 'and chop-chop, or we'll miss all the best swings.'

'Off out?' came a voice. She looked up from buttoning Lou's coat. It was Robbo, standing at the top of the stairs in only his underpants.

Revolting, Josie thought. How could her sister let that thing go near her? 'We're just off to the park,' she told him, grimacing as he stood and scratched his balls. 'We won't be long.'

'Oh, be as long as you like for me!' he called down gaily.

She didn't have a clue what he was on about – she rarely did – but when he started stumbling down she hotfooted it out of the door with the children. No length of time would be long enough, frankly.

It was something to do, at least, Josie decided, as they walked down to the park. It was at the bottom of the estate and had been there since long before she was born; a huge scrubby grass area surrounded by woodland – a place of secrets and adventures and many a childhood gathering. It also had a play area, complete with swings and a slide and a rusted iron climbing frame and a roundabout that, since going on it once and throwing up, she had always avoided like the plague.

There was also a big duck pond, which rarely saw any sort of wildfowl, but which, despite being full of old tyres and shopping trolleys, would become the estate's impromptu paddling pool during the summer. Despite the scummy brown water and the unmentionable things floating on it, the local kids were always happy to strip down to their underwear and have a splash about on any half-decent dry day.

Which today wasn't. It was cold and cloudy and threatening drizzle, so as soon as they arrived, Robbie split off to join a group of boys playing football on one of the pitches, while the girls raced ahead to join the queue for the slide.

Josie found a spot on the grass where she could keep an eye on all of them, happy to at least half-drift off into the world of her own reveries. At least she was out in the fresh air, rather than staring at her four bedroom walls, and being with Robbie and Sam and Lou always lifted her spirits.

Not that she could relax too much, not here. Horton Park wasn't just a place for kids to enjoy innocent pleasures. People were regularly mugged walking up here, night *and* day, and it also had the unofficial status, through years of tradition, of being the place to be if you wanted to arrange, or view, a fight.

It had been that way for years – for as long as Josie could remember, certainly – if you had a grudge match in mind, and you wanted it played out in public, you'd put the word around and get yourself an audience.

It was generally something of a big social event, as well. If it was between two big rival families, and the weather was fine, supporters would even bring picnics and tartan blankets and make an afternoon of it.

And it was much the same if the exchange took place between kids, only with boiled sweets, rather than cans of beer being passed around. Barley sugar, Josie remembered – that was always a favourite. And her favourite Yorkshire mixture, too. The kinds of sweets that were guaranteed to last the length of a good meaty fight.

It was quiet on that front today, however, just overrun with kids, which kept her three occupied for a good couple of hours. Which suited her perfectly, because it meant they'd be worn out, which was always a good thing. It meant that when she put them to bed they'd be out like a light, and she'd have free rein over what to watch on telly, because the idiot would be either spark out or actually out, down the Bull.

Hopefully the latter, she thought, as, with the sun beginning to sink towards the horizon, she started the usual process of 'just one more swing/slide/go on the climbing frame' before she was able to prise them away. It didn't take too long, however, as with the darkening sky came the cold, and as they headed back Sammy and Lou's hands were like ice-pops in hers.

'Can we have hot dogs and chips?' Lou wanted to know as she skipped along beside Josie.

'We'll have to see what your mam has in her cupboard, mate,' she said. They'd not even asked where their mam was, much less when she was coming back. Which was sad, Josie decided. If she ever had kids herself, she'd hate to think they wouldn't be looking for her, wondering why she wasn't there. 'I tell you what,' she said, 'if there's nowt, we'll get some money off Robbo to get some. How's that sound?'

Lou looked up her. 'You might have to ask me nan then, Auntie Titch. Me mam says he never has any money.'

'It's okay,' Robbie said, jogging along beside them, 'I can get some. If there's none in I'll go and nick some from the Paki shop. I could get some of those special bread rolls as well if you like.'

'There'll be no need for that, Robbie,' Josie chided, looking at him sternly. 'I'll make something nice for tea for us, *whatever* we find.'

That was sad, too. That Robbie already knew all about stealing. It wasn't right. But, as luck would have it, there was no need for any further debate on the subject because there was a tin of hot dog sausages in the cupboard in any case. No special bread buns but they were just as good rolled up in white sliced anyway and, as there were a few potatoes too, she also rustled up a big pan of chips. There was even a bottle of ketchup, which made it feel like a feast, which they all ate gathered around the coffee table, watching the cartoons on TV.

She didn't ask, because she really couldn't have cared less about anything he got up to, but Josie's guess was that Robbo, though he did at least have clothes on, had barely stirred since she'd left him to go to the park. And though it felt completely normal to be cooking for him too – and he wolfed it down appreciatively – she couldn't help but wonder how a grown man could spend quite so much time doing absolutely fuck all, day after day after day. If she had to live like that, she decided, she'd go mad.

'Right,' she said to the kids once the last plate was licked clean. 'You've got quarter of an hour while I clear all these plates and stuff away, then it's upstairs for bath-time and stories and bed.'

'Yayyy!' they all chanted, piling their plates into her waiting hands. 'Yayyy, Auntie Titch!' as if she'd just told them she was Father Christmas. All that for a story. They were that short on being read stories. Did their mam ever read to them? She doubted it.

It turned into four stories, naturally. Three for Sammy and Lou, from their big nursery story book, and a big chunk of *James and the Giant Peach* for Robbie, which he'd recently got from the library. He loved this book with a passion and would always ask Josie to read a certain passage out loud, no matter which chapter she was currently reading. *'And James Henry Trotter, who once, if you remember, had been the saddest and loneliest boy that you could find, now had all the friends and playmates in the world.'*

Reading that line always saddened Josie. And she knew why as well – because it made her realise that little Robbie, too, was searching for something but, unlike James, he didn't know where to look.

She'd been upstairs a good hour before they were all tucked in and settled and she was ready to go back down. She'd be sleeping on the couch, so she'd brought her long nightie and her maxi-cardigan – as much to cover herself up as keep out the cold. She'd hoped he might have gone out, but knew he hadn't

– she'd have heard the door go, almost certainly – and that being the case hoped he'd do what he tended to do most evenings: quickly smoke himself into a stupor.

He was certainly on the way when she got back down and joined him in the lounge. He was sprawled out on the rug in front of the fire, his pipe beside him and his drugs paraphernalia laid out in the hearth.

Seeing her come in he pulled himself up onto his knees. 'You want a quick blast on this, Titch?' he asked as he raised the milk-bottle pipe up towards her. 'It's good stuff. Black Leb from Paki Mo. Gives you a right fucking kick, it does, this stuff.'

She looked down at him in disgust. She'd rather give him a right fucking kick up the arse. It was clear from both the look of him and the pungent smell that enveloped the room now that he'd wasted no time in getting started once the kids were out of the way. How could he live like that? How could anyone want to live like that? She shook her head as she sat down at the far end of the sofa. 'Nah, mate,' she said, 'I can't be doing with that shit.' She reached around her to grab the blanket Lyndsey had left out for her on the sofa back. 'I think I'm just gonna get my head down on here and watch a bit of telly if it's all the same to you.'

Robbo laughed at her, as she arranged the blanket over her, exposing his raggedy row of teeth. They were stained just like his fingers, an unpleasant shade of yellow. 'Suit yourself, you big baby,' he said mildly. 'Go ahead, and don't you mind me. I'm gonna get through this little stash and then I'll be off up to bed myself. Mind you,' he said, grinning at her, 'that looks proper cosy. Aww – you want me to come over there and tuck you in, little sister-in-law?'

He'd put on a stupid voice – as if he was speaking to one of the children. Except he never spoke to the children in that way, much less ever stir himself to tuck the poor little bleeders in. And 'sister-in-law'? Yuck, she thought. *I don't fucking think so.* 'Fuck off, Robbo,' she said to him, equally mildly. 'Shut up and smoke your pipe. I'm trying to watch *Dad's Army.*'

She wasn't sure what time it was. Only that she was dreaming. Was in that weird place halfway between the dream and the reality, her consciousness ebbing and flowing in languid waves. She'd drifted off to sleep at some point – she had no idea when. Was only aware that with the air so thick and fuggy from the drugs, she'd had the thought that she might even be very slightly stoned as well. You breathed some of it in, didn't you? Whether you wanted to or not.

And now she was where? She was … yes, she was with Mucky Melvin. He was there – right there. Right in the room with her. He'd been offering her ciggies, trying to coax her to get into his fetid bed with him. 'Come on,' he was saying to her, in his phlegmy old man's voice. 'Come on. You know you like it *really.*'

And he was stroking her. Weirdly, he was stroking her and laughing. Not laughing loudly. More laughing to himself; finding something funny. And he wasn't being rough with her. Why wasn't he being rough with her? Why wasn't he pinning her down? Swearing at her. Panting. Because he wasn't. Whatever he was doing was actually rather nice. Kind of soothing and rhythmic and gentle.

Yet there was something wrong, even so. What was the something? She struggled for a moment or two, trying to gather her thoughts. That was it, she realised. That whatever was happening, nice and soothing as it was, was something that shouldn't be happening; that whatever she was feeling was something she shouldn't be *feeling*. Not if this was Melvin …

she tried to clear her head … open her eyes … *That* was it, she decided. She needed to *open her eyes*. She needed to wake up. Wake up and *see* what was going on.

She rolled then. Turned over on the couch, wrestling with the blanket. Except it wasn't the blanket. That was gone. It was her nightie she was wrestling with, because something seemed to be stopping it from changing position with her. And with the knowledge came another, much more awful realisation – that the reason her nightie was swizzled up beneath her was because Melvin's hand – *no, no, Robbo's hand! Fuck!* – was inside it and trying to get in between her legs.

'What the fuck are you *doing*!' she yelped, trying to wriggle herself away from him, panicking. Taking in the scene – him kneeling up so close to her, his eyes so unfocused, his arm still trying to wriggle its way along the sofa with her, a hot urgent presence against her thighs. And then the hand – his other hand – which seemed to come out of nowhere. Which landed square on her mouth, clamping down hard.

He pushed her down, back into the cushion. 'Shush,' he whispered, his breath hissing close to her ear, 'shush. It's all right, babe. Just lie back and enjoy it. I won't hurt you.'

Josie felt tears begin to squeeze from her eyes. And at the same time, a rage begin to surge from her belly. The fucking *bastard*. She was *not* going to let him do this. She found some strength from somewhere and was surprised to find it more than sufficient. For all his determination, he was no match for her now she was truly riled. As soon as she began to flail her legs, he released his hand for long enough that she could kick him away bodily, and she did. Upon which he sat back on his heels again and smiled at her. 'What the fuck is up with you?' he wanted to know. 'I thought you were enjoying it. Correction. You *were* enjoying it. Don't say you weren't.'

'Get the fuck away from me!' she yelled. 'I'm telling our Lyndsey about this, I swear I am. You dirty fucking bastard. You *filthy* fucking bastard!'

Robbo stood then, and she didn't know what he was going to do next. It was only then she realised just how stoned he really was. He seemed to hover there, his eyes scanning the room, his head dipping and nodding, before his gaze came to a halt at the wall above the fireplace.

She followed the line of it. There were crossed samurai swords hanging there. Been there for ever. Been there so long that you didn't really even notice them any more, except in a vague 'what a wanker, thinking he's so hard' sort of way that she suddenly remembered Vinnie once remarking.

Oh, shit, she thought, watching petrified, as he lurched and staggered towards them. Oh shit, he was really stoned. What the fuck was he going to do? He made a lunge towards them – what the fuck *was* he going to do? Try to rape her at fucking sword-point? And she took the opportunity to leap from the couch, cover the two steps to the TV, and grab the first heavy object she had managed to lay eyes on – a large, multicoloured, glass fish. She wasted no time – there *was* no time – in thinking about it further. Just took her opportunity, as he wrestled with the handle of one of the swords, to bash him over the head with it as hard as she could.

He went down at once, like at least a half a ton of bricks, with the sword, which he'd just managed to free from the wall, still in his hand. It clattered against the coffee table while he half-hit the sofa, landing awkwardly with his face and one arm resting across it, while the rest of him slumped chest down, on the floor.

And she'd drawn blood. She could see it begin to darken and dampen his hair. Could see it – *shit!* – begin to trickle down his neck. Fucking hell, she thought, moving closer, bending down, crouching beside him. Was he breathing? *Oh, shit*, he had to be breathing. She couldn't have killed him, could she? Surely she couldn't have *killed* him. Not just like that.

His chest heaved, as if in answer to her unspoken question; a sudden and massive inhalation, quickly followed by an out-breath and a groan.

Momentarily relieved, Josie exhaled too. Then she saw the blood again. How much there was of it; all red and slick and glossy. He might be dying. *Oh my God*, she thought, *he might be bleeding to death in front of me!* She scrabbled to her feet and flew from the room. Then she yanked open the door.

Then she ran.

Chapter 18

She had no idea what the time was, only that the house was in darkness. Though it wasn't bitterly cold inside, as the fire, not long died, was still glowing red. The lounge was empty, though, as was the kitchen. Only the grease-laden stale smell of chip-paper lingered. She ran back into the lounge and looked up at the clock. It was now almost 11 o'clock at night.

Maybe her mam and dad had just gone to bed. The thought cheered her. 'Mam!' she called, hitching up her nightie and taking the stairs two at once. 'Mam, you up there? *Mam*! Mam, I need you!'

There was no response, and putting her head round her parents' bedroom door confirmed it. The Bull, she thought wretchedly. They'd be at the sodding Bull, having a fucking lock-in, wouldn't they? She had to fight down an urge to just drop to her knees and sob. It was *her* who had to go round and fucking babysit – even though they were her mam and dad's fucking grandkids – while they went and got pissed with their mates. How was *that* fair? And what the fuck was she supposed to do now?

Auntie Maureen, she decided, trying to gather her wits and think rationally. She'd go there. She didn't hold up much hope of having any luck with Moira next door – she'd be at the Bull with her mam, probably. No, better to dash to Maureen's and pray that she was there.

The cold of the lino was seeping into her feet now. She needed shoes, she realised, her slippers being still round at Lyndsey's, where that bastard Robbo was probably still lying right now. And perhaps still bleeding, too. The thought galvanised her. She could go to prison, after all, couldn't she? Be done for murder! She ran into her bedroom and scrabbled around under the bed till she found both of her plimsolls, then rat-a-tatted her way back down the stairs.

She'd already cannoned into Vinnie by the time she saw him.

'Whoah!' he yelped, jolted back against the coat hooks on the wall. He was obviously as surprised to see her as she was to see him. He'd clearly just come in from somewhere – he smelt of cold crisp night air. 'Vin!' she cried, grabbing his forearms. 'Oh, shit, Vin – you've got to help me! You've got to come with me, right *now*!'

'Whoah,' he said again. His arms were pinned by his sleeves. He must have just been about to take his coat off. 'Hang about,' he said, shrugging it back onto his shoulders again. 'Come with you where?'

'To our Lyndsey's,' Josie gabbled at him. 'Quickly, Vin – it's Robbo. I think I've hurt him.'

Vinnie pinged on the hall light, flooding the small space with a bright yellow incandescence that made Josie squint.

'*Hurt* him?' Vinnie asked her. 'Hurt him *how*?'

Josie pushed past him and pulled the front door open. 'Hurt him badly, I think. I hit him. Vin, come on – we've gotta go there. I could have *killed* him!'

Her brother didn't seem to need any further explanation, thank goodness, and, snapping the light back off, he followed her out of the door, down the path and into the night.

'What d'you hit him with?' he wanted to know, as he followed her the short distance up the street to Lyndsey's.

'That fish,' she called back, 'you know – the one they have sitting on the telly? Oh, Vin,' she said, swerving onto their front path, though the gap in the fence where the gate used to be, 'I hit him so hard – I just went for it, but it was so heavy ... I didn't quite realise. I just grabbed it in a panic, and ...'

'But *why*?' he wanted to know, grabbing her wrist just as she was about to push their door open. He held it firmly, his eyes glittering in the light from the street lamp as he took in the nightie, the woolly cardigan, the grubby plimsolls, her tear-stained face. She could see him computing it; his agile mind coming to conclusions, calculating, waiting for an explanation. 'What did that fucking *shite* do to make you hit him, Titch?'

There was a fraction of a second when she could see where this might lead; and it was enough to still her tongue momentarily. But his gaze was so direct and probing that her brain couldn't quite unscramble. There was absolutely no question of her lying to him. He had this way of making you tell him the truth – something she'd long forgotten but now remembered. There was no question – and, besides, that bastard Robbo deserved everything he had coming to him, didn't he? He just mustn't be dead. She shuddered. She just mustn't have killed him.

'He tried it on, Vin,' she told her brother. 'He tried to feel me up when I was sleeping. I just woke up and he was, like, looming over me ...' She felt herself reddening under Vinnie's stony-faced scrutiny. 'And he had his hand, like, inside my nightie, and ...'

She didn't need to say any more. Vinnie let go of her arm, mounted the step and pushed the front door open.

Josie followed. 'So I hit him,' she explained, 'on the back of his head. And there was just so much *blood* – I never expected that, I mean, I just meant to *stop* him ... I never meant to split his skull open, to –'

'Shh!' Vinnie cautioned, putting a finger to his lips, 'or you'll wake the kids up.'

She mouthed a sorry and followed him into the living room, where Robbo was lying exactly as she left him. Seeing the amount of blood again made her start, but she was quickly reassured, seeing that his chest was rising and falling steadily. *Oh, thank God*, she thought. *Thank God he isn't dead.* Though she could see from the set of her brother's jaw that he might soon wish he was.

Vinnie strode across the room and squatted down beside him, lightly touching his hair so he could peer at his wound. Then he stood up and, glancing at Josie, slowly took off his precious coat, before draping it carefully over the back of one of the dining chairs.

He nodded towards the kitchen. 'Get me some water,' he told Josie quietly.

Josie hurried out and looked for a glass. She'd tidied the kitchen earlier but Robbo had obviously been banging around in there after she'd gone to sleep, and she could see a plastic beaker half-submerged beneath the beige surface of some old washing-up water. She reached in and retrieved it, feeling a perverse determination not to treat him to a clean one from the cupboard. She was also conscious of being quiet because of the children sleeping upstairs, and the sound of banging cupboard doors would go straight up through the floorboards. They'd obviously not been woken by the struggle as there was no sign of the three of them. Thank heavens for that at least, she thought.

She swilled the beaker around in the tepid water then turned the tap on so she could rinse it and fill it, wondering as she did so quite what was going to happen now. It was only beginning to hit her that perhaps Vinnie wasn't the best person to have encountered and brought back here. Had it been her mam, it would have been one thing – she'd have been merciless with him, certainly – but this was Vinnie and, if she'd noticed one thing about him in the short time he'd been back, it had been this new edge he had to him; an unfamiliar tension, a kind of simmering aggression that she didn't know the reason for. It wasn't directed at her, and she was certain it never would be, but still she felt it, and it made her uncomfortable.

Thank God he wasn't drunk at least, she decided, taking the beaker of water back into the lounge. No, he probably wasn't quite sober – he'd obviously been out and about with his mates, too, and perhaps to the Bull – but at least he wasn't drunk, so hopefully things wouldn't get too nasty.

But as soon as she got into the lounge she realised she was wrong. She'd just been thinking of asking Vinnie if he thought Robbo might need stitches from where she'd hit him, when she saw there'd be nothing like that going on.

Not tonight, anyway. The first fronds of a new anxiety began to stir within her. The water she'd been asked to get obviously wasn't intended for Robbo to sip. Far from it. Vinnie was kneeling on the floor now, in the middle of gagging him.

It seemed pointless to ask him what he was doing. So she just stood stupefied as she watched him stuff Robbo's mouth with something. A hankie? A sock? There were plenty of both lying around – just stood clutching the water as Vinnie then wrapped another piece of cloth – black, this time – round his mouth. He then tied it at the back of his head. Josie looked around. What was that? Where had he got it? Did he just have this sort of stuff on him? It was a question she couldn't answer, and it bothered her.

He tied it tightly, too, Robbo's previously slack mouth yanked back into a kind of rictus, then fixed the grim bandana only an inch or so above the wound. He then pulled Robbo round so that he was lying face up on the floor, and held out his hand for the beaker.

Josie handed it to him, clutching the edges of the cardigan together with her free hand, and realising that the gag was a pair of Lyndsey's tights. She then winced involuntarily as her brother did exactly what she now expected; threw the contents of the beaker over Robbo's face. She shivered. It was mains water, and she'd let it run, so she knew just how cold it was.

The effect was instantaneous and surprising. Having failed to wake up at any point during Vinnie's ministrations with his gag, Robbo blinked into consciousness immediately. It was shock, Josie supposed – shock then compounded by terror, as he realised he was unable to cry out.

He raised his arms as if to shield himself, but Vinnie grabbed his wrists and brought them down again. Robbo just stared then, transfixed. He didn't try to raise them again. 'Vinnie –' Josie began, as Robbo blinked at her too, his fear now palpable.

'What?' Vinnie said mildly, turning to look at her.

She lowered her gaze. 'Nothing. I mean, Vin, you know, you don't need to …' she tailed off. Didn't need to *what*? She didn't even know what he was going to do to Robbo, did she? And whatever it was, well, she knew speaking to him was going to be pointless. There was something in his expression that said everything his voice wasn't. He'd do what he wanted to do, whether she liked it or not.

'Bring me that chair,' Vinnie commanded. 'That one over there.' He pointed. And as she went to get it, he hauled the now wide-eyed Robbo effortlessly to his feet. He'd become so strong since he'd been away. So unexpectedly big and strong. And though Robbo was Vinnie's height, he was so emaciated and feeble from all the drugs that he looked like a bag of skin and bones in comparison. Why had she been so scared of him? She could probably have knocked him out with a punch. And now, instead … She swallowed hard. Now what?

'What the fuck is that?' Vinnie said suddenly, as he plonked Robbo down onto the chair. He wasn't even resisting, Josie noticed. He was flopping about like a rag doll.

'What?' she said, following Vinnie's gaze.

'That fucking sword there!' Vinnie supplied, pointing at where it lay on the carpet.

'He got it down,' she told him. Her voice felt scared and shrunken. 'He got it down off the wall, but I was too quick for him. Like I told you, I grabbed the fish, and –'

Her words were drowned by the thunderclap of Vinnie's palm hitting Robbo's cheek. 'You fucking cunt,' Vinnie snarled at him. 'You fucking *cunt.*'

Again, Robbo made no defensive move to stop it, but even so, Vinnie wrenched his arms roughly behind the chair back and, grabbing a length of rubber tubing that was coiled in the hearth, deftly secured his wrists to the dining chair. Yet again, Josie looked on in a kind of stunned fascination. Robbo, whose drug-smoking paraphernalia had just been used to tie him up, seemed reactionless, like a shop-window dummy. He was that stoned. That defenceless. That inert.

A sudden thought gripped her. Was he brain damaged? Had the fish knocked out some key part of his mind? She opened her mouth to speak but Vinnie was already on the move, stalking past her and out into the kitchen. She went to follow him, but just as she did, she became aware of a noise upstairs. She listened harder. It was one of the girls, crying.

'Vinnie, that's Lou or Sammy,' she began nervously. 'And if they both start up, they might wake up Robbie, and ...'

'So go up and sort it, little sis,' he said. He wasn't even looking at her but his tone was clear. Go. He was now rummaging in the cutlery drawer.

It was as if it was the sign she'd been waiting for. An escape. She rushed from the room and hurried up the stairs.

Vinnie looked at the excuse for a bloke that his sister was inexplicably still shacked up with and felt a small fizz of something like excitement in his chest. He couldn't have played it better if he'd tried to. Robbo really was the biggest piece of shit, he decided. And an even bigger idiot than his name already suggested. He had put himself exactly where Vinnie wanted him by sticking his filthy, shitty hands up his sister's skirt.

Vinnie brought the knife from behind his back and raised it slowly in front of him. Actually, it hadn't been her skirt, had it? It had been her nightie. Her fucking prim little-girl nightie, while she'd been asleep. Vinnie swallowed, feeling the disgust rising up through him like a kind of nausea. Robbo had known, even. Known what that fucking pervert Melvin had done to her – had even been fucking touching him for money, the bastard. And not content with that – not once considering how she'd already been so *fucking* defiled – he thought he'd try and grab himself a bit of her as well.

Or perhaps it was *because* his little earner had dried up. Was that it? A kind of 'so there!' revenge? Or was it nothing more thought out than the sort of shitty, opportunistic grope blokes like Robbo made their speciality? Vinnie focussed his attention firmly in the present, grinning manically at the shivering wreck he now had at his mercy, and who he'd enjoy giving some abuse to in return. 'You fucking cunt,' he whispered, advancing on him. 'You want to see something stuck somewhere you don't want it stuck, do you?

As the knife glinted in Vinnie's right hand, Robbo attempted to shuffle back into his chair, grunting like an animal trapped in a pen. But Vinnie had that sorted; he sank down towards the floor in one movement, his knees coming to rest on top of Robbo's bare feet. He smiled indulgently as Robbo let out a low, muffled groan, presumably in anticipation of the pain that was soon to come.

'What's that you say?' Vinnie asked softly, still grinning. 'Only it sounded like you said "Please, Vinnie, stick it to me". Is *that* what you said, you fucking pig?'

And while Robbo stared at him, singularly failing to provide an answer, Vinnie sank the blade of the knife into the middle of his scrawny thigh. Robbo lolled in his seat, then, head tipped back, jaw clenched. He was such a stoner that Vinnie wasn't even sure he really felt it, but, just to be sure, he slid it out again (oh, dear, those loons would be ruined – pity) and sank the knife into his other thigh for good measure.

'I think they call that a double whammy,' he said conversationally, as he removed the knife the second time. 'One for tapping that cunt Melvin for cash when you were supposed to be fucking *beating the shit out of him* for what he did to my little sister, get it? And the other is for her as well, for being the fucking piece of shit *you* are as well. For daring – for even *daring* to suppose that a spastic like you would have a chance in a zillion of having any fucking decent woman anywhere near your disease-ridden *prick*.'

The reaction was pleasing. Robbo's face was a picture, and Vinnie badly wished he had a Polaroid on hand, to capture the expression for posterity, especially when his gaze (not to mention the hand with the bloody knife in) moved slowly but surely towards his groin.

'You can stop shitting yourself now,' he said conversationally, while the blood seeped from Robbo's matching leg wounds. 'You got off pretty lightly. I'm done with you.'

He inspected the knife and then wiped it clean across a dry patch of Robbo's jeans. 'Well, at least for the moment, anyway.' He rolled his eyes heavenwards. 'Cos you got nippers to take care of, you see. Nippers that I *care* about, you fucker.' He stood then, considered the knife again, then jabbed it towards Robbo. 'Which, let me tell you, is the only reason I haven't kicked your fucking balls in as well.'

Josie whimpered on the bottom stair, her hand stuffed in her mouth. She'd settled the girls a while ago and had crept back downstairs again but, unable to bring herself to go back into the living room for fear of what she'd find there, had been trapped in the hallway ever since. She couldn't leave. Not with her being the one who'd dragged Vinnie round there in the first place. But at the same time she couldn't bear the thought of witnessing her beloved brother doing whatever he was doing to Robbo.

So, she hadn't seen it – 'it' being whatever torture he'd inflicted. But she had certainly heard it. An important part of it, anyway.

And Vinnie knew about Melvin. Shit. How could that be? Her fucking sister; that must be it – her fucking sister must have told him. Even though she promised. And what was all that about Robbo tapping him for money for it? What was that about? God, she thought, wishing she'd never told anyone *anything*. Now she'd caused all this to happen. What the fuck was she going to do now?

Her head started banging; a steady thumping in her temples. She didn't even know how this night was going to end, let alone try and work out the future.

She could hear Vinnie chatting to Robbo again now. Conversationally. Amicably. As if he was an old friend, catching up on his news. So it was safe to go in, perhaps. And she couldn't sit here for ever, could she? Decided, she stood up and walked back into the lounge.

She was just in time to watch Vinnie settling Robbo onto the settee. A pale gag-less Robbo, a bloodied, trembling Robbo, who, as well as the wound she'd inflicted on him earlier, now had two burgundy patches blooming on his thighs, stark and shocking against some sort of bandaging. She didn't like to think … No, no, she decided – she must make herself *not* think.

'There you go, mate,' Vinnie was saying, 'Think we'll leave you to it for now.' He turned and grinned at Josie then. 'Ah,' he said in greeting, 'you about ready for the off, sis? Only Robbo's feeling a bit tired now, aren't you, mate? Oh, and he says he's really sorry about that stupid business earlier. Fucking drugs pickled his head a bit, ain't that right, Robbo?'

Josie lowered her head as Robbo nodded. She couldn't bring herself to look at him. She was ready to go, alright. She wanted to run for miles and never stop. Just keep running and running till her legs burned and her chest heaved. But somehow she had the feeling she wouldn't get anywhere. All she could see was herself being propelled onto a giant roundabout. One from which she'd never be able to get off.

Chapter 19

Josie had seen all sorts. She really had. It wasn't like she was a complete wimp or anything. She'd seen June and Jock going at it hammer and tong, and witnessed some major tear-ups on the estate. She also knew what it was like to be at the receiving end of violence; something she'd worked hard to tuck away in a corner of her brain and forget. She hadn't managed it. She knew that. She wondered if she ever would now. Because it still had the power to creep up on her and ambush her – catch her unawares while she was thinking about something completely different, and kind of overtake her body. It would make her heart thump and her nerves jangle, as if she was transported right back there – it really could be that intense. At times like that she could feel his strength as he gripped her, and hear the sound of his calloused hand rasping up her thigh. She could even smell the pillow; the oily muskiness of it, the bacterial soup under his arm, the whiff of stale pee.

But these days, for the most part, she could quash it. It was the aftermath of it that was troubling her, because she'd created it. She'd told Lyndsey and because of that she had now created violence. *She* had. She had – what was it the police said? Incited it? Yes, that was the word. She'd done that. And the thought that she'd done it really sickened her. Why had she told Lyndsey? Why?

Caz was wrong. It wasn't the right thing or the best thing at all. It was just about the stupidest thing she had ever done.

She stared at the ceiling, trying to gauge what the time was. It was fully light but there were birds singing, so she guessed it must be early. And the house was silent. Well, almost. There was just the one sound. The low, familiar rumble of her dad snoring.

She wondered if Vinnie was at home now. He'd walked her back, and his mood had been odd – disconcertingly buoyant – as he reassured her she'd have nothing more to fear. Though he'd said nothing about Mucky Melvin and what he might have learned about what had happened to her, and she'd been much too frightened to bring it up. Too scared of him questioning her, making her tell him stuff.

So she was still none the wiser about what he did know or didn't know. And having dropped her, he'd gone straight back out again.

Where had he gone? What had he gone to do? It was this that had woken her repeatedly throughout the night, she knew. Waiting and wanting to hear the sound of his return. Had he gone to Melvin's to torture him too, for answers? She still couldn't get her head around what she'd heard him say to Robbo – that he knew he'd been tapping him for money. She couldn't believe Robbo had been doing that.

No, actually, she could *easily* believe he'd been doing that – it was exactly the sort of thing he would do. But what about Lyndsey? Did *she* know about the money? She couldn't have, surely. She'd never let him do something like that, would she?

The questions swirled, filling her head, making her anxious. What if Vinnie had gone to Melvin's? What if he'd gone round there and hurt him – what if he'd even *killed* him? The way he'd been last night – actually, the way he'd been since he'd come home from borstal – she was frightened for him. Frightened of what he might have become. She didn't care about Melvin. He deserved every single horrible thing in the world to happen to him. But what about Vinnie? If he did something – *anything* – bad to anyone, he'd be sent back to prison, and she couldn't bear to think about that. Oh, why hadn't her mam been in last night?

She threw the blanket off and kicked it away. She needed to do something. She wasn't sure what she could do about Vinnie exactly, but there was something she definitely knew she *could* do. And would do. She needed to fight her own battles, starting today.

St Luke's hospital was in Little Horton, just a 15-minute walk away, and though that was obviously too far for her sister to go on foot, for Josie it would be a much-needed chance to use up some energy – burn off the tension that had wound her up so tightly.

Dressing quickly and quietly, so she wouldn't wake her parents, she tiptoed out to the landing, poked her head round Vinnie's door – it seemed he was home, and she was relieved – then made her way slowly down the stairs, avoiding the creaky ones, and slipped out and off up the road.

She knew where she was going because she'd been there before. She'd been there to visit her mad Uncle Charlie, who'd been in there some time. He'd been badly burned by a fire that got out of control and nearly killed him, at some squat he was living in with a bunch of druggies. They'd run away and left him, of course, because that's what druggies did, and she shuddered to recall just how horrible he'd looked. But that was drugs for you, she thought. Made you mean. Made you mean and made you stupid with it.

The hospital was huge. That she did remember, just as soon as she clapped eyes on it; huge and posh – just as she imagined a five-star hotel might be like, all grass and trees and flower-beds, currently full of red and yellow flowers – and completely at odds with its grim grey surroundings. You almost wanted to get ill, she thought, just to have a chance to stay here. Not too ill, obviously, but just ill enough.

But she didn't know where to go, and didn't really know where to start either, so the probability of getting lost was pretty high. And she thought she might well do – after all, she was at a loss as to what to head for. What sort of ward did someone having an abortion get put on anyway? She discounted maternity, because it surely wouldn't be that, would it? And then, scanning the many signs hung from the ceiling on the main corridor, she saw a name she recognised. Halcyon Ward. She was sure her mum had mentioned that. Halcyon, she thought, heading off in that direction. Didn't Halcyon mean something about good times and parties? How ironic that it should be that.

Josie had worried that they might not let her see Lyndsey. She didn't know what the visiting times were and thought she might be too early, but when she spoke to the nurse at the nurse station at the ward entrance, she didn't seem to mind and waved her through. It was quiet, half the beds empty, so perhaps that was why; she passed four devoid of patients before reaching Lyndsey, who was halfway up the ward, under a window. The view was as pretty as her sister looked grim. Though not especially grim – these days she looked rough most of the time, much like everyone who smoked heroin seemed to do.

She was reading. Sitting up in bed flicking through an old copy of *Look-In*. It had Donny Osmond on the cover, she noticed. She quite liked Donny Osmond. Though today it was as if he was looking right at her – his teeth grinning out at her like an accusing white beacon. Donny Osmond, who was a

Mormon and never seemed less than perfect. Donny Osmond who had probably never done a bad thing in his life.

She watched Lyndsey glance up incuriously as she approached, presumably expecting a nurse. She then did a double-take, realising it was actually her sister walking towards her. 'Titch!' she exclaimed, throwing the magazine down on the bed. 'What the hell are you doing here? What's going on? Has something happened to one of the kids?'

She looked genuinely anxious, and Josie quickly shook her head. 'Not the kids, Lynds,' she said. 'No. It's not about them. You feeling okay?'

'Then why are you here?' she said, clearly not interested in pleasantries. 'Shouldn't you be home looking after them? Don't tell me you really came all this way to see how I was doing. No danger of that, eh?' She laughed without humour, then abruptly stopped and scowled. 'Fuck, I need a smoke.'

'Have a smoke, then,' Josie suggested.

'Not *that* sort of smoke, Titch. Don't play dense. No point in asking you though, is there?'

Josie tried to feel sorry for her. She really did. She wanted to care. She tried to be reasonable as well. After all, her sister was bound to have a face on. She'd just been though God knew what surgery to get rid of the baby. Plus she didn't have her gear with her, so she was likely to be ratty. Though not *that* ratty – odds on she'd have sneaked something in.

But it was Lyndsey's tone, really. Did she actually give a shit about her? No 'Hello', no 'Nice to see you', no 'Are you alright, Josie?' No 'Thanks for helping'. Was that the drugs, too, or just how she'd always been?

'I want to ask you something,' she said, pulling up the chair that was parked by the bed. It was heavy and squealed in protest as she dragged it across the floor.

'What about?' said Lyndsey, wincing at the noise, looking irritable. She'd look more than irritable in a minute, Josie thought wryly.

'It's about what I told you about Mucky Melvin,' she said. 'And about what you told Robbo.'

Lyndsey's brows pulled together. 'What about it?' she said.

'Like I said, what exactly *did* you tell him, Lynds?'

'What you told me. Just like I said I would.'

'And what did he do?'

Lyndsey's expression changed again then. She looked wary as well as tetchy. 'He did what I said he'd do. Put the frighteners on him. Like you *asked*.'

'And did you go?'

'Go where?'

'Did you go *with* him? You said you'd go round with him, remember?'

Now Lyndsey looked properly flustered. She picked the magazine back up and relocated it to the top of her locker before answering.

'No, I didn't in the end, I – look Titch, what's this? Twenty questions? He put the frighteners on him, just like I said he would. And that was that.' She paused then, and her eyes narrowed. 'Has he been bothering you again? Is that it? Is that what this is all about?'

Josie shook her head. Did Lynds know or didn't she? She couldn't make her mind up. *Oh, well*, she thought, *in for a penny in for a pound*. She swallowed. 'No,' she said. 'No, he hasn't been bothering me, and it's not because Robbo's put the frighteners on him. It's because he's been fucking *paying* him, Lynds. Paying him to keep quiet.'

She'd kept her voice low, so not to draw attention of the patients in the nearby beds, but she could feel her voice rising in her throat. And she knew the answer, now. She knew because the look on her sister's face had told her. She *did* know. She knew all about what Robbo had obviously been up to with Melvin. It was there, it was a fact, it was right there in her face.

'He's been blackmailing him, Lynds. How could you let him *do* that? You know, I've been thinking and thinking. Lying there all night, just thinking. How could he *do* that? Earn money out of something like that? Get his *fucking gear money* off that perv, on my account!'

Lyndsey regarded her with an expression she found difficult to read. 'What the fuck do you expect?' she hissed finally. 'What the *fuck* do you expect, Titch? Where d'you think you're living – fucking Hollywood? This is the real world. And what difference does it make to you anyway? He's left you alone, hasn't he? So it's worked!'

'Christ, Lynds – that's not the point!'

'That's exactly the point, little sister,' Lyndsey snapped back at her, throwing off the hospital sheet and blanket. 'That's *precisely* the point.'

Josie felt tears begin to prick at the back of her eyes. To think she'd allowed herself to believe Lyndsey hadn't known. That she'd told Robbo to go round and give Melvin a proper pasting and that as far as she'd known that was exactly what he'd done. How stupid had she been? How naïve?

'You've been getting money off him, that's the point,' she said, sniffing the tears back. 'And it's wrong!'

'Oh, I get it,' Lyndsey said, swinging her legs around and putting her feet on the floor. Her skin was all mottled and she was wearing ankle socks that didn't match. Christ, she looked like a mental patient. 'Jesus,' she said, combing hair out of her eyes with her finger. 'I have to get out of this fucking bed. She didn't move though. Just glared at Josie. 'You *want* some of it? You want some of the money? Is that it?'

'No!' Titch protested. 'That's the last thing I want! It's sick, it is, doing that. As sick as he is!'

Lyndsey flapped a dismissive hand. 'Well, that's just as well, mate, because that ship has sailed now.'

'I know,' Josie said. 'And now *Vinnie* knows as well!'

This failed to stir anything approaching concern in her sister's face. She leaned across to her locker, opened the door then slammed it shut again. Whatever she was looking for, it obviously wasn't there. 'Yes, Titch,' she said, 'I already *know* that dear Vincent knows all about it. Took him all of two and a half minutes to know about it, because that div of a bloke of mine can't keep his fucking trap shut.'

'And that doesn't *worry* you?'

'Worry me? Why should it worry me?' Lyndsey shrugged. 'Like I just told you, that ship's already sailed.'

'No, no – I don't mean that. I mean you're not worried about Vinnie?'

'About Vinnie? Since when did anyone *ever* have to worry about Vinnie?'

'About what he might do! Don't you *get* it? About the fact that he might end up going back to prison! And it'll be because of *me*! God, I wish I'd never told you. You've ruined everything!'

Lyndsey's eyes widened. 'Me? What the fuck have *I* got to do with anything?'

Josie sat forward in her chair. Her stupid sister wasn't even getting it. 'Everything! You told Robbo, and I let you, and he's ruined everything. If he'd just done what you promised he'd do, none of this would even be happening! It'd be over. But instead he's been blackmailing him and shouting his mouth off and

now Vinnie knows about it, and now something even *worse* is
going to happen. And it's all *your* fault! *All* of it!'

'Hold up,' Lyndsey said. 'What exactly *is* going to happen?'

'Vinnie'll beat him to a pulp. I know he will. You don't realise, Lynds. You don't know what he's like now. He'll –'

Lyndsey laughed again. Loudly. 'Trust me, sis, I *do* know
what he's like now. He's a fucking animal now is what he is. But
you don't need to worry about that in any case. Melvin's
scarpered.'

'What, gone somewhere? You mean he's not in his house any
more?'

'No.'

'But where's he gone?'

'Haven't a clue. The moon? Scunthorpe? How should I
know? Just know he's gone and holed up somewhere else now.
Somewhere our "avenging-angel" fucking brother won't be
able to find him.'

'When? When did he go?'

'I imagine it was the minute he knew Vinnie was out, don't
you? He's a lot of things, Melvin, but he's not a complete idiot.
Probably saw him, didn't he – just like everybody fucking else
did – swaggering like Prince Charming down the fucking
street.'

'But he didn't *know*, Lynds. How'd he know Vinnie even
knew anything about it? How did he? That's what I can't work
out. *How?*'

'How the fuck should *I* know?' Lyndsey said. 'Why you looking at me? For fuck's sake, can't you leave it? He's gone. Vinnie
won't find him. So no harm done. Your precious brother will
stay out of clink – well, in *theory* he will, anyway – and that's
the end of it. And you can stop getting on your high fucking
horse for a change.'

It was Robbo, then. It had to be that fucking idiot Robbo who'd told Vinnie, and her stupid sister just couldn't see it. Just like she couldn't see an inch beyond her nose about anything where he was concerned. End of it? That was hilarious, that was. That was really fucking funny. There would never be an end to it – not for her.

'I'm not,' she snapped, hating her now. She really didn't care, did she? 'For your information, I came here for a reason.'

Lyndsey had picked up her magazine again. 'Which is?' She now looked bored.

Well, not for much longer, Josie thought, *and she can't say she didn't ask for it*. 'To tell you you'd better discharge yourself, because I'm not going back.'

'Going back where?'

'Back to yours.'

Lyndsey sighed. 'Oh for God's sake, Titch. Can't you just –'

'No, Lynds, I *can't*. I'm not going back because that fucking idiot of yours tried to feel me up last night. And it wasn't the first time, either. *That's* why.'

Now she was interested again. She put the magazine down and looked daggers at her. 'What the fuck are you on about?'

Josie made herself hold Lyndsey's gaze. 'You heard me. And you don't need the details. But you know what? I was asleep, Lynds. *Asleep*. And he was trying to grope me. That's why I'm not bloody going back, okay?'

Her big sister had once been so pretty. Long-limbed and doe-eyed and make-the-boys-cry pretty. And now ... Now that sister was long gone. It was sad. It felt tragic. But it was true, even so.

'Oh, *great*,' Lyndsey said, after what seemed an age had passed. 'Made you feel better, telling me all that, did it? Great.' She sat back against the pillows and waved at Josie as if dismissing her. Lying there like some princess and just swatting her away. 'You go ahead,' she said, 'you go ahead and desert the sinking fucking ship, why don't you? Christ, it's not even like you haven't been touched before, is it? But go ahead. Blab all you like. Thanks a *lot*.'

Josie stared at her sister, open-mouthed. There was so much she could have said. About Robbo, about Vinnie, about what Lyndsey would be coming back to. But she decided to say nothing. There was really no point, was there? It was done now. All out there. So she stood up and left.

Lyndsey didn't say a thing to try and stop her.

Chapter 20

It was Saturday evening, and the Bull was pretty crowded. It wasn't anything special in terms of Saturdays, but it had been one of those stupidly warm early September days when you were tricked into believing that Bradford was still going to get a proper summer. Everyone kitted out in the warm weather gear they'd almost given up on, which, in the case of the blokes, involved some pretty dodgy shorts. Though in the case of the girls, it meant an explosion of cheesecloth shirts knotted round their midriffs and hot pants, which was reason enough to celebrate, Vinnie reckoned.

It was still hot even now, at half eight in the evening, and Don, the landlord, had a grin on his face that could have stretched all the way to Bridlington, even if he was sweating buckets trying to serve a bar queue ten deep and the ice machine had long since given up.

Most of the pub's young crowd had spilled out on to the street, and the atmosphere was buzzing outside. Half the estate seemed to be there, which was all to the good, because somewhere there would be someone who knew something about Mucky Melvin; it wasn't like he was overrun with friends on the estate, was it? Someone would give the address up, Vinnie was sure of it.

'He might have buggered off altogether,' Brendan said. 'I fucking would if I was him, mate. Wouldn't you?'

Vinnie shook his head. 'And go where? To sleep under a viaduct? Nah, he'll be around. He'll have found some crony or

other to take him in. They like to stick together, nonces –
that's what they're good at. Someone's taken him in. Someone
local. Some other low-life who's into child-snatching, probably.
It's just a question of finding out who.'

But it seemed like it was going to be Vinnie's lucky night
because another mate, Steve, had come to join them. He was
a part-time taxi driver at his uncle's firm, and he also worked at
the local scrap yard now and again. So he got about a bit, and
because he had his nose into everything he knew a lot about a
lot – including something that might potentially speed up the
hunt.

'You know Debra Nicholson?' he asked Vinnie. 'Used to live
over on Canterbury Front?'

Vinnie nodded. The name was instantly familiar, even
though she was a girl he didn't know particularly well. She'd
been in the year below him in school and he remembered her
as being the sort of bird who swanned around with her nose in
the air, like the girls from Canterbury Front generally did.

'What about her?' he asked.

'Well, I was just thinking about what you were saying. She's
having a bit of a party at hers later, or so I'm told, and I'm betting
there'll be a fairly good chance Mikey Harris might be there.'

'Mikey Harris?' That was a name Vinnie didn't know.

'Good friend of hers,' Steve explained. 'Going out with her
best mate.'

'Course!' Brendan said. 'I know him. Of *course*,' he said
again, nodding. 'That's a really good point, mate. He's Mucky
Melvin's nephew, Vin, that's who Mikey Harris is.'

'Not that I think he has anything to do with him,' Steve
added. 'For obvious reasons. I mean, would you? But you never
know. If anyone's got an idea where he might be hiding out, I'd
say he's a prime candidate, wouldn't you?'

Vinnie tipped his head back and drained his pint in a couple of swallows. Then he placed the glass down on the already crowded pub window-sill. 'Right lads,' he said. 'Who's for getting tanked up? I feel a bit of a party coming on, don't you?'

It turned out that Debra Nicholson didn't live on the estate any more. She'd moved to one of the roads down at the town end of Little Horton Lane, which was some distance away. It was a good half an hour walk and Brendan was whining about getting a taxi, but with four pints already inside him, Vinnie barely noticed. That was one thing about borstal life, he supposed – and, weirdly, he missed it; the relentless obsession with PE. And much as he moaned about it (everyone moaned about it because moaning was what you did) it sharpened you up being so fit; kept you strong and on your toes. As did having a good reason for going where you were going, and that was one thing he definitely had in spade loads.

His rage about Titch had not abated. It sat there inside him like a low rumbling presence. Like the beginnings of an earth-quake or volcano, stirring just under the surface, ready to blow.

She didn't deserve it. She didn't deserve any of it. She'd done fuck-all but be nice to everyone – fucking *everyone*. Wouldn't say boo to a goose and got shat on by all and sundry. He wasn't stupid enough not to realise how things worked. He was the prodigal fucking son just by virtue of the fact that his mam thought the sun shone out of his arse. Perhaps she wouldn't think that any more – not if she'd seen some of the rucks he'd got into. But he could see just by the way she simpered round him – specially in public – that his 'holiday' at her majesty's pleasure had only served to make it shine even more.

Which left no room for his little sister. Which was just like it had always been, only worse. She was just there and expected to get on with it. And with that no-hoper, washed-up selfish druggie of a sister, she must have felt pretty lonely, all told.

He knew he'd frightened Titch the other night, and he felt bad about it. But fuck, whenever he so much as thought about what had been done to her, he saw red. He couldn't help it. He wanted blood. He craved it. So having to deal with that fucker Robbo had actually been a gift. Vinnie held him personally responsible for turning his sister into a smackhead, so he'd had it coming to him since the day he clapped eyes on Lyndsey. So what that she might have been doing dope before she met him? He was a bloke and a decent bloke would have helped sort her out – not get her on heroin, knock her up, spend her fucking family allowance money. Not get so feet-under-the-fucking-table secure that while his girlfriend was in hospital having a fucking abortion, he thought helping himself to a bit of younger skirt was an acceptable fucking way to carry on.

No, Robbo had got off lightly. Literally, in fact. He'd been Vinnie's light entertainment; the warm-up act before the main show.

'Hold up,' Pete puffed, 'I gotta stop and have a slash. How much further is this fucking house, anyway?'

Vinnie laughed at his mate. He was beetroot and sweating. 'You're such a fat lazy fucker, Pete,' he said, boxing him play-fully on the upper arm. 'You want to get in shape, mate. Leave off the pies. Take a leaf out of my book.'

'What, banged up doing porridge?' Pete said, as he peed into a dusty buddleia. 'No fucking thanks. I'd like to keep my arse in one piece, thanks.'

'I know,' Vinnie shot back, 'because you need it to fucking talk out of!'

Vinnie grinned as he dodged Pete's retaliatory stream of piss. He was enjoying tonight. He could almost sniff Melvin on the breeze now. Catch the scent of revenge in the shifting summer air.

Things were going to shape up well. He could feel it.

'Look, I can't let you in okay? There's already a million people in here. And the place is getting wrecked as it is.'

Debra had grown. That was for sure. She was in a vest and a pair of shorts that left almost nothing to the imagination, and though she'd daubed on enough lipstick to look uncannily (and slightly unsettlingly) like his mother, Vinnie decided that, actually, she was really pretty.

Pretty but arsey, and currently blocking their way. Brendan clearly lacked any sort of skill at charming birds of any kind – out of trees or into letting blokes into their parties. Edging him and the others aside, Vinnie mounted the doorstep and thrust his bottle of Double Diamond in her direction.

'Alright, Deb?' he said, nodding appreciatively. 'Long time no see.'

She stared at him for a moment, obviously taking in the shiny hair, the luxurious tache, the confident grin, the cool threads – and he had the same sense of self-confidence that he'd felt a lot since he'd been home. People treated him differently now, and he knew it wasn't just because he was older. He'd been inside. He had a status that his mates could only dream of. Particularly when it came to certain types of girls. He knew in that instant – that one when she realised who she was looking at – that she was going to allow them to go in.

'Vinnie?' she squeaked, blushing almost as pink as her lipstick. 'Shit – Vinnie McKellan! Bloody hell!'

Vinnie turned and smirked at his mates, as she stood to one side to let them in. 'Watch and learn, lads,' he whispered. 'Watch and learn.'

They naturally made straight for the kitchen. There was a kind of through lounge, separated by an arch, but Vinnie ignored it. It was a solid sea of bodies, most of which were jigging around to Roxy Music, heads bobbing like corks, looking like dicks. No, the kitchen would be where it was at because it always was at parties, so they threaded their way through, acknowledging the odd familiar face – though, in doing so, Vinnie felt the width of the gap that had opened up now; the lads seemed to know people he'd never even clapped eyes on. The world could change a great deal in three years.

'There he is,' Pete said, nudging him, as they went through the kitchen doorway. 'That is him, isn't it, Steve?'

Steve nodded.

Vinnie cast an eye over the lad standing in the far corner, by the fridge, chatting to a bloke he didn't recognise half-in and half-out of the back door. He looked like a regular bloke – longish hair, bit of a hippy, twenty-ish, generally unremarkable, and Vinnie wondered what it must be like to have a filthy pervert sharing the same blood as you did. Was that sort of thing in your genes?

There was the usual mess on all the horizontal surfaces. He didn't know what the deal was – most likely that her parents had buggered off to Blackpool for the weekend – but he had the impression the party had been in full flow since the middle of the afternoon. There were Tupperware bowls scattered around, empty except for crisp shards and crumbs now, and an assortment of beer and cider cans – big and small – plus rows of plastic bottles, most of them empty, of cream soda and lemonade and cola.

It was fuggy, too, a haze of grey-blue sitting just above eye-level, regularly topped up by smoke from cigarettes and joints. There seemed to be two main groups of lads, but few girls in the kitchen currently, as some sort of competition seemed to be taking place in the garden involving a bunch of empty beer bottles and a lot of giggling. Vinnie glanced around him as he began looking for a bottle opener among the detritus. You could almost smell the testosterone.

The lads in the kitchen were beginning to notice them now too, and, taking in the various unfamiliar faces that were scrutinising him, Vinnie again felt this sense of wired disconnectedness – this sense of needing to keep alert and at the ready. He was, in every sense, very far from home turf. He was only just settling back into the pecking order of his own area, after all, and he could tell his mates were feeling it too.

No, the natives might not be entirely friendly. But then they weren't here to make friends. Neither were they here for the Slade that was now blaring from the living room. They were here for a purpose and there was no time like the present. Finding a bottle opener, he opened his beer, and took a long thirst-quenching swig. Everything felt more manageable with a beer in your hand. And even more so when in your stomach.

As it turned out, the natives weren't unfriendly. Pretty soon it was established that the guy standing with Mikey Harris was the cousin of a bloke Steve had done a bit of work with, and that they'd actually met a couple of times before. So it wasn't long before they all started drinking together, and the initial tension began to melt away.

Though, information-wise, it soon became clear, at least to Vinnie, that Mikey Harris might be a bit of a non-starter. For one thing, it seemed he had a pretty large group of mates with him, any or all of which, being that bit older than Vinnie and *his* mates, would also need taking on or taking out. And for another, Vinnie reckoned himself to be a pretty good judge of character, and this Mikey Harris guy seemed alright. Odds on he felt the same as everyone else did about his uncle, which meant that, odds on, he wouldn't know where he was.

Course, he could just ask him, but 'Where's your bastard uncle hiding out?' wasn't the sort of thing you could just slip into party conversation – not without drawing attention to the reason you wanted to know. And if the guy genuinely *didn't* know – well, that was the tricky one. Because the one thing he didn't want to happen, at least in the short term, was for anyone outside his immediate circle to know how much he wanted to track the bastard down.

No, much better, he decided, to simply watch – to watch and learn. No point in anything kicking off until it needed to.

But it looked like that wasn't his choice to make. Time had passed now – quite a lot of time. It was fully dark. The beer they'd brought had all but gone now, and the energetic partying in the garden had become more of a sit-in, the participants only spottable via the glowing tips of their cigarettes. The crowd in the kitchen had swelled a bit too, and some more characters – older guys neither Vinnie or his mates knew – had arrived out of nowhere and seemed to be holding court.

And one of them seemed to have his eye on Vinnie. He wasn't a big guy, but the way he carried himself suggested no one had pointed that fact out to him, and when he spoke it was clear he was on something too.

'Vinnie fucking McKellan!' he said, loudly and jocularly, causing several heads to swivel round to see.

Dispensing with his stock answer – who the fuck wants to know? – Vinnie merely nodded an acknowledgement as the guy approached. And was then surprised when the guy grinned and thrust an arm towards him.

'I've been hearing about you,' he said, pumping Vinnie's hand enthusiastically. ''bout time someone showed that smack-head Robbo what was what.'

Vinnie was aware of Pete and Brendan exchanging nervous glances next to him. They obviously knew who this character was even if he didn't. But this probably wasn't the moment to ask them. Or, come to that, ask how this bloke even knew who he was, much less what he knew – assuming he did, and it certainly seemed that way – about what Vinnie had done to Robbo in the week. He was also short of a response, so he searched for one.

'Glad to be of service,' he replied, thinking furiously. How the fuck *did* this guy know? And who *was* he?

'I'd offer you a drink,' the bloke went on, 'only there seems to be shit-all left here.' He grinned again then, revealing a row of alarmingly brown teeth. 'Though I've got other stuff, if you're interested, like.'

'You're alright,' Vinnie said evenly. 'I try not to.'

'Leave that to your half-wit of a brother-in-law? Very sensible.'

Vinnie couldn't detect an edge in the guy's voice, but felt he had to clarify even so. 'He's not my brother-in-law.'

'Sorry – my mistake,' the bloke conceded. 'Your sister's "boyfriend". Anyway, since you seem to have his ear now ...' – he stopped to laugh, and his cronies all joined in, as if on cue – '... perhaps you can remind him when you next see him that I'm only going to be feeling indulgent for so long. You know what I mean?'

He was a dealer, then. That figured. The bloke Lynds and Robbo got their smack off? 'No,' Vinnie said, 'but as an educated guess, I'm assuming he owes you some money.'

'Got it in one,' the bloke answered. 'Anyway, extremely nice to meet you. Nice to know there are like-minded folk out there. And if you ever need a job, lad, come and find me, okay?'

He winked at Vinnie and squeezed past, then went into the garden, the long tail of his retinue dutifully following. There was an almost audible mass outbreath when they'd gone.

'Well, that was, um, interesting, to say the least,' Brendan ventured. And it was at that point that things went horribly wrong.

Looking back the following day, Vinnie recalled what happened next in a kind of inevitable, not to mention sickening, slow-motion. And a blurry one, too: perhaps it would come back to him in time, but right then he couldn't quite recall the exact point when 'bad' turned to 'very, very bad'.

What he did recall was that immediately following the drug dealer's exit, everyone seemed to start talking at once. It seemed the guy was well known to almost everyone but him, and that it wasn't at all surprising that he knew about Vinnie, since he would have been round to Robbo's regularly – or so the theory went – and seeing him in a state would have natu-rally wanted to know why. And he would have had no trouble finding out either. This was Robbo. It wouldn't take much, after all.

And it seemed everyone else wanted filling in now. This had been bemusing for Vinnie, and not a little pleasing. He was being talked *about*, as well as talked to, and with a new level of reverence, so he was only too happy to hear his punishment of Robbo being described in such awed and respectful tones. Reputation was everything, after all.

But then he heard a single word that changed everything. 'Josie'. And suddenly his ears were the sharpest they'd ever been. And also focussed, which meant an exchange by two guys across the kitchen – neither of which he'd ever seen before – did not escape his notice. Not a word.

'Josie McKellan?' one was saying.

'Yeah, I *know*,' said the other.

'Christ!' said the first, laughing. 'That's fucking smack for you!'

Vinnie was not meant to hear it. That much was obvious. But the words floated across the crowded kitchen towards him even so, as if propelled there by an unseen angry force.

He looked towards the source of them, but not before Brendan had as well, and who, being closer, was quick to answer.

'Hey,' he said, 'watch it, mate. I'd keep your trap shut if I were you.'

To which the lad, presumably because he hadn't realised who was who – not to mention *where* Vinnie was – answered, 'Oh, come *on*, mate – would *you*? He must have been pretty fucking desperate.'

Vinnie was aware of only one face at that moment, and moved towards it as fast as the crush of people allowed.

Which was fast. He was nose to nose with the lad in seconds. 'You want to say that again, mate?' he asked him quietly. 'To *me*? Only I'd feel bad smashing your face in just on hearsay, you know?'

And perhaps at that point, it still could have been dealt with. At that point there was still scope for apology, for reparations. Perhaps at that point the best thing either of them could have done was to take a step back, breathe deeply and walk away.

But it wasn't going to happen, and for so many reasons. Reasons of drink, reasons of face, reasons of sheer unbridled anger. And mostly because the lad's friend was an arsehole.

'Come on, mate,' he said to Vinnie. 'No need to overreact, is there?' At which Vinnie slammed his forehead into the guy's nose.

What happened after that was blurry, as, his head throbbing, Vinnie lunged for the other guy. Fists flew, there were shouts, glasses shattered, girls screamed and at some point, this being a kitchen, the inevitable happened. Someone opened a drawer and pulled out a knife.

It wasn't Vinnie. That much he did recall. It wasn't him that had had that particular bright idea. All he knew was that somehow, at some point, he had taken possession of it, and that somehow he had stabbed the guy, twice.

'Shit, Vinnie! *Shit*! What the *fuck*!' It was Pete's voice. It seemed to soar above him – even above the cacophony of female screams. He could hear someone else shouting, too – no, several people, yelling. 'Call the police! Someone call a bloody ambulance, for God's sake!'

'Shit!' Brendan screeched at him. 'What the fuck did you do *that* for? Christ! Pete, come and help me. *Jesus*, Vin – you idiot! Christ, we have to get out of here now!'

And somehow, without him consciously knowing how they'd got there, the four of them were running down the road, their feet pounding, the sound of wailing sirens at their flank.

Chapter 21

June woke up with a start and she wasn't happy. That bleeding husband of hers, she thought irritably, as she was jolted into consciousness. When he'd been on a heavy session, his snoring could wake the dead. The dead, the bloomin' undead, and half of Bradford while he was at it. And now she was awake she knew there was little chance she'd get back to sleep anytime soon.

She pushed him hard enough to make him grunt and then roll over onto his side, but in the ensuing silence – Jock only snored when he was flat on his back – she realised that it might not have been his snoring that had woken her. She could hear something going on downstairs. Vinnie, no doubt, home from his own evening out, and now banging around in the kitchen, probably making toast.

June smiled to herself. And doing a bad job of trying to be quiet, by the sound of it, in that way everyone did when they were bladdered. She sighed contentedly, happy to just lie there and listen, perfectly at ease with her sleeplessness. It was so good to have her boy back. The house felt whole again.

If a lot noisier. 'What the *fuck* is going on down there?' Jock growled, his voice in the darkness startling her. He rolled back over towards her, gusting beer fumes in her face.

'It's just Vinnie,' she told him, fanning them away irritably. 'Stop your bloody mithering.'

'*Me* stop?' he railed. 'Bloody racket going on at this hour! VINCENT?' he yelled. 'Shut UP! People are trying to fucking sleep up here, in case you hadn't noticed! Go to BED, you noisy little bleeder!'

'Oh, for God's sake!' June said. 'You'll have our Titch up as well now. Just go to sleep.'

'What, with that racket going on? Fat chance.' He poked her in the ribs. 'Get down there and tell him to shut his bloody noise up.'

'Me? You're the one making the bleedin' fuss about it!'

But even as she was saying it, June was pushing back the covers. She was wide awake now. She was more than happy to go down and see what Vinnie was up to. They could have a nice cup of tea and a natter.

Titch was running up the stairs just as June started going down them. So she'd obviously been woken up as well.

'What the bleeding hell are you doing up?' she said, tying up her dressing gown.

'Oh, Mam …' Titch began.

'Oh, Mam what?' she said, moving aside to let her pass. 'And are you coming up or going down now? And keep your voice down.'

'Mam, it's Vinnie,' she said, turning round, 'I was coming up to get you …'

June followed her down the rest of the stairs. 'What about him? What's he been up to?'

Probably something and nothing, she thought. Typical of Titch to be over-dramatic. But once down in the hall, with the light spilling out from the kitchen, she could see the panic in her daughter's stricken face. 'Oh, Mam, he's in trouble,' Titch said, her chin wobbling. '*Bad* trouble.'

June felt a stab of anxiety. 'Trouble?' she said, following Titch into the kitchen. 'What kind of trouble? What's he –'

And then she stopped, because she saw the livid swelling on Vinnie's head. And then the blood, quickly after it, smeared on his cheek and on his jeans. Then the vivid patch of it on his shirt – one of his few smart shirts, too. That hit her like a slap around the face.

She quickly assessed him. He was sitting on the kitchen stool, staring at her, though she wasn't convinced he was really seeing, with his elbows on his thighs, and his mouth set in a thin line. His eyes were glazed, but he didn't seem to be hurt. Well, not bar the red swelling slap-bang in the middle of his forehead. And he didn't look to be bleeding, not obviously. And his hands, which he held clasped together between his knees, were pale and clean. Must have washed them, she noted distractedly.

'You been in a ruck, son?' she said.

He nodded. 'You could say that, Mam,' he answered quietly.

She moved towards him. 'Let me take a look at that head of yours – you been headbutting someone or did you walk into a bleeding wall? Honestly, Vin, when are you ever going to learn? Titch, I think there's half a bag of peas in the top of the fridge. Grab them for me. And you'd better get that shirt off, so I can put it in to soak,' she said, gently smoothing his fringe back. 'Might not work, but –'

'Leave it, Mam,' Vinnie said, removing her hand with his own. 'There's no point.'

Titch hadn't moved yet either, June noticed. 'No point?' she said, looking from one to the other. 'You're just going to go out and buy a new one, are you? What with – fucking shirt buttons? Anyway, what happened? Where'd this kick off? Where'd you go when you left the pub anyway?'

'I said *leave* it, Mam,' Vinnie said, standing up and nudging past her so he could get to the back door and open it. 'I've got to think.' He reached into his jeans pocket, pulled a packet of Woodbines out and calmly lit one.

June spread her hands. 'Think? Think about what? What's going on, Vin? What are you *on* about? Is someone after you? You been in a brawl? You expecting trouble? *What?*' She placed her hands on her hips. 'Because if there's one thing –'

'Vinnie, for God's sake just *tell* her!' said Titch. Her voice was an angry rasp of recrimination. 'Mam, it's much worse than that. He's stabbed a lad. Badly.'

June felt something shift in her stomach. 'You fucking *what? Vinnie!*' she barked at him. 'Stop standing there staring at the fucking moon for five minutes and tell me what's going on here!'

'He got into an argument and stabbed a lad and everyone saw it and everyone knows it was him and –'

'Shut up a minute, Titch, will you! Vinnie, *who?* Who'd you stab?' She spread her hands again. '*And why?* What the fuck were you *thinking?* You stupid little bleeder! *God* – so where was this?'

Vinnie launched his half-smoked cigarette into the air and turned around to face her.

'It's no one you know, Mam,' he said. He sounded as calm as she felt frantic. 'It was at a party over on Little Horton Lane.'

'Little Horton Lane?' June's mind was working now. 'Shit. What about the bizzies? They turn up?'

Vinnie shook his head. 'We didn't see any but we legged it. An', Mam, it wasn't my fault, okay? I didn't fucking start it, and I didn't get the fucking knife out. Someone else did. This wasn't just me, okay? This was – Jesus. That *cunt!* I could – *fuck* –'

Vinnie trailed off, shaking his head then slammed his fist hard into the masonry beside the back-door jamb. '*Fuck!*' he said again, spitting the word out. '*Fuck!*'

He then pulled his fist back, spread his hand and looked at his knuckles, and, before June could stop him, did the same thing again.

Titch let out a sob. '*Vinnie*,' she screamed at him. '*Stop it!*'

June threw herself at the space between his fist and the wall. 'Vinnie, leave it! *Stop* doing that! You'll break your bloody knuckles in a minute!'

He looked past her, glassy eyed, and for a gut-wrenching moment she thought he was going to cry, but the only sound came from Titch behind her, weeping.

'Look at the state of your fucking hand!' she said, pulling his wrist up to inspect it, and wincing to see the blood beginning to ooze out of all the grazes. This time he didn't try to stop her. She pulled him towards the sink then and turned the tap on. 'You stupid fucking bleeder – Titch, will you shut up with your bloody wailing! We need to think here! – You think they'll have called them? You think they'll be round after you?'

'Oh they'll be round, Mam,' he said as she held his hand under the water. 'Sooner or fucking later they will. Ouch, that fucking hurts!'

June held Vinnie's hand under the tap for a full minute then wrapped it in a tea-towel, pressing down hard to stop the flow. What the hell *should* they do? Was there any point in him trying to wriggle out of it? Self-defence, maybe? Her mind was working nine to the dozen now. Yes, that's what they'd do. She'd have that shirt off him – dump all his clothes in a bin somewhere and clean him up. And then he'd have to lie low for a while – maybe go and stay at one of his uncles … And just deny it. They couldn't argue with that, not without actual evidence. 'We'll just say you weren't there,' she said. 'We'll get you cleaned up and out of here, and I'll be your alibi. That's what we'll do, Vin.' She began scrubbing harder at the new blood across his knuckles.

'Ouch,' Vinnie yelped. 'Easy, Mam! That fucking stings, that does.'

'You're lucky not to feel the sting of my hand across your stupid chops!' she retorted. She felt close to tears herself now. The stupid fucking idiot. Putting her through all this stress again.

'And mine!' Titch suddenly said, causing them both to turn around. She was standing there, clearly seething, jabbing a finger in her brother's direction. 'You couldn't do it, could you! You couldn't keep yourself out of trouble for *five fucking minutes*! You come back here – all full of yourself, shouting your mouth off to everyone, being the big hard man, stomping into stuff you had no business stomping into and causing trouble for everyone!'

'Titch,' Vinnie started. 'Titch, *Christ* – you think I *meant* this to happen?'

'It doesn't matter whether you meant it to happen – it *has* happened! You could have walked away –' she stepped closer to him, jabbing her finger right in his face – 'but you didn't. You never do. You're so *fucking* full of shit, Vinnie!'

'Titch, pack that in right now!' June snapped. 'We've got to get your brother sorted and out of here. And we can't concentrate with you screaming at him, you hear me?'

'No, I won't pack it in!' she screamed back at June. 'You're just a selfish bastard, Vinnie. You don't think about anybody but yourself and how "cool" you are. Well, you're not cool. You're going to get done again, and that's not cool. That's just bloody stupid. An' then you'll be gone again. Five minutes you're home, and you just rake everything up again. And you'll be gone again. And we're all just supposed to get on with it again! I hate you! You're the worst brother anyone *ever* had, and I HATE YOU!'

'Hate who, for fuck's sake?' said Jock, who had now appeared in the doorway. 'And pipe down will you?' he said, hoicking a thumb back towards the hallway. 'There's a cop car just pulled up outside.'

'Oh, shit,' June said. '*Shit*. Jock, It's Vin. He's got himself in a bit of a mess and –'

'I can see that,' said Jock, looking his son up and down. 'What the fuck have you been up to this time, you fucking idiot?'

June watched her son wince at Jock's words. She wanted to punch Jock in the face. It was already almost too much to take in. The bloody cops outside, now, too, and Vinnie still covered in blood …

'Been in a fight,' she said. 'Stabbed a lad. Yes, been a stupid bloody idiot, but –'

The knock on the door was loud and emphatic. Three strikes, a gap, then three more.

'Shit,' said Vinnie, looking at her. Looking more seven than 17 suddenly.

'Mam!' Titch demanded. 'What are we going to *do*?'

'Do?' she answered. 'How am I supposed to know, you dozy mare? Ask your idiot brother. Vin, you think you can make a case for yourself – you know, self-defence?'

Jock rolled his eyes. '*Think*? Only bloody option he's bloody got!'

The door was struck again. 'So we'll say you got in, and you were hurt, and you'd been chased, and –'

'Shut the fuck up, June,' said Jock. Then he turned around and went to answer the front door.

Titch was becoming hysterical now, sobbing freely, her shoulders shaking, sucking air down in gulps. 'They're going to take you back now, I know they are,' she was saying to Vinnie. 'They're going to take you back inside again! Mam – we have to *do something!*'

Vinnie, in the middle of it all, seemed uncharacteristically stuck for words. 'Titch,' he kept saying. 'Titch, *please* – look, I'm sorry, okay?'

'Jesus Christ!' June snapped. 'Will you just pull yourself together, girl! What else d'you think is going to happen? Of course they're going to take him away, because he's been a *stupid little bleeder!* There's nothing to be done, okay?' she finished, glaring at her daughter, and swallowing hard to stop the sob that was trying to escape from her throat.

She wasn't going to give the bastards that much.

1974

Chapter 22

March

Vinnie ran his fingers through his hair, and tried to steady his jangling nerves. Today was the day, finally. His day in court. Bradford Magistrates Court. *Again.* Six months it had taken; six interminable months on remand, and his (seriously belated) Christmas present was a brown paper parcel from home, hand delivered by the solicitor who'd come to see him yesterday. His name was Mr Cordingley and he'd been very specific.

'From your mother,' he'd said. 'And she insists that you wear them.' The 'them' being his beloved Crombie, clean and carefully folded, together with a brand new shirt and tie, which he knew she could probably ill-afford. 'It's serious, son,' the lawyer said, passing the already opened package across the visiting-room table to him. 'You're almost 18 now, and with your previous, make no mistake – they'll intend to try you as if you were an adult. And if you mess up and it all goes pear shaped you could be looking at a long stretch.'

'Thanks a fucking bunch, Mr Cordingley,' Vinnie replied, grinning. 'A right barrel of fucking laughs, you are. You fill me with so much hope. *Not.*'

Mr Cordingley shook his head and sighed. 'Vinnie, lad, even if I tried to give you any hope it would be false. I know I'm good, lad, but Jesus Christ himself couldn't get you off this charge – and, remember, he walked on fucking water, son!'

Vinnie grinned again now, as he swung his legs around and got up from his bunk. It had been such a shock, hearing a solicitor coming out with a funny like that, and he had a new-found respect for the bloke. He'd already heard that he was well known and liked amongst the criminal fraternity, and now he was starting to understand why.

He stretched and pulled the brown-paper package from his locker. It was a decent shirt, with a striking green and beige paisley pattern on it, which would look good with the mustard kipper tie his mam had chosen to go with it. Topped off with the Crombie, he knew he'd look pretty sharp. She had a good eye for fashion, no doubt about it, did his mam, though think-ing about her filled his mind with the same dragging sense of guilt that had dogged him every day of the last half dozen months. He couldn't give a fuck about the bastard who'd started what he'd eventually had to finish (and couldn't have given a fuck when told he'd made a full recovery, except in so much that it made things better for him), but when it came to what it had put his mam and Titch through, he felt terrible.

But there was no time to dwell on what had already happened, so he put it out of his mind and tried to concen-trate on the coming day as he washed and dressed. He just wanted to get the thing over with. He'd been on the remand wing at Thorp Arch prison for what felt far too long now and he just wanted to know where his next home might be. It would be another prison, rather than a borstal; of that there was no doubt: he certainly wasn't expecting to be allowed home yet. But he would be in time, he hoped, and in the shorter term for some home visits, maybe, and one of the likely places – the main prison here – was a little too far from home. His hope was to get sentenced to a few months in Armley nick, because, being in Leeds, it was only a short train ride to Bradford, which meant his mates and family might at least be able to visit him.

If they wanted to, that was, and, in Titch's case, he was doubtful. Her parting words to him – basically, 'I hate you – you're not my brother' – rang in his ears all the time, even if the person who screamed them at him had not spoken a word to him since. Where Titch was concerned, the pang of guilt was more like a stab to his heart. Because she'd been right. Whatever the justification – and that cunt had definitely had what was coming to him – she'd been right. He'd let her down unforgivably. No surprise that she wouldn't, then, was it?

And might never – not unless he did something to redeem himself. He remembered how helpless he'd felt when the coppers had cuffed him, trying to make her understand, trying to get her to accept his apology. But as they'd dragged him off, his mam in tears by then, his dad shaking his head, all he could see was the expression on his little sister's face, as she stood watching his departure, stony-faced. There had been no love in that face, no care or compassion. No, all he'd seen had been hatred and scorn.

That had hurt. But it had also served to concentrate his mind. Every day of his remand he had played the game and kept his nose clean, so he could serve his time peacefully and uneventfully, and get home again, so he could right the wrongs he'd failed to right before.

Mr Malvern, the cockney screw, appeared at the cell door. 'You ready, son?' he said, unlocking it and giving Vinnie a once-over. 'You're looking dapper, young McKellan. Let's hope the judge is a young lady, hey? Because you'll knock her socks off in that get-up, and no mistake.'

Vinnie smiled. He liked Malvern. He was one of the few screws in Thorp Arch that had any time for the lads. 'You after my arse, sir?' he said. 'Only it sounds like you fancy a bit of this for yourself.'

Mr Malvern laughed loudly. 'You cheeky young tyke! Come on then, lad. Let's get you down to security. You can say your goodbyes on the way.' He paused and clapped a friendly hand across Vinnie's back. 'And I mean this with all sincerity, young Vincent; I hope I never have to see you again. Know what I mean?'

Vinnie nodded. He knew what was meant and he appreciated it. He also hoped he could make it a fact, too.

'Good luck, Vin!' came the shouts of the lads along the corridor as the pair of them made their way out. He returned their greetings – he'd made some good friends in here these last months – and also took the trouble to stick two fingers up at the screws he passed and didn't like, before being transferred to a waiting van, cuffed to another screw and driven to court. Another four or so hours, he thought, and the waiting would be over. And another step on the road to being free again, thank God.

It had been four hours, too – almost to the minute. He'd worn his cool threads, and his family and friends had turned out in force to support and speak up for him, yet in just four hours since departing Thorp Arch, he was given the depressing news that he would be heading straight back there. And then the even more stupefying news that it would be for three fucking years! He couldn't take it in. He'd been expecting a few months. But the judge had just sat there, banging on about making examples and how he had no choice but to come down hard when it came to his background and how he should have learned his lesson, and then had hit him with it: *three fucking years!*

The whole courtroom had been stunned into silence. A silence that was only broken by his mam starting to cry and, while she began sobbing loudly into a white handkerchief, a low rumble of dissent that soon became a cacophony, as relatives and friends started shouting obscenities from the gallery. And in the middle of it all was Titch, standing beside her mother clutching the metal handrail, white as a ghost and seeming to be saying something to him. He was trying to work out what it was when the judge banged down his gavel, startling both of them, and calling for order in the increasingly disordered court.

Vinnie's gaze settled on his solicitor, who also looked stunned. He'd told him to prepare for the worst, but that it would be this worse was obviously a big shock for both of them. Three *years*? Three years for *that*?

It couldn't be happening, could it? Except it seemed it was when Vinnie felt himself being tugged by the security guards who had been standing behind him, jolting him back into reality. 'Come on, lad,' one of them said. 'We need to get you downstairs to the cells. Your mates and family aren't doing you any favours, here. Come on, let's go.'

Vinnie wrenched his wrists from the security guard's grip. 'Get your fucking paws off me,' he snarled. 'Don't you dare fucking drag me. Not in front of my fucking mother. I'm coming, okay?'

The officers shared a glance and then stepped slightly away. 'As you wish, lad,' the other guard said, 'but move it all the same. Your mother will be told she can have a short visit with you, but for that to happen we need you downstairs, so this lot calm down.'

Feeling slightly calmer himself at the prospect of seeing his mum, Vinnie dutifully turned and followed the officers out of the courtroom and down the narrow stairs to the cells. He could hear his mother wailing as he went. 'He's only a boy, you dirty bleeders!' she was yelling at the judge. 'You can't give him three years!'

But apparently they could, and they had. And as he'd waited in the tiny holding cell, Vinnie could only shake his head in wonderment. It was a fight, that was all – one he hadn't even started. How could they do this? *Christ*, he thought, *how had eveything changed so dramatically?* It had never really occurred to him, not even when Cordingley had pointed it out, that coming close to 18 had implications other than just meaning he was almost a man in the eyes of the law. It clearly also meant they dished out longer sentences, the bastards, as if it made any difference to what had happened that night. He wiped his palms on his trousers to get rid of the sweat that had formed on them. He felt suffocated, panicky, and ripped at his tie to loosen it while he paced the holding cell floor. He hoped his mam would come soon, and maybe bring Josie with her. Would she be allowed? She'd looked so pale, and the thought of not seeing her really troubled him.

He heard June before he saw her. And it cheered him up a little, listening to her running commentary as she rattled down the steps. She was really ranting at the officer who had the job of bringing her to him. 'I don't need you man-handling me, thank you very much,' he heard her snap. 'You're nothing but an arsehole in a uniform, if you want the truth. Now just show me to my bleeding son, if you don't mind.'

The cell door opened and Vinnie was invited to step outside. 'Um, your mum's here to see you,' the officer told him. 'I've come to take you to the visiting room.'

Vinnie straightened his tie back up and walked across the cell, taking care to keep his chest out and shoulders straight.

'You want to be careful of my mother, mate,' he told the officer. 'She'd have your throat slit as soon as look at you, so I wouldn't give her any shit if I were you.' He then made a big show of sauntering out past the now red-faced security guard, and walked towards another tiny room down the corridor, aware of the fast clippety-clop of his mum's shoes as she followed. He knew where he was going. He'd been here often enough before. Let the fucking guard come running in his wake.

'Where's our Josie?' he asked as he walked to the table and took the seat he was directed to by another scowling security guard.

June sat down opposite him. 'These prats would only let *me* come,' she answered. 'She's alright though, Vin, really. Told me to tell you that, she did – oh, and that if you write her a letter, she promises she'll write back.'

Vinnie nodded. Perhaps there was still hope, then.

'Tell her I will, Mam, and that I'm sorry. Tell her I'll sort it when I get out, I promise.'

'I'll tell her no such fucking thing!' June snapped, raising a hand to jab a finger towards him angrily. 'It's you trying to fucking sort things that's got you into this mess. Don't think I haven't heard all about it. Don't you ever learn, son?'

Vinnie leaned close to June then and raised his own finger. 'If you've heard all about it, Mother,' he said in a low voice, 'then you wouldn't even fucking *question* what I did!' He then straightened up and sat back in his chair. 'So if I were you, Mam, I'd just leave it at that, okay? And pass on my message to my sister, alright?'

June looked like she was about to say something but thought better of it. 'Okay, mate,' she said. 'Keep your hair on!'

So she didn't know all of it. That was his guess, in any case. Or didn't want to know, which amounted to the same thing.

'Anyway,' she went on, 'we haven't got long, so is there anything you need sending in? I've got a bit put by. Not much, but if you need any baccy or owt, I can at least manage that till you sort yourself out.'

Vinnie played the game. He was good at that. His mother clearly wanted small talk for the ten precious minutes they had, and if that was so, then it suited him just fine. She was a master, he'd learned gradually as he'd grown up, at doing that. Hearing only what she wanted to hear and disregarding the rest. Which had once served good purpose as far as he was concerned – when neighbours, social workers and police had been banging at their door, he'd always been able to count on his mam to hear only his side of things. Now though, it got on his nerves. He wasn't a boy anymore and it annoyed him that June probably did at least have some idea about what happened to Josie. But she didn't care enough to act on it, that was the bottom line. Let it lie would have been her motto – sweep it all under the carpet. Much better than causing trouble for her and hers. And right now, with the prospect of a three-year stretch ahead of him, it looked like she was going to get her way. But after that … No, after that, things would change.

Vinnie arrived back at Thorp Arch a couple of hours later, having promised to both write and to keep out of trouble. He looked up as the transportation van turned into the entrance and was being checked in through the gates, seeing the place anew – as if arriving for the first time.

It looked so bleak. And it was something he'd never thought about before, not while he was working on the assumption that it was just a temporary stopover. *Fuck*, he thought. This place was to be home for the next three years and, while most lads could guarantee that their sentences would be cut, sometimes by as much as half, he wondered if he had a hope in hell of doing so himself. He'd never done so before. Could he now? Could he hold himself together for long enough? He hoped so. But he wasn't stupid. He knew himself well enough to know the odds were stacked against him. You were a certain way, a certain person, and trouble had a habit of finding you. He stared out into the darkness at the forbidding, cold walls that would hold him. *It looks like a castle*, he thought, as the van moved slowly forward, *like the one Edmond got shoved in.*

The hero of *The Count of Monte Cristo* – possibly his favourite book ever – had been an innocent man, imprisoned for 14 long years before he managed to escape and play out his revenge on the ones who had wronged him. And if he could wait that long, Vinnie decided, then he could wait three. *Yeah, he could wait*, he thought as they swept inside.

Chapter 23

Vinnie stretched out on his bunk, pressing his feet against the cold bars that served as a foot board, balancing the desire for another five minutes in the sack with his increasingly pressing need to pee. Above him, his cellmate Gordon was, he knew, going through the same ritual in his own bunk. That was prison life for you: ordered, predictable, full of small but important decisions. He chose the latter and lifted his blanket from his legs.

'Another day,' he called up to Gordon brightly. 'Another dollar!'

His cellmate groaned. 'S'fucking alright for you, lad,' he answered. 'You've got it cushty in the fucking library. Some of us in this place have to do real work!'

Vinnie laughed and sat up. As cellmates went – given that you got what you were given – Gordon wasn't too bad. He was a long timer – a big bloke of about 50, heavily tattooed, who'd already done ten years for manslaughter and expected to serve another five. And who seemed to be doing so with an attitude that Vinnie envied. Nothing fazed him and he accepted his lot without moaning about the injustice of it all, unlike the majority of the arseholes that Vinnie was banged up with.

Vinnie went to take his slash. 'You know what I say, Gordon. If your face fits an' all that. I can't help it that you've been tarred with the ugly brush, can I?'

'You cheeky cunt!' Gordon replied, laughing as he jumped down onto the floor. 'I'll be out freezing my bollocks off, as per,' he moaned. 'While you're nice and warm in there, doing your sissy girl's job, pretending like you can fucking read or something.'

'Oh, shut up mithering,' Vinnie said, playfully punching Gordon's muscular arm. 'I don't hear you moaning when I nick you all those picture books you like, do I?'

Gordon was right though, Vinnie thought, as they both pulled on their trousers and waited for the cell door to be opened, mugs in hand. He did have it good at Thorp Arch. He'd found his feet quickly, making a smooth transition from remand prisoner to full-time inmate, and had soon learned how to manipulate his way into a coveted job at the library. It had involved a bit of intimidation and a lot of his precious baccy – bless his mother – but it had paid off: he now spent his days exactly where he wanted to be.

No such luck for Gordon. He spent most of his time in the prison gardens, and was currently busy cutting back trees and big shrubs in preparation for the long, biting winter that would soon begin to set in. Rather him than me, Vinnie thought. Though, in fact, Gordon loved it – he just liked taking the mick.

Titch had been as good as her word. He'd written to her – a long impassioned letter, trying hard to make things right between them (if that were even possible, which Vinnie doubted). And, as she'd promised, a letter soon came winging back. But for all his excitement at receiving it, it was a dry, unemotional two pages. A series of 'I've been here', and 'I've gone there', interwoven with bland commentary about who was doing what and where back in Bradford. Of what he'd done and what had been done to her there wasn't a single mention. When it came to the subject that burned so fiercely still inside him, she could just as easily have written 'no entry'.

Her second letter, in response to another lengthy one from him, was no less lacking in anything that really mattered. He wanted to know how she was coping – he couldn't stop thinking about how being violated like that must have hurt her, and he wanted to know she was going to be okay. But she was absent – she might as well have been writing to a fucking pen friend. It was all school – her coming CSEs and O Levels, her plans to stay on and actually fucking take some – and Caz, and her problems, about which Vinnie didn't give a fuck. He wasn't stupid, though. His sister's real message was obvious. He'd failed her and now she'd shut him out. And he knew there was only one way he could earn the right to be let in again.

And that wasn't going to be happening anytime soon. Right now, it was a case of getting up and getting on with it, day after boring prison day. Not that all days at Thorp Arch were as boring as others. Some, it had to be said, were positively entertaining.

He and Gordon had made their way to the canteen for breakfast and were now 'enjoying' what passed for a fry-up from the serving counter, but only saw the inside of a decent frying pan in its dreams. The atmosphere had been jovial to start with. The usual cacophony of sounds synonymous with prisons everywhere – the clanging of trays onto tables, the random shouts of the inmates, the odd whistle to maintain order and the scuffle of chairs being scraped back and forth.

As a long-term prisoner, Gordon was tuned into all these sounds, and with an acuity that was better than most. And Vinnie was learning from him all the time, becoming better at reading him; tuning in himself to those times when Gordon's demeanour signalled that things might be a little off-key. Today was no exception. So when Gordon leaned across the table to whisper to him, he was unsurprised by his expression. It looked like something was kicking off.

'Vinnie!' he hissed, nodding towards a table to the side and a couple of rows back, to where a black guy was sitting by himself. 'See that cunt over there?' he asked.

Vinnie half turned and nodded.

'There's gonna be some bother, mate,' Gordon continued calmly. 'And I think it's going to happen today. He's in for raping some lass, and apparently she was nine months pregnant. Almost ready to drop, by all accounts. Anyway, Martin Healey – well, turns out he knows her.'

Vinnie knew Martin Healey. He'd had an encounter with him too. He'd tipped Vinnie the wink only a couple of weeks ago, in the washroom. Said he'd been watching him, and had liked what he'd seen and heard about him. Vinnie didn't know what that was but he'd felt puffed up with pride that such an established older con had singled him out for praise. He felt a surge of adrenalin. A rapist. A rapist *cunt*. A man who deserved a fucking battering. Which he'd be only too happy to dispense fucking personally. One that would *surely* impress Martin Healey.

'So he's going after him?' Vinnie asked Gordon. 'Like, *now*? Just like that?'

Gordon tipped his head a quarter of an inch. 'Oh, he's been planning it awhile. I've been keeping an eye, lad. He's been having some tools made up.' He picked up his fork and scooped some beans into his mouth. 'That cunt's going to get it,' he said, scanning the room as he swallowed. 'And it looks like it's happening today.' He leaned forwards again and waggled his fork in Vinnie's direction. 'Just keep your nose out and your head down and you'll be alright, lad.'

Vinnie scanned the room as well, trying to pinpoint the key players, aware of a dull thudding starting up in his chest. It was almost an unconscious thing with him these days, he realised. He'd see some cunt – like this black bastard sitting just down the way – and he'd have this physical thing, this blood lust, take him over. So far he'd controlled it, but it was like the word 'rapist' threw this switch in his head. The *cunt*. It was taking over now, as he checked out where all the screws were – thought they seemed oblivious – and honing in on the individuals that were now beginning to identify themselves, albeit unwittingly, because they were acting out of character. Martin Healey, for instance, who was sitting way across the other side of the canteen, away from all his usual cronies – prisoners who were stationed in odd locations themselves.

Keep my nose out and my head down? Vinnie thought for a moment. *Yeah, of course I fucking will.*

He turned back to Gordon. 'What's the blacky's name?'

His friend considered him for a little while then shrugged, almost imperceptibly. 'What, you after a ruck, lad?' he asked Vinnie quietly.

Vinnie met Gordon's eye and nodded, equally imperceptibly. Upon which Gordon carefully put his knife and fork into his trouser pocket and slowly tipped his remaining sausage and beans onto the table. 'He's called Claude,' Gordon said. 'And I'm told he's a hard bastard. So you best be carrying if you're after getting into Healey's good books.'

It was in that moment that Vinnie recognised an inescapable truth. This wasn't just about reputation building, about getting Healey on side. Perhaps it never had been. Perhaps it wasn't about that at all. All he knew was that, right then, he wanted to hammer that rapist bastard, and to hell with the consequences.

'I'm only interested in myself really, Gordon,' he whispered. 'And I don't need no tools.' He nodded towards Gordon's empty plate, which he held in his hands. 'That your weapon of choice, mate?' he said, beginning to be conscious that the mess on the table was attracting the attention of the nearby lads, if not the screws.

Gordon smiled. 'I could take out that black cunt with one punch,' he told him. 'Nah, lad,' he said, 'this is to give a couple of the screws a slap with when they go after you. Which you know they will, too.'

Vinnie laughed. 'On three then, okay? Three!'

And before Gordon had even had a chance to stand up, he'd leapt up, jumped the two tables that separated him from the bastard rapist, and had him on the floor before Healey could so much as hoick his jaw back up. He might not be able to do a great deal about the rapist back home, but he was clear-sighted and confident about what he *could* do. He could nuke this fucking cunt or die trying.

Claude fought back. Fought back hard, but had been caught by surprise and Vinnie knew he had the advantage. And he planned on capitalising on it, as well. He had space, too, the other prisoners instantly grouping to form a solid barrier between the screws – who were suddenly a lot more observant – and their batons, and the unexpected turn of this morning's entertainment.

Claude was a big bloke, and at least three stones heavier than Vinnie. He was older too – maybe mid-twenties – and Vinnie guessed he was the veteran of a fair few fights already. But that was less a problem than a challenge. And Vinnie did love a challenge, wrestling hard to keep Claude on the ground – though face down, eating shit was what he really deserved.

Fuck tooling up for a lark, he thought as he succeeded in clambering astride Claude's chest – teeth were generally his weapon of choice. In fact, his mouth was now practically watering at the thought of taking a bite out of the guy's ebony skin.

The crowd were closing in, now, tightening the barricade to stop the screws breaking through, and Vinnie was aware he only had a few seconds left. He deftly manoeuvred his body, shook his hair back out of his eyes and leaned in towards the cunt's face.

'One shot, mate,' Claude taunted, wriggling and defiant and grinning. 'And you'd better make it a fucking good one, cos after this is over, I'm taking your fucking head right off.' He spat, then. 'You got that, Bradford boy?'

For a second, Vinnie felt a moment of pride that this prick even knew where he came from. But then he got straight to the task in hand. 'You'll take my head off, will you, you cockney cunt?' he spat back. 'Well, not till I've got myself a bit of you first, *you fucking rapist!*'

He howled like an animal as he went in for the kill, a blood-curdling sound that was the result of all his anger filtering down into this one intensely charged moment. He lunged forward and the gasps of the other inmates were audible as he clamped his teeth together around Claude's left ear. He bit down hard, till his mouth flooded with the metallic tang of warm blood, then, tasting it, bit down even harder. He kept on ragging at the ear, tearing it away from the side of the bastard's head, and then, just as he thought he had a decent chunk free, the crowds parted and the batons rained down.

He was done. Shielding his head from the blows with crossed arms, Vinnie opened his mouth and, trying to stand

now, spat a pool of blood onto the floor. He could barely feel
the pain because the adrenalin was coursing through his veins
now, as he looked at Claude writhing in agony on the canteen
floor.

He knew things would be bad now, but he still felt triumphant. And a kind of release – a blessed release – from a tension
he hadn't realised had been as bad as it clearly had. It wouldn't
last. He knew that. Till the day he dealt with Melvin it would
always be there, coiling ever tighter till he released it again.
But for now he felt good. Good for him, good for that poor
fucking girl, righteous. And good knowing he'd sent out a very
important message to his housemates: *go on, try me if you like.
Fucking bring it on!*

They dragged him from the canteen, still raining blows over
his back and shoulders, while a bemused Martin Healey looked
on. Vinnie didn't care. He couldn't feel them – he was cush-
ioned by elation. Bolstered by the response of his fellow inmates
as he passed them, by the cheers, by the clapping, by the
respect.

Charles Rawson, the prison governor, listened intently.
Listened without commenting as his senior officer, Robert
Malvern, read out the background report. Pausing before
putting the file onto Rawson's desk, Malvern cleared his
throat. 'I know it looks bad, sir, and it is, no doubt about it.
All I'm saying is that McKellan must have been provoked.
Or,' he paused, 'put up to it. That's a distinct possibility.
Because I can honestly tell you that in all the time he was on
remand – and it was a good six months, sir – we never had a
peep out of him. Not one. Model prisoner, really. A bit of a
lad, yes. But not a bad 'un. I think his heart's in the right
place.'

The governor pinched two fingers at the bridge of his nose and looked at Malvern through metal-framed reading glasses. 'I hear what you are saying, Robert. And I've also seen the background file on this young man. And I'm afraid to tell you that, with respect, you're wrong. The lad's an out and out thug and always has been. Granted, you're right, he did behave himself on remand, but so would any half-intelligent kid hoping to get off lightly, wouldn't they? No, I'm afraid he showed his true colours in the canteen last week – and my only question, if indeed I even had one about this lad, would be quite why it took him so *long*.' He closed the file. 'Robert, we have to be firm here. It's important we send out the right message. We said a fortnight on the block and we must stick to a fortnight. We can't be seen to capitulate, can we?'

Malvern couldn't hide his sigh of frustration, although he tried to. He didn't even fully understand why he felt the need to defend Vinnie, he just knew that he liked the lad – always had, in fact – and knew how much this solitary spell would be harming him. He was a book lover, a free spirit, and clearly a bit of a party animal. And, okay, so he was a criminal – they all were, in here – but not, as far as he could see, the sort of animal the governor had him pegged as. 'No, sir,' he said. 'I get that. I just wanted to put it to you as an option, now that I've seen him. He's done a week now, and we could always put him on another landing, if you thought that might help. I just can't see what good it's doing keeping him down there. The lad's a reader, sir – a bit of an intellectual, which is the thing that most worries me. He's got fuck all down there except the Bible to fill his time and, from what I've heard, he's using that to wipe his arse with. I just think that if we leave him any longer we're asking for more trouble, not less; that we'll have a riot to deal with on top of everything else. I have to tell you, the other lags are doing their nuts, sir. It's getting volatile. They are saying McKellan was provoked and tormented, for one thing, and that this attack wasn't a case of empire building. Sir, if you've read the whole file then perhaps you already know that apparently his own sister was attacked in similar circumstances. That she was raped – and, under those circumstances, I don't know many men who *wouldn't* have done what he did, do you?'

Malvern sat and waited while the governor deliberated. It was a longish wait, and he wondered if he'd made any difference. He was a hard man, was Rawson; a bit of an unknown quantity as a governor, and Malvern couldn't second guess what he'd decide. Probably to stick with his 'two weeks, no let-offs', he judged, which meant he was surprised when Rawson finally spoke.

'You're right, Robert. Yes, you're right, of *course*. I suppose he *could* be forgiven for such an act given the circumstances.' He took his glasses off. 'Yes, okay then, we'll do it. Bring him back out of solitary, though not back to B. No –' he consulted some paperwork on his desk. 'He can go onto D block. And, let me see … yes, have him banged him up with the new inmate up there. Name of Joseph Devanney.'

Devanney. It wasn't a name Malvern recognised. But then if he was new there was no reason why he should. He stood up and nodded. 'Right, sir. Devanney. Anything I should know about him?'

The governor, who had already picked up his pen by way of dismissal, perched his reading glasses back on his nose and looked at Malvern over them. 'What? – Oh, no. No, Robert, nothing that I'm aware of. Now, if there's nothing else, I really need to get on.'

* * *

Vinnie scrubbed his skin in the shower until it burned. He'd been on the verge of cracking up when the two screws had come to collect him – and with a new understanding of what solitary meant. It had been hell. Seven days of hell, no doubt about it, and he could see how the blinding, all-consuming monotony and silence could, given long enough, be enough to send even the hardest of men over the edge.

Locked in that tiny, cold cell for 23 hours a day had been a killer. Though righting the wrong that bastard Claude had done kept him going early on, Vinnie knew he couldn't have hacked it for much longer. He couldn't bear the lack of human contact, or the sensory deprivation, and vowed that from now on he would have to conduct his business in a more controlled manner and in less conspicuous places.

He was a little miffed that he was going to D wing, however. He'd just started to enjoy himself on B and had been making friends. Oh well, he thought. He'd at least see them in the library and during yard time. The good thing was that he was out of the fucking hell-hole, and perhaps the switch to D would only be temporary. And the one thing he wasn't going to do was mention it. After all, it might be the result of some administrative fuck-up, and he was definitely not going to point that out to them.

Dressed in fresh clothes he was soon taken up to a corridor on D wing. 'Here we are,' said the screw, who had a particularly irritating smirk. The sort of smirk that needed wiping off, ideally.

There was already someone in there. He was an unremarkable-looking man, perhaps in his fifties, and as soon as he saw Vinnie, he stood up and extended a hand.

'Alright, lad?' he said pleasantly as Vinnie shook it. 'You must be young Vincent. I've heard all about you.'

And you've grabbed the fucking bottom bunk, Vinnie thought. He turned to the screw. 'This is where I'm staying, then?'

'Not up to your standard, McKellan?' the screw said mildly, having probably noticed that too. 'Ah, diddums, but don't worry, it's probably only temporary. Now get your fucking arse in there and say hello to your new bum chum.'

Vinnie stepped inside. The cell was identical to the one he'd left the week before apart from the fact that there were no pictures or photos on the walls. He guessed his new cellmate had only recently arrived too. 'The name's Vinnie,' he said as he let the hand go, 'Not Vincent. And you are?'

'Joe. The name's Joseph, but I go by Joe. What you in for?'

Vinnie laughed. So he *was* new. 'You don't ask things like that, mate. This your first time inside?'

The man blushed. Actually blushed. 'Yeah, first time, lad. Last as well, I hope. Can't say as I like the fucking place much.'

'You'll get used to it,' Vinnie answered, as he set about unpacking. He didn't have the energy to bring up the bunk situation right now. He'd just get his stuff out and around him, make his space seem more homely. His gear had beaten him to it; a big bundle sat on top of his locker. Bar his own clothes, stored ready for when they spat him back out again, all he currently had in the world. His worldly goods, in fact – his photographs, his small sheaf of letters from his mam and sister, his posters and his precious dozen or so books.

Joe watched him unpack, yapping on inanely about nothing in particular, and right away Vinnie knew they were not going to be friends. It wasn't his age – Gordon was the same sort of vintage – just that he knew they'd have nothing in common. The man was a lightweight, a divvy, a bit of a girl. Topping all that, however, was that he was trying much too hard, and, not wanting to have someone fawning all over him like some tragic cling-on, Vinnie knew he'd spend as little time with him as possible.

Starting now. 'Listen, mate,' he said, putting his pile of books on one of the empty lockers, 'I'm not being funny or owt, but I've just come up from the block, and all this small talk is giving me a headache. Nothing personal, but I wouldn't mind half an hour of privacy while I get my head back on, if that's alright with you.'

Joe nodded with the irritating anxious-to-please demeanour of a class new boy who was still trying to find his place. 'Of course. Suit yourself, lad, I was only trying to be friendly. I suppose I could go down to the rec area for a bit. If that's what you want.'

Vinnie nodded. 'I do, mate. Thanks for that.' He climbed up to his own bunk with a paperback and lay down on it. 'I'll be sorted once I've got my bearings again.'

Joe left the cell and Vinnie sighed. This was going to be hard. He'd never shared a cell with someone he didn't really like before, and if they didn't move him, the next couple of years were going to be hard. And he felt restless, too, unable to relax and perhaps doze. Perhaps a smoke would help settle him down.

As soon as the thought hit him, his craving for tobacco intensified, and he climbed down again; perhaps he'd go for a wander and see if he could find someone he knew well enough to bum a roll-up from. Though there was a thought. It was odds on that this Joe character smoked, and while the cat was away – well, why the fuck not? He'd have his baccy stashed here somewhere, so it was only a case of looking, so he set about doing so right away.

A quick riffle through drawers and lockers revealed nothing, but that was perhaps to be expected. Green as he was, he'd know enough to know to hide the things he valued, and baccy was of value – it was currency, for fuck's sake. It was just a question of where, so he carried on till he was rewarded, which didn't take long. He found the baccy tin in the corner of the foot end of the bunk, under the mattress.

The tin had been painted black and had an engraving etched onto it. A childish attempt at a duck, by the looks of it. But it wasn't just the baccy tin that was stashed under the mattress, there was a porn mag as well – so far, so par for the course – and, slipped inside it, a soiled and well-thumbed manila envelope.

Working on the basis that the more you knew the better off you generally were, Vinnie took the lack of a seal as an open invitation – it was probably a letter of no interest, but no harm in reading it even so. It was all potential ammunition, after all. But, what he pulled from it wasn't a letter, it was three Polaroid photos.

He took them out and turned them over and felt the blood begin to pound in his temples. Three photographs, all of the same girl. A young girl – a very young girl. Four perhaps? No more. And in the most vile, disturbing, provocative, sick poses he had seen in his young life. In one she was in a party dress, staring blankly for the camera, lifting the dress up at the front to reveal she had no underwear on. One was of her sitting in a chair, legs splayed at either side, resting on the chair arms – again, without underwear – and the third ... Vinnie gagged as he looked at the on the third picture: she was naked, full frontal, wearing nothing but scarlet lipstick, her tiny mouth circling a peeled banana.

Vinnie couldn't breathe. He threw down the photos as

though they had burned him. Then put them back where he had found them along with the baccy tin and porn mag. He couldn't quite believe it but it was true even so. They'd put him in a cell with a fucking filthy nonce.

Chapter 24

Keeping calm, that was the thing, Vinnie realised. Devanney would be back soon, and he needed to have his head straight. He needed space – that was the main thing. Space to gather his wits and think about what the fuck was happening here. Space to deal with the hammering that had started inside his chest, the rising nausea, the sheer disgust he was feeling, as the images kept flashing in his brain.

Why? Why had they put him in with this character? They knew about the sicko. They must do, because they always, always did. *Think, Vinnie, think!* He kept telling himself. He needed to get out – put himself among friendly familiar faces – so he headed off down the corridor, to the melee of regular guys, even though he hardly registered the many welcome greetings that accompanied his progress through the wing. He'd head to the library, he decided – familiar, reassuring territory, where, among friends, he could cool down and decide what to do.

Rounding the final corner, he cannoned into Malvern. 'Whoah, lad,' said Malvern. 'Where's the bleeding fire?'

'Oh, sorry, sir,' he said automatically, realising who it was.

'I'll live,' Malvern joshed. Then he looked at him more carefully. 'You settling in your new cell alright?'

'It's alright, sir,' Vinnie told him, lowering his eyes, wanting to keep schtum.

'And your cellmate, McKellan – he alright as well?'

Vinnie shot his head up. He knew something. He fucking knew something. 'Why d'you ask, sir? Is there something I should know?'

But Malvern's face was telling him nothing. Actually, no – not nothing. It was telling Vinnie that he knew nothing. 'Not that I know of, lad,' he said, and Vinnie judged that he meant it. 'Just asking if he's alright, that's all. To your liking.' He smiled then. 'We don't want you getting yourself back into trouble, do we?'

Vinnie took a deep breath. He'd learned nothing of any use here. 'Right, sir. Um, no we don't. But I need to get to the library, if that's okay. I just want to know my timetable now I'm back.'

Malvern stepped aside amiably and let him through.

Once at the library Vinnie was pleased to see his mate Eddie Ruddock manning the front desk. He was an old timer, in his sixties, and was apparently part of the furniture. He'd been heard to joke that he'd been living at Thorp Arch so long, that no one even remembered what he'd got sent down for. He had no desire to go back to the outside either. Prison was his life and he liked it that way. He grinned his toothless grin when he saw Vinnie.

'Now then, young ginger,' he said, 'nice to see you back in circulation. You come to give me a hand, voluntary like?'

Vinnie flashed him a smile. He felt calmer now, seeing him. 'Not today, Rudders,' he said, 'but I'll be back, don't you worry. Meantime, though, mate, I need a big favour.'

'Name it, lad,' Eddie said. 'If there's owt I can do, you know I'll do it.'

Vinnie told the old man what he'd found and, as he did so, felt a plan start emerging in his mind. Well, not so much a plan as a compulsion. A juggernaut of a decision that – this being prison and nonces being nonces – his old friend would no more have tried to talk him out of than fly. In fact, he was keen to help. Nonces had it coming and it needed to come from somewhere, after all. 'Leave it a bit,' he said. 'Wait till just before lock-up, then go and look behind the toilet in the shower block. You'll find what you need waiting for you there, lad.'

The hours dragged, particularly when it got to evening. Dragged as only hours could drag when the first thing on your mind every time you left it to its own devices was a naked four-year-old girl posing for a Polaroid. If the heat in his mind could have been matched by a similar heat in his body, he would have burned through his mattress straight onto the animal currently lying in the bunk below.

He'd been and retrieved what Eddie Ruddock had arranged for him and since getting hold of it – a shank; a crude knife made in this case from a razor blade tightly tied to a length of wood – it was all he could do not to attack Devanney on the spot. It, too, burned, from its position under the pillow his head was resting on, but he must wait. He mustn't move till they were well into the small hours and the nonce beneath him was in a suitably deep sleep.

Vinnie flexed and unflexed his knuckles in the darkness. Whose daughter was it? His? Or – another sickening thought – his granddaughter? There was no danger of him drifting off.

Devanney's screams, when they came, could be heard all over the prison, because Vinnie had beaten him almost to a pulp.

It hadn't taken long, either, because Vinnie had been in such a frenzy, tearing at his skin with his nails, gouging at his face, biting him repeatedly, and then, when he had finally knocked all remaining fight out of him, the pièce de résistance, the appropriate grand finale. He took his bloodied shank, used it to tear down Devanney's pyjamas and then started hacking at his balls.

The blood was everywhere. Went everywhere. Fountained from the writhing man's groin, covering Vinnie from head to toe with its squirting mess. He didn't care. In fact, by now, he felt calm, almost detached. Detached enough to notice, out of the corner of his eye, the two screws who were just outside, doing nothing.

He even glanced at them and experienced a weird kind of satisfaction to see them quickly dodge back out of sight, into the shadows. He had been set up. And perhaps he'd always known that. Because as he slashed the knife repeatedly at the mush he'd made of Devanney's testicles, it all made sense. The early release from the block, the screw telling him he wouldn't be long in his new cell, even Mr Malvern acting all fucking CID about his cellmate. Even Mr Malvern. So perhaps he'd read that wrong.

He stopped hacking and stared at Devanney, who was whimpering and barely conscious. 'You're one lucky fucker,' he said to him, 'you dirty bastard nonce. You were gonna die tonight. I'd have done fucking life for you, you know that? But not for these fuckers –' He raised his voice. 'You hear? Not a fucking chance. Sleep well, *Joseph*, because when I spread the word about you, trust me – you're gonna wish I *had* finished you off.'

He climbed off the bunk then, wiped the blood from his eyes and face, and, plastering a smile on his face, raised his arms high. 'Right, you fuckers,' he called, dropping the shank and clasping his hands behind his head, 'I'm ready for you now! Come and fucking get me!'

Finally, *finally*, the machine rumbled into action. Whistles blew, feet stamped, shouts and clanking keys could be heard. Then light, then the batons, then oblivion.

Robert Malvern – on early duty the following morning – stood and listened to Stuart Halliwell filling him in on what had happened overnight. Halliwell was a junior officer, relatively new, and Malvern could see he had been badly shocked by the night's events. So it was his job to set an example. To maintain the cool professional detachment expected from a man in his position; something he'd developed over many years.

Even so, something about it made his jaw clench. 'I'm taking the block breakfasts down,' he told his young colleague. And Halliwell, clearly keen to knock off and get away from the place, wasn't about to object.

Malvern had been in the service for long enough to have seen plenty. He'd seen things he'd rather not have seen and things he was glad he *had* seen; the prison service was certainly good at giving you life lessons. But opening the cell door that morning was to be greeted by a sight that, gruesome as it was – and, shit, they'd clearly gone to work on him – just made him feel overwhelmingly sad.

Vinnie was covered in blood. There was barely an inch of him not stippled or smeared with the stuff, and Malvern, both sickened and familiar with the way of things in prisons, looked immediately and keenly at his chest. The boy was face up, and it was rising and falling in a slow steady rhythm, and Malvern exhaled, not having even consciously realised he'd been automatically holding his own breath. McKellan, probably exhausted, was simply asleep, eyes swollen tight shut, hair matted, body beaten and, given the shit he was going to wake up to, sleep, Malvern decided, was the best thing for him.

Malvern looked around, then, and taking in one of the long walls of the cell, realised that something had been daubed in blood along the length of it. He looked again at McKellan, homing in on what he thought he'd probably find. A particularly nasty gash on his forearm, congealed now and glossy, and almost definitely very purposefully self-inflicted.

Squinting slightly in the gloom of the windowless room, he followed the line of large, carefully painted words on the wall. *I am what you designed me to be*, he read, taking time to make the words out. *I am your blade. You cannot now complain if you also feel the hurt.*

Malvern put the breakfast tray down carefully, so as not to wake the sleeping prisoner, and took a moment to re-read the message. It was apparently by Charles Dickens – Vinnie had scrawled that beneath it – and it took Malvern's mind immediately to the lad's small stack of books, his precious library job, his unquenchable thirst for reading and learning. And it bothered him – even humbled him – that he didn't know the quote himself. But mostly he stood there and tried to take in the bloodied mess of the young man currently sprawled on the floor beneath it.

On some days – on most days – Malvern was proud of his profession. And on others … He squatted down and thought about his own son, just nine years old. Well, on others, he decided, he fucking wasn't.

1979

Chapter 25

March, Josie decided, was probably the very best time imaginable to have a baby. Yes, it had its negatives: it had been hard being so pregnant in the bitterest part of winter, waddling around, always scared that she might slip and fall, but to have had her daughter at the start of spring meant enjoying it with her – the expanding days, the sunshine, the knowledge that summer was just around the corner. And best of all, having someone of her very own who loved and needed her.

She was on her way to the post office, a trip she made every Monday morning; a short and currently sunny walk through the cul de sac at the top of the estate. It was there that she picked up her family allowance, usually pushing little Paula, all snug in her pram, more often than not dressed in something Eddie's mum had knitted for her.

Eddie and his family had saved her, there was no doubt about it. Meeting Eddie three years back had felt like nothing short of a miracle for Josie, not just because the unimaginable had happened – that a boy, a lovely boy, actually wanted to be her boyfriend – but because she felt something she'd never before felt in her life; that she wanted to be with him too.

Though it had taken many months to get to that point. At first she'd shunned him, just like she'd vowed she'd shun any male, ever. But Eddie had been patient. Patient to a fault. It had been an Easter Monday when they'd met – three years next month, in fact – when he'd sprung to her defence down the youthy one evening when a gang of older girls from Southfield Lane were being mean to her and Caz. He'd been a proper knight in shining armour, just like in the fairy tales.

For which Josie had been grateful, albeit a bit grudgingly, because she had a rule: she didn't need any rescuing. Well, not once they'd been seen off and she'd regained her composure and reminded herself that, while it was kind of him to step in, she really didn't need *anything* from a bloke. So by the time Eddie asked her if she'd go out with him, back in the youthy a few days later, she had no hesitation in refusing him; he'd only be after what every other bloke was after, after all. And that was something she wasn't giving anyone.

'So can we be friends, then?' he'd suggested, and had looked so doe-eyed about it that she felt mean in refusing that too. And that was how it had been, for the best part of the following year; they'd see each other often, going for walks, going swimming down at Grange Baths, and now and again, when they had some money, getting the bus into Bradford to see a film at the Odeon. Which was all fine, as far as Josie thought, until one day it hit her that, to the outside world, anyway, she apparently wasn't being fair.

And it seemed she was about to have competition. From Janet Hawkins, one of the girls who lived on Canterbury Front, and who'd told her at a youth club disco, and in no uncertain terms, that if Josie didn't want him, she *did*.

'He's a catch, he is,' she'd said to her. 'You must want your head testing, Titch!' And that had been a shock, that. A *big* shock. Not the fact that someone fancied him; after all, he was tall and nice looking, and he also had a good job as a painter and decorator, rather than idling around the estate doing fuck all, like so many of the lads did once they'd left school. No, it was more the shock of how she felt about the idea of him getting a girlfriend, which was something she'd not thought about before. So she did think, and realised that she felt pretty strongly; that if Janet Hawkins went near him – if *any* girl went near him she would ... what? Threaten them? Send them packing? She wasn't sure. All she knew was that she was feeling something pretty physical about it and that, annoyingly, it wouldn't go away.

Josie looked into the pram at her brand new baby and she smiled. She had her dad's curly hair, and his big smiley eyes and – well, if you were to believe her mam's opinion on the matter, anyway – her granddad McKellan's 'bleeding great conk of a nose'. Which she might have – as the health visitor had said, it was too early to tell yet. But Josie didn't care anyway – her dad's nose was fine. And though she'd never say so to June, not wanting to give her mam anything to sneer about, she thought baby Paula also looked quite a lot like Vinnie.

She parked the pram outside the post office carefully, so as not to wake her sleeping baby. It really didn't matter who she did or didn't look like. To her and Eddie, she was perfect in every way.

Josie put the brake on and rummaged under the rain cover for her bag. She had a letter she needed to get in the post today as well. It was for her brother, her first in a while, what with having the baby and everything, and she couldn't wait for him to get it – particularly the photos. She'd borrowed Caz's Polaroid to take them, and couldn't wait to see his face when he saw his baby niece, and realised she had inherited their wiry ginger hair.

She felt a rush of excitement at the thought of Vinnie meeting Paula. Excited at the thought that, if he managed to stay out of trouble, he'd be home again in less than six weeks, and she was counting the days.

It had been a long time, such a very long time. And for a long time she'd raged, unable to forgive him for leaving her, unable to feel anything but betrayed and abandoned by the only person (bar Caz – whose pragmatism was sometimes infuriating) who knew what she'd been through and cared.

But not enough, clearly. This had fuelled her anger constantly, and she found it hard to imagine ever forgiving him, until the day when, a year or so after them first being together, Eddie had told her something that blew everything away.

He had been at that party, and he'd seen what had happened, and like everyone on Canterbury Estate – bar, it seemed, Josie – knew what the fight had been about: *her*. And Eddie hadn't wanted to tell her, obviously, because who *would* want to tell their girlfriend nasty stuff like that? But, oh, once he had, how she'd wished she had known. Why, for God's sake, hadn't *Vinnie* told her?

'Christ, Titch, Why do *you* think?' Eddie had asked her, exasperated. 'For the same reason I didn't. Because that's not what you do! You're so hard on him, love, but he was only trying to protect you.'

'But he shouldn't have done!' she'd railed anyway, refusing to be mollified. 'I can fight my own battles! Christ, I haven't had much choice, have I?'

And Eddie had told her to grow up, and he'd been right.

Josie was just closing her purse when she felt a tap on her shoulder. She turned around to see an elderly lady standing behind her, who was gesturing back through the shop to the front door. 'There's a little 'un out there,' she said, 'Wailing fit to bust, she is. Might it be yours, love?'

Josie thanked the woman and hurried back outside, thinking, as she always did, that it was completely ridiculous that you couldn't take prams into shops. It was indeed Paula; she could now hear the cries for herself. Another of June's great pronouncements (and this *was* probably true) was that her latest grand-daughter had a great pair of lungs on her; something she, being a bit of a singer, invariably took credit for. Whether Paula could *actually* sing, like most of her mam's side of the family, was something else they wouldn't find out for a while yet, but in the meantime, she was doing a good job of practising.

Paula was scarlet and furious when Josie got back to her, and her plaintive cries had even attracted a small audience; a scraggy-looking terrier, straining at the lead that was tethering it to a nearby drainpipe, and a couple of boys of about eight, both in school shorts and shirts, who she thought she recognised but couldn't place. Whoever they were, they were wearing the sort of expressions that made Josie sure it had been them who'd probably set Paula off.

Seeing lads like these two hanging about really got to Josie these days. Seeing any boys looking shifty tended to get to Josie these days, and not because they always put her in mind of Vinnie – and that didn't take much – but because of little Robbie, her once-lovely nephew, who was no longer so little and no longer so nice. He was 16 now and dealing drugs, which was really no surprise to anyone (given doing drugs was his mam's full-time occupation these days) even if that idiot Robbo had been long since kicked out. And when he wasn't dealing, Robbie was usually out robbing round the estate with his gang of cronies, and she could find no way to reach him anymore.

Josie narrowed her eyes at the pair of lads that were now observing her. 'Shouldn't you two be in school?' she said, scooping the angry pink bundle from her pram.

'None of yer business,' one of the boys answered.

'How d'you know it isn't?' she asked. 'It might be.' She clutched Paula close against her shoulder, cradling her head into her neck, and jiggling her up and down a little to try and soothe her. 'How d'you know I'm not a teacher?' she added. 'How d'you know I'm not the Board man, for that matter?'

'You're not, though,' the other answered cockily. 'Cos you're a *girl*. Anyway, we already know who you are. You're Titch McKellan, Vinnie's sister, ain't you?'

It was a statement rather than a question. Which was no surprise either. You were never quite so notorious as when one of your family was holidaying at her majesty's pleasure. Not round Canterbury, anyway, which made her sad. That and the fact that made her big brother a kind of hero to these two. Which was all wrong even though a part of her knew it was also right – and trying to decide which left her head in a mess every time. He'd always been *her* hero, and he shouldn't have gone back inside, that was all. It was just such a terrible *waste*.

Paula was quietening down now, probably because she could smell her mum again. And it might have been the dog that set her off, truth be told, Josie decided. 'Is that so?' she said to the boys, carefully placing Paula back into the pram again. 'Well, makes no difference, anyway. You should still be in school. How you ever going to make anything of yourselves if you don't go to school and learn anything?'

'School's for sissies,' one of the boys said. 'You don't learn nothing useful. You learn much betterer stuff on the streets.'

'*On the streets*'? *Listen to them*, she thought. If only they could hear themselves. 'Such as?' she wanted to know, placing a hand on each hip. She was actually rather enjoying this. 'Like how to nick stuff, how to dodge the bizzies, how to play knock-a-door-run and drive everyone up the wall? Oh, that's *really* clever, that is. That'll really serve you well in life. Just like thinking "betterer" is a proper word will, as well.'

''Tis a word!' the shorter of the two boys protested. 'It means good, an' that. And …'

'And what?' she said, using her foot to snap the brake off the pram, while he thought.

But the boy wasn't thinking. He was now looking past her. He'd obviously seen something of greater interest than her. So she went to turn as well, and just as she did so, heard a loud, phlegmy cough close behind her. It was a sound she hadn't heard in years – how many years now? But that, chillingly, she remembered very well.

He was almost beside the pram. Almost in smelling distance, as well as seeing distance, and she instantly recoiled. Melvin. Mucky Melvin. Here. Now. Just the sound of the name felt like a physical assault on her. And the distance of years – and how long *had* it been now? Six? – had suddenly shortened; snapped back to almost nothing at all.

He bent slightly to peer into the pram. 'Well, well,' he said, his voice like wet sandpaper. 'Little girl, is it? I bet she'll be a stunner when she gets older.'

Josie felt her hands gripping tightly to the pram handle as she pulled it back, lifted the front wheels and turned it full around. Even the idea that he was looking at her baby revolted her.

She started to walk away from him, aware of the two boys still looking on. Though they'd moved a few steps away now, to a new, safer vantage-point. She could tell that seeing Melvin up close had rattled them a bit as well. But though she felt frightened too, there was another feeling welling up inside her. Rage, that was what it was. A powerful maternal rage.

She turned back to him again, sickened and shaking with fury. 'You,' she said, raising a hand to stab a finger towards him. 'If you ever come near me and my family again, I'll make sure you fucking pay for it, you hear me?'

Melvin stood his ground, unabashed by her. Brazen, in fact. How dare he! Then his features, always grisly but now etched with a network of deep wrinkles, rearranged themselves to form a lecherous smile.

'Oh, it's a bit late for that, lass,' he said, licking spittle from his lower lip. 'Your Lyndsey's little Sammy does my shopping for me these days. Little angel she is.' He paused, the smile splitting his face further. 'Oh, yes,' he finished, 'she's *always* happy to oblige.'

Then, as Josie watched, disgusted, he cleared his wattly throat. He spat then; producing a green globule that fell and glistened on the pavement, before he hobbled, chuckling, into the post office.

Josie stood rooted to the spot for a moment, unable to move, much less think rationally or speak. Sammy? Lyndsey's *Sammy*? It couldn't be, surely? Wherever Melvin lived now it was nowhere near where they did. He'd been re-homed at the other end of the estate – and good riddance – and she thought she'd seen the last of him. She *had* seen the last of him. And as far as she knew, he'd not been seen on their part of the estate in years. So how could it *be* that … She felt a jabbing in her side. It made her jump. It was one of the two boys.

'You know who *that* was?' he asked her, chest puffed out, chin jutting. He was clearly proud to be able to deliver such important intelligence. 'That was Mucky Melvin, that was,' he said solemnly. 'He lives in a haunted house, and he's a perver.'

'Yeah, he's a perver,' the other boy agreed, 'and you shouldna spoke to him. Me mam said. She said he likes doing things you don't want to know about. Things like sexing stuff, an' that. He's a very bad man.'

Josie looked from one boy to the other, her mind whirring horribly. She nodded at them. 'I know,' she said. 'I know.'

Josie walked home from the post office the long way. Eddie's mum was at home and for the moment she wanted to avoid her. She loved her to bits; she and Eddie's dad had been so good to them, always, but right now she needed space and time to think.

Sammy. Could it be true? She hoped to God it couldn't be. Hoped to God it was just him trying to rile her, just for the hell of it. But her nieces were 13 and 12 now, making Sammy – and she could hardy bear to think about it, really – almost exactly the same age as she had been when Vinnie had been dragged off to approved school and she'd made the worst mistake ever in setting foot in that filthy bastard's house.

And Sammy had been acting funny just lately, too. She saw lots of the girls – they'd both been such a help with Paula – but over the past few months, since a while before she'd had the baby, come to think of it, Sammy had seemed different – quieter, less full of life, a bit withdrawn. Josie had put it down to her being a teenager, starting her periods, being a bit moody, but as she walked and pondered she felt a chill coming over her; like when a door suddenly blows open, allowing you to see what you couldn't see before.

And Josie didn't like what she was seeing. It repulsed her. The question was, what to do? Who to tell? Lyndsey would be worse than useless; she was always worse than useless, because she was off her head most of the time these days. No, perhaps she needed to pop round when Sammy got home from school, take her out for a walk or something and ask her outright. *Fuck*, she thought. Melvin wasn't gone and forgotten after all. He'd been forgotten but he had *not* gone. Just moved away and *moved* on. And it was going to be up to her to stop him. Starting now.

She looked again at her baby daughter, now gazing up at her with her huge, thick-lashed eyes. *A little stunner*, he'd said. Josie tightened her grip on the pram handle. She just hoped she wasn't too late.

Chapter 26

Vinnie took a long slow look around his cell, and realised that what he felt was ill at ease. It was an unnatural feeling for him, being so nervous, and he didn't like it. Even so, he couldn't seem to shake it off.

Six years. Six long years he'd called Thorp Arch his home, and now he was leaving it he felt strange. He'd had quite a few cells now, on quite a few landings, but though the company had been different – sometimes good, sometimes not so good – each cell had been basically the same.

Gordon was long gone – since over a year back, his time served. And even he – twice-round-the-block old timer that he was – couldn't believe they'd made Vinnie serve every single day of his sentence. It was practically unheard of, and though Vinnie didn't like it – who would? – it at least gave him a certain cachet, a certain notoriety.

Which was about to depart along with him. He was someone in here. Whereas out there ... well, if he didn't have such a solid, focussed plan on his mind, he might be feeling even more nervous than he already was at the probable uncertainty of his new social status.

His thoughts were interrupted by the familiar sound of heavy boots on hard floor.

'Now then, sir,' he said, as Mr Malvern stepped into the cell and joined him. 'I don't want no tears when I'm gone, okay? I know how cut up you're going to be without me, but try to hold it together won't you, sir?'

Malvern laughed and sat down on the bunk alongside him. 'I'll try my best, son,' he said. 'Though I can't make any promises. How long before they come for you?'

Vinnie shrugged. 'Dunno, sir. They said it would be just after dinner but that was over an hour ago. I wish they'd hurry up, though. I got my mate Brendan coming – driving all the way from Bradford and all to fetch me – and he's not going to wait all fucking day.'

In truth he would. Of course he would. He was as solid a mate as anyone could ever wish for, and thinking about seeing him stilled Vinnie's nerves a bit.

Malvern nodded. Then he cleared his throat. 'Listen, son,' he said, looking at Vinnie intently. 'I know we've had our ups and downs in here and our little misunderstandings, but I hope you know how much I mean what I'm about to say. I really hope you're going to try hard to stay out of here – and places *like* here – from now on, Vinnie. It's not worth it, mate. However much you think it might be when push comes to shove, it really isn't. And you're a good lad, son. I know you are. You're worth more than this.'

Vinnie grinned, and Malvern smiled, knowing exactly what he was referring to. *Little misunderstandings? That was the understatement of the fucking year!* He had, for a long time, laboured under a massive misunderstanding. That Malvern had been a key part of that set up with Joe Devanney. The cunt was long gone himself now, and good fucking riddance. Hopefully to some prison hell-hole for sub-human species. But his sense of injustice had burned. And along with it had certainty about who'd stitched him up. That it had been the governor *and* Malvern. That Malvern had been responsible for that long period of isolation he'd endured. For the fact that he'd emerged from it such a different, broken person; with that leaden feeling that something vital had snapped inside him, and lacking the will to care about anyone or anything.

He had almost lost his mind and had definitely lost his will and it had taken many months and lots of proof before Vinnie would allow the possibility that, actually, Mr Malvern had had nothing to do with it. Had been as blind to the set-up as he had.

He would miss him. Along with Gordon, he was the closest thing to a fucking father he'd ever had in here. Yes, he thought as Malvern stood up, he would miss him.

'Don't you worry, sir,' he reassured him. 'I've had enough of bang-up. I'm 23 now – nearly 24! I need to find a bird and settle down a bit. And anyway, sir, you've met my mother. You think she'd let me? She'd chop my fucking hands off if I started getting up to no good.'

Mr Malvern smiled and stepped outside again. 'Good to hear it, lad,' he said. 'Anyway, I'll go and find out what's going on for you. Make sure you've got everything, won't you? You done the rounds? Said all your goodbyes and fuck-offs yet?'

Vinnie nodded. 'Said all I had to say yesterday. Not many of my mates left in here anyway, sir, are there?' he winked. 'And I've sorted out the ones that matter.'

Malvern nodded. Vinnie knew he understood.

Since the business with the nonce, and the punishment that had ensued, Vinnie had done a great deal of soul-searching. And one of the things that had struck him most forcibly was that, for however long he had left – and it had, after that, become a long time – that he should trust no one. Not on the inside and not on the outside, and it simplified life enormously. If you worked on the basis that no one gave a fuck about you, it absolved you of the responsibility of giving a fuck in return. Gordon was excluded, of course – he was his only real fucking friend in here – and, to a certain extent (he was still a prison officer, working to rules) Mr Malvern too. But Gordon – *fuck* he missed him, because, in truth, he had saved him. He'd been the only port in such a fucking ugly shit-storm. And that was because he knew that, despite the permanent grin and the ready bravado, Vinnie *had* been a broken man – hardly a man at all, looking back. A busted kid – literally – after they'd finished with him. Left him with his broken bones, his chipped teeth and his burst eardrum. A busted kid who, protected by Gordon (who peddled the line that he was as fit as ever and not to be messed with), needed a great deal of time and space to heal, and a place of safety in which to find his resolve again.

But he had, he was proud to note, scored a victory. It was soon clear that no nonce would be tolerated on normal landings. Not when Vinnie was about, anyway. And the other prisoners soon got behind him in their droves, leading to what seemed revolutionary at the time, but three years on had become routine: segregation of sex offenders away from the normal landings.

Several other prisons – more forward thinking, perhaps – were already doing this, Vinnie later found out, to the benefit of all. But, even so, from time to time, the odd one or other found their way to a cell with a more run-of-the-mill prisoner, and from time to time – as night followed fucking day, in fact – the nonce would end up getting a beating.

No one would ever convince Vinnie that these episodes weren't planned. Which was fine as far as he was concerned – nonces got what they deserved – but only if the designated avenging fucking angel wasn't the one who ended up paying the price.

He stood and stretched. And now it was done. He was free. He was free and going home – 'home'; what a weird concept that was – and to his mam, who he knew would be just the same as when he'd left. Still slapping on the lippy in front of the mantelpiece mirror, still giving his dad shit about nothing.

But no Titch at home now. *Christ*, that seemed unbelievable. Unbelievable to think she was a fully grown woman, let alone one with a bloke and a job and a fucking baby. He pulled her letter from his jeans pocket and unfolded it carefully, smiling at the sight of the two snaps of his latest niece. *Poor little bleeder*, Titch had written. *Looks just like you, ha-ha.* And Vinnie liked to think she did, too.

It would be weird seeing Titch again, all grown up, all sorted out now. Because she was. She so obviously was. You could tell that from her letters. She'd got things together, clearly. Put the horrible stuff behind her – though, how the fuck *did* you put shit like that behind you? Being raped by a fucking nonce when you were 11?

Vinnie didn't know how she'd done it – and maybe she hadn't. Maybe she'd just done a good job of burying it. Something Vinnie'd not managed himself. In fact, there was only one thing Vinnie *had* put behind him – any idea that he should do what the psychologist wankers wanted. Move on in life. Let bygones be bygones. Forget, forgive and all that kind of shit.

He hadn't forgotten and he would never forgive. He was going home to unfinished business.

* * *

That Vinnie hadn't been able to finish off Joseph 'call me fucking Joe' Devanney had, for a time, angered him greatly. It had always been a long shot – and something of a poser in the planning, too. It was tricky having to balance hurting him so hard and fast that he finished him off quickly and doing what his heart said was what really needed doing – and could anything be bad enough for the cunt who was responsible for the photographs of that wide-eyed little girl that still burned so brightly and repulsively in his head?

And perhaps, all said and done, it was good that he survived. Survived fucked up and with his genitals beyond repair. That was good. He survived as a warning to every other cunt like him. And that he survived held another important positive. Had he died then Vinnie would have been done for murder rather than ABH, and those extra three years he served would have been substantially longer. Perhaps long enough that another nonce – the one he really wanted – would have popped his clogs before Vinnie had the chance to take the matter of his demise out of his filthy, child-molesting hands.

It was a watershed moment for Vinnie, deciding on his destiny. Once he'd reached the conclusion that taking Melvin out was the only practical course of action, life in prison had become something of a breeze for him. Once he'd emerged from the ashes of his former self, healed both bodily and mentally, it served simply as a period of time in which to prepare and focus. He ate well. He exercised regularly. He was in the prime of his life and his body responded by becoming fit and lithe and strong and dependable. He played the game – so much so that Gordon would often clap a fatherly hand across his shoulder, saying 'That's the way, son' whenever Vinnie did the mature thing and walked away from bother – and he did that all the time now.

He made 'friends' superficially, smiled when social cues dictated it, became angry when circumstances dictated it was expected, settled scores as and when safe and appropriate.

He had become, to all intents and purposes, a version of himself. One that was fit for purpose in any given prison situation, and the only time he was his true self was when he was alone, with his nose and heart and head inside a book. Though he guarded this version of himself diligently. His prison self would do just as the other inmates did, and trade baccy for porn mags, so he had a small stash for recreational purposes. He rarely looked at them, though it was all about conforming to type, obviously, so if you passed his cell you'd see just what you expected to see: an inmate, lying on his bunk, porn mag open in front of him, thinking the same unrequited carnal thoughts everyone else did.

What they didn't know was that out of sight there would more often than not be a real book – *Great Expectations*, *The Count of Monte Cristo* or *The Adventures of Tom Sawyer* – carefully concealed between some slut's wide-open thighs.

'You ready, son?' Malvern said, interrupting Vinnie's thoughts again. 'Or d'you love it so much you want to do an extra week or two? Only they've asked me to fetch you and escort you down to pick up your things and get processed out of here.'

Vinnie laughed and slapped Malvern across the back. 'Get me things? I was still reading the fucking *Beano* when I came in here, sir, so I doubt there'll be anything much I'm going to want to take with me.' He grinned. 'Mind you, if anyone's messed with my Crombie or owt, *they*, sir, are going to be a dead man.'

They made their way along the landing down the stairs, and through the process of being processed, and Vinnie was pleased to see his precious Crombie still fitted him. Slipping it over his shoulders felt like slipping on a whole new persona and, once he was into it, he found he actually rather liked it. It had the benefit, he thought, as he signed the various papers, of beautiful simplicity.

'Now, lad,' Malvern said, as he prepared to finally release him, 'do you have any plans for the outside?'

Vinnie looked at him, feeling he was at least deserving of his honesty. 'Not really, sir,' he said. 'Not anything you'd want to hear about, anyway.'

And then he was gone. Led out of the main gates and waving across the road to Brendan, who was leaning against the bonnet of a battered green Cortina.

Vinnie walked across to meet him and he didn't look back. He didn't want to see Malvern's look of disappointment. Didn't want to weaken his resolve.

Chapter 27

Vinnie took a final drag on his ciggie and yawned as he slid into the passenger seat of Brendan's car. It had been a long night for both of them, but in a good way – the best way – and he was grateful to his mate for being so brilliantly organised. Though who'd have imagined he'd been so clued up about the red-light district in Wetherby? That had certainly been a turn-up.

It had been a good decision to hold off driving back home for a day. It had been a good way to spend his resettlement allowance, not to mention a way of thanking his best mate, but mostly it had re-orientated him, and, yes, settled him. Set him up.

'I take it you enjoyed your night with the Whore of Babylon then, mate?' Brendan said, chuckling, as he pulled back out onto the street to begin the long journey home.

'I've had better, our kid,' Vinnie answered, grinning.

'You've had better?' Brendan snorted. 'Fuck off! I'll bet that place was a fucking riot compared to all the pillow biting you've been doing for the last six fucking years!'

Vinnie reached across and cuffed his mate round the back of the head. It was so good to be back. And he intended making the most of it while he could. 'So,' he said, once they were back on the motorway to Bradford, 'before I throw myself into the fray, what's going down? Anything?'

'Not a lot,' Brendan said. 'Same characters doing the same shit as always. Gerard and Martin have been in and out of

Armley nick for the past couple of years, oh, and Martin's had a kid. You know that Lizzie Conley? Well, she's bringing up his sprog. They're not together, like, but I think he still goes round for a bit of how's your father. Like I said,' he chuckled, 'nowt much has changed really.'

'Speaking of nothing changing, you seen anything of our Lynds?' Vinnie asked him. 'What's she up to? No sign of that freak Robbo sniffing around again, I hope?'

Brendan shook his head. 'Not sure he even lives round here any more, to be honest.'

'And she's not shipped in another smackhead or got herself knocked up again, has she?'

'No, don't worry. No danger of that, mate.' He paused. 'Look, don't take offence –'

'As if. I don't give a flying fuck what she gets up to.'

'– but she's not good these days, Vinnie. If it weren't for your Josie, those poor girls of hers would be living a fucking awful life. Well, Robbie already is – but then you know that already. But, well, you'll see soon enough, I suppose …'

'Honestly, mate,' Vinnie reassured him, 'don't worry about it. There's not a lot anyone can do about it, is there?'

'Though actually,' Brendan said, 'there *is* probably something you should know.'

'Which is?'

'Mucky Melvin.' He glanced across at Vinnie.

Vinnie felt himself stiffen. 'What about him?'

'I don't know if it's actually true or not, mate …'

'What?'

'Well, you know I told you when I wrote about him approaching our Kelly's little 'un on the street a while back? Well, and like I say, I don't know if it's actually true or not, but someone told Kelly they'd heard – and I don't know who from

– that your Lyndsey's Sammy's been running errands for him lately. Like I say, it's all a bit Chinese whispers, but, well, I thought you ought to know, mate.'

Vinnie digested this piece of information as if it was a piece of particularly resistant gristle in a prison stew. It lodged half-way down and it was a real act of will to swallow it. He'd taken in the information about Brendan's sister's girl with a degree of detachment. It was entirely what he'd expected because Melvin was a fucking nonce and that's what fucking nonces did. It wasn't so much a guilty one-off as a fucking career for them. And there was always another little 'un on the production line to target. He also knew that Brendan's sister would keep her little one safe. But as for Lyndsey … He stared ahead for a bit, thinking.

For half a second he thought of telling Brendan the whole story about his own sister. He knew about Robbo trying it on with her, of course, and that Melvin had as well, but no more. And Melvin had tried it on with every child in a fucking skirt, hadn't he? But something stopped him. Something instinctive. And something rational as well. Would it help anything for Brendan to know? No, it wouldn't.

'Cunt,' Vinnie settled on finally, as a response. 'Anyone know where he's hiding out these days?'

'He's not been hiding, mate. Last I heard, he was in a squat somewhere down the bottom of the estate right now, or so I'm told. Though something tells me that he might want to now.' Brendan glanced across at Vinnie. 'You thinking of going after him? Giving him a bit of a pasting?'

Vinnie smiled at his friend. 'Can't think of anything I'd like to do more,' he said. 'Well, I can, but right now I'm all shagged out. Anyway,' he said, reaching into his pocket for his Woodbines. 'I need to speak to our Sammy first, don't I?'

And hopefully not hear the same sickening tale about that cunt, that ... no, he thought. Don't think the worst yet. Remain positive. After all, he didn't doubt that, with what they had for a mother, his nieces were far too savvy to set foot in the fucker's lair. 'But not a peep about it, okay? I don't want that cunt getting wind that I'm back.'

'Not a peep,' Brendan promised. 'But don't you do anything without me, Vin. I mean it.'

Vinnie smiled at his friend. He was the best mate anyone could wish for – always had been. He was as loyal as they came, Brendan. A bloke with a really good heart. But you needed more than a heart for what Vinnie had in mind – a bloody strong stomach, for a start. No, there was no way he'd involve his oldest friend, not in a million years. Vinnie didn't want that kind of shit on his conscience.

'Don't you worry, mate,' he lied. 'Scout's honour. I do nothing without my fucking side-kick tagging along, don't you worry.'

'Side-kick?' Brendan chided. 'You cheeky bastard!'

Nothing had changed. Nothing. It was like he'd got stuck in a time-warp. Or been shot into one of those worm-holes they were always going through on *Star Trek*. Only with crap instead of asteroids for company.

He got out of Brendan's car, grabbed his case, and thanked his mate for coming to get him.

'See you in the Bull later?' Brendan asked. 'Or you stopping in with your mam tonight?'

Vinnie laughed. 'Is the pope fucking Catholic, mate?'

He waved Brendan off and glanced around the empty mid-afternoon street, feeling a heaviness come over him that wasn't just about his raucous night last night or the fry-up they'd wolfed down at the motorway services. Six fucking years, yet nothing seemed to have altered. The world had changed so much, yet up here, it was like they'd forgotten to tell anyone. As they'd driven into the estate it was like he'd been transported straight back to being a teenager. Same peeling houses, same broken fences, same littered, overgrown gardens – did no one ever think to trim a fucking hedge here? He smiled to himself, thinking back to Thorp Arch and the extensive grounds there. Thought of Gordon and how proud he always was of his fucking shrubberies. And how order and cleanliness and routine and discipline had been something he now took so much for granted that coming back felt like entering a shit-hole.

Looking up at his sister's house, he noticed the bathroom window was still broken. How long now – nine years? I could fix that for her, he thought. Well, in a different life, a different circumstance. As it was, it would probably have to stay broken.

He walked the length of the short path in less than half a dozen strides, gave a quick blast on the front door then turned the handle. It wouldn't be locked, he knew, because it never was.

He then stepped inside and, ready as he was to see whatever state his sister might be in, he had to do a bit of a double take, seeing his nieces. He wasn't even sure that he'd have recognised them.

They, however, certainly remembered him.

'Alright, Uncle Vin?' Lou said – least, he *thought* it was Lou. Yes, yes it was. Lou was the older one. Must be what now? Thirteen?

'Alright as I'll ever be, I suppose, love,' he said, smiling. 'How about you two?'

Sammy smiled shyly at him. 'I'm okay,' she said.

Lyndsey got up from the sofa where, it seemed to Vinnie anyway, she might well have sat since the last time he saw her, without ever once getting up.

'Grown a bit, haven't they?' she slurred.

They had definitely done that, Vinnie conceded. And changed a bit, as well. And in ways Vinnie wasn't quite comfortable with. The pair of them were plastered in make-up. Bright blue eyeshadow slicked like chalk marks across their eyelids, thick black lines painted round their eyes. The way they dressed, too – he knew fuck-all about fashion, but it must have had some major shift since he was banged up, because the pair of them looked like something out of fucking Shalamar, putting him uncomfortably in mind of the ministering angel who'd attended to his baser needs last night.

It wasn't a comfortable thought. *Christ*, he decided. *If this is what happens when you let a fucking bird run the country, she could fuck right off again.* He sat down across from the girls, still trying to take them in. 'Well,' he said to Lyndsey, 'you going to make me a cup of tea, or what? That's what normal people do when they have visitors, I've heard.'

'Fuck off,' Lyndsey said, but she shuffled off to the kitchen anyway, leaving the girls sitting looking at him self-consciously.

He waited till he could hear Lyndsey banging around – hopefully constructively – then turned to Lou. 'Do us a favour, babes,' he said. 'Run and give your mum a hand. I just remembered I forgot to tell her I don't take sugar in my tea these days, and she'll probably bung three teaspoons of the stuff in. Oh, and some biscuits. See if she's got any? I know it's a long shot but I'm starved.'

Lou leapt up obediently, as he'd expected. They were bound to feel embarrassed about being stuck with this virtual stranger. Six years was a long time when it was half your lifetime, after all.

But he didn't have long, so he needed to get to the point. 'Sammy,' he said, 'I know this will come as a bit of a shock, but I've got to come out with it. I've been hearing stuff on my way home today. Has Mucky Melvin been bothering you?'

Her eyes widened and her face answered the question for her, reminding him painfully of how it must have been for Josie at that age. She shook her head immediately. 'No.'

'Love, I know about him,' Vinnie persisted, experiencing that same leaden feeling as before. 'And you're not in any trouble. I just need to know. I've heard some things. Not just about you. About a couple of other girls too. And I heard you'd been running errands for him. Getting his shopping for him? Is that it?'

Sammy shook her head. 'I don't, Uncle Vin, I swear.'

'Don't what?' Lyndsey was now standing in the doorway.

'Don't go anywhere near Mucky Melvin,' she said, looking from her mother back to Vinnie. 'Honest, I don't.'

Lyndsey rolled her eyes. 'Christ, Vin. You as well?' She walked across to her baccy tin and picked it up. 'What *is* all this with Mucky Melvin? First Titch and now you …'

'Titch?' Vinnie said, shocked. 'What about her?'

'Coming round here a few weeks back, doing the same as you.' She waved a hand towards her younger daughter. 'Honestly, Vin. You really think she'd be so fucking stupid? She's a fucking McKellan.' She rolled her eyes again. 'You really think she's that wet behind the ears?'

Vinnie turned to Sammy then and even beneath the caked on layers of make-up, he watched the answer spread across her cheeks. Yes.

Vinnie had a present for his mam, and he was proud of it. Not quite the show-stopper that his gypsy caravan and shire horse had been, but a beautiful thing, made with just as much love and care. Not by him – he'd lost interest, though his mam didn't really need to know that – but by Gordon; it had been his parting gift to Vinnie.

It was a baccy tin, an ordinary baccy tin; nothing special, but what was on the lid *made* it special, because it was a very intricate affair. There was a decoration on it made from matchsticks, just like the caravan, but in this case they were soaked in a solution beforehand which made it possible to form them into shapes. In this case, the ornamentation took the shape of a rose, created by layers of moulded petals, which were then set with varnish, and glued to the top of the tin. It had then been painted gold and just beneath the flower was the carefully etched inscription 'mother'. It was a work of art, and Vinnie knew she would love it.

But that would have to wait now. He needed to go and see his little sister. Find out exactly what had been going down. And, he decided with a kind of frisson of grim excitement, perhaps he also needed to change the timescale of his plans.

Once he knew what he needed to, he hadn't wanted to press it. Whatever had or hadn't happened, there was nothing that could be done about it anyway – well, not that wasn't going to be happening in any case. And when Lyndsey started interrogating Sammy, he wished he'd never even asked her, because it was clear Lyndsey had up to now believed Sammy's denials and – probably out of guilt, which was pretty fucking appropriate – now obviously felt the need to come over all concerned parent for his benefit. Which was pretty bloody rich, even for her.

He felt sickened thinking about what might have been happening to his niece, and could only hope that it hadn't been as bad as it could have been. And he was at least reassured by the fact that Titch had obviously taken action. Thank fuck those girls had her in their lives at least. But, shit, did that cunt have a particular thing for the girls in his fucking family, or what?

He walked the long way round to Eddie's parents' place to avoid passing his mam's house. *Well*, he thought grimly, *not any fucking more.*

Josie had changed too. But in a better way. The best way. She was obviously older, but he'd already seen a recent picture of her, so looking at the young woman she'd now become wasn't a shock. But what impressed Vinnie most was something maybe only he would have noticed. For the first time he could remember, she looked happy.

'Thought you'd have had some balloons out, at least,' he said, as she opened the door and whooped with delight.

She hugged him tightly before letting him go and dragging him into the house. 'And I thought you'd have lost that spazzy moustache!' she retorted. 'Oh, God,' she said, startling him by throwing herself on him again for another hug, 'I am *so* glad to have you home again, Vin.'

'So,' he said, following her into a living room that looked like Buckingham Palace compared to his mam's (though it did lack a guitar clock) and thinking how pleased he felt that she'd fallen on her feet, 'where is everyone? And where's my latest niece?'

'Eddie's mam and dad have gone into Bradford, and Eddie's at work,' she told him. She grinned. 'As in doing a job. I know – a shock,' she added, laughing. 'But it's what some people do. Maybe you could try it now you're out.'

He grinned. 'You cheeky bleeder! I'll have you know I've worked pretty much every sodding day of the last six years.'

'Yeah, you told me,' Titch laughed. 'Sitting in a library? That's not work. Not for *you*. Anyway, sit yourself down. I'll go up and fetch Paula.'

Vinnie took in more of his surroundings as he waited, and felt the heaviness of earlier lifting a little. Though he didn't know Eddie well – he'd been away six years after all – he remembered the nice lad he'd been before he went in, and Brendan had confirmed it as well. He was a good solid bloke, and would take care of his sister, and that was all that mattered.

'Here she is,' Titch beamed, coming back with the baby in her arms. 'Paula, this is your uncle Vinnie. You're going to love him.'

She held the bundle straight out to Vinnie then, startling him for a second time. But he took his niece gladly, even though he felt a bit cack-handed doing so. He'd not seen a child – particularly a baby – in so long, that he was scared he might hold her wrong and start her off crying.

But as soon as he had hold of her, such worries melted away. You didn't forget that stuff, after all, and it suddenly seemed like no time at all ago that he was cradling Lyndsey's three in exactly the same way.

'Sammy and Lou have grown,' he said, lowering himself onto the big chintzy sofa.

'Haven't they just,' Titch agreed with him. 'Though – hang on – you mean you went there before coming here? Charming!' she huffed. 'I suppose you've already been round mam and dad's too.'

He shook his head, cursing his stupidity in telling her. Why had he done that? 'Nah,' he said. 'And I only nipped in to check the house number of this place. Had to come and see this princess first, didn't I?' he looked down at the baby, who was gazing up at him with enormous blue eyes. 'Christ, though,' he said, 'poor little bleeder's got my nose!'

'Mam said it's Dad's, and Eddie's mam say's it's her auntie's – you know, I've decided everyone sees what they want to in babies.' She smiled. 'And I agree with you.'

Vinnie smiled back and crooked his little finger so that Paula could grip it. Which she did, gurgling at him as if she knew exactly who he was, and that she knew she was safe in his arms. He sighed, feeling chuffed she wasn't crying for her mother and, remembering the job he'd vowed to do – and *would* do – wondering when there would be a chance to feel this peaceful again.

One thing was for sure. No girl in his family – including this one snuggled right here in his arms – was ever going to have to fear that cunt ever again.

Chapter 28

His room was pitch black, silent and freezing when he awoke and for a moment he couldn't work out where he was. The noise was shrill though, so he leaned across to his bedside and switched off the tin alarm clock: 3 a.m. He sat up, disorientated. He was in his cell surely, but if so, why couldn't he see? Where were the dim landing lights?

But then it hit him. He wasn't in prison any more. He was in his old bedroom at home. Hence the cold. So he leapt out of bed and started to limber up, both to keep warm and also because it was part of his routine; keeping fit was second nature to him now. He tried to be quiet though. He didn't want to wake up his mam and dad.

He let his thoughts wander as he pushed out some sit-ups. He thought of Brendan, but he didn't feel guilty. He knew Brendan would be angry, but that was tough shit. If all this was to come on top, he didn't want to take his best mate down with him.

Vinnie pulled open his bottom drawer carefully, mindful of the broken runner, felt around and pulled out a sweater. It was still dark but now his eyes had adjusted, he could see just how enormous it was, and he grinned. Fuck knew just how big his mam must have thought he'd grown, but it was sweet of her to find some old thing of Jock's to fill his drawers with, bless her. He pulled it on over the T-shirt and jeans he'd fallen into bed in. It would certainly do fine for tonight anyway.

All that remained now was to push his feet into his beloved dealer boots, now a bit stiff and worse for wear. Then his Crombie – he couldn't countenance going anywhere without his beloved Crombie, and he was done. He crept as silently as he could down the stairs.

It had been 24 hours, almost to the minute, since he'd crashed in, drunk as fuck, after his first night back home. It had been quite a night – had there been anyone who hadn't bought a drink for him? – and though his head was reasonably clear, tonight's return visit to the Bull had topped up his alcohol levels, even having spent much of yesterday asleep in bed, and with a plate of his mam's stew and dumplings on board.

But perhaps a little alcohol was important, he decided, making his way out through the back door to the coal-hole to retrieve the black bin liner of stuff he had hidden there. Stone cold sober he might be tempted to think more pragmatically about everything, forget how it had burned in him, this determination for justice, and that was the last thing he wanted to happen.

Walking through the estate streets, Vinnie didn't keep to the shadows and edges. He walked purposefully down the middle of the road. He didn't give two fucks who might see him and wonder – in fact he hoped some people might. He knew the police wouldn't be knocking about around the estate at this time – not without an invite – and as for everyone else … Well by morning, they'd all have a fair idea who had done this in any case.

He grinned as a sudden thought popped into his head. Mr Malvern had once been discussing Charles Dickens with him, and came out with a quote that had stayed with him: *Charity begins at home, and justice begins next door.* Well actually, sir, Vinnie thought, flexing his fingers around his bin bag, justice begins in about five fucking minutes, down the bottom of Dawnay Road.

The squat that was currently home to Mucky-fucking-Melvin naturally had no locking doors. It was an abandoned house of a kind which could be found all over the estate, the last official residents having done a runner. The council being the council – i.e. fucking inefficient in most departments – often took months to cotton on to these empty homes. And in the meantime – the residents of Canterbury Estate being generally resourceful – they were put to good use. They provided places to stash stolen goods, throw an all-night party, take a bird for a quickie or, in Melvin's case, somewhere to live when you needed to leave your own home for some reason.

Most of the squats had boarded-up windows. This was a ruse by whoever was using them, to give the police or any particularly nosey neighbours the impression that the council knew about them and were working on them. Number 12 Dawnay Road, however, didn't. It was a dump, out and out, a proper hovel – with its front windows sporting several broken panes, held together only with the torn-up bin bags that had been taped across the holes.

Vinnie entered silently, though had to swallow hard to stop himself gagging because the stench was horrendous: a vile cocktail of stale food and shit and piss. He trod carefully, grateful for the light coming in from the nearby street-lamp to help him, which also illuminated a filthy mattress lying on one side of the front room, on which Melvin was currently lying, snoring.

Vinnie glanced around, taking his time to get his bearings. A kind of fire had been built in the middle of the floor and he could still see a half-burned chair leg sticking out from the ashes. That'll do for starters, he thought, stepping across the crap on the floor to get to it, and leaning down to pluck it from the ashes. He inspected it more closely as he quietly put down his bag of kit, then roughly poked the middle of the sleeping form. Melvin coughed once, then tried to pull up the overcoat covering him, apparently unaware still that he had a visitor.

Vinnie poked him again and then squatted by the mattress, directly in front of him, then, as his eyes flickered open, poked him again.

'Rise and shine, you filthy old cunt!' he said brightly. Upon which Melvin, wide-eyed now, tried to sit up.

Vinnie didn't let him. He shoved him back hard onto his makeshift bed, ensuring he was now lying flat on his back and could clearly see who it was who'd come to visit. The old man looked up at him, his eyes first filled with fear then, a moment later, with a kind of acceptance.

He cleared his throat again. 'Didn't think it would be long before you came calling, McKellan,' he said. He laughed mirthlessly. 'Come to talk, have you?'

Vinnie laughed as well, then gripped Melvin's flaccid throat in his hand. 'That's right, old man,' he said. 'Come for a nice cosy chat, I have. Starting with what you did to my sister. Then perhaps, over a cuppa, we could move on – how does that sound? To what you've been doing to my niece.'

Melvin wriggled, but it was pointless, and he soon even stopped trying, instead rasping, 'I never touched your fucking niece! And your sister? Christ, McKellan – don't tell me you believe that fucking nonsense? I never went near her. And if she says so she's a fucking liar!'

Vinnie felt his lips begin to quiver. He knew the feeling and he welcomed its arrival. This cunt was actually making him feel physically sick. He could feel it rising up within him, like

a tide. He cleared his own throat and was rewarded by a mouth-
ful of phlegm, which he spat with precision into the old man's
face.

Melvin tried to twist away, but Vinnie's grip was too strong
for him, and as he watched the glistening phlegm make a track
across his mouth, Vinnie tightened it further, watching with
pleasure as Melvin's face, engorged with blood, grew redder and
redder and his eyes began to bulge. But, pleasing thought it
was, it was too soon to have the cunt pass out on him. He
relaxed his grip. 'You calling my sister a liar?' he said. 'You
scummy piece of fucking shit. Are you really that stupid, old
man? And did you think you could hide from me? Did you
really fucking think I wouldn't hunt you down? I've spent fucking years fantasising about what I was going to do to you,
Melvin, and now you have one chance – one fucking chance
– to admit what you did. You're going to die tonight, and no
mistake, you only have two options. You're going to die slow or
you're going to die slower. Up to you, old man.' He squeezed
again, smiling down. 'Up to fucking you.'

Vinnie could see the resignation begin to dawn in Melvin's
eyes. He knew what his fate was going to be tonight. He must
do. But no harm in pressing the point home, Vinnie supposed,
feeling as calm as he had in a long time. Leaning back, he used
his free hand to grab the bin bag from where it sat, then tipped
it out to spread the contents on the floor. That done, he
grabbed a handful of Melvin's hair, to twist his head round, so
that he could see the contents for himself: a large carving knife,
a pair of pliers, a litre pop bottle of petrol and a box of Swan
Vestas.

'I don't hold with safety matches,' he said conversationally.
'Where would the fun be in that? Anyway, take a good look,
old man, before I punch your fucking lights out.'

Melvin looked and even as he did so, Vinnie could feel his hands start twitching, and gripping the hair tighter, he released Melvin's neck, then started smashing his fist repeatedly into his face. It was a full minute before he paused to draw breath. Melvin's eyes were already swelling and his mouth was pouring blood, and he was limp as a doll when Vinnie released his hold on his hair.

'Fag break,' he said, standing and reaching into his coat pocket for a cigarette, and giving Melvin another slap as he reached down to grab the matches. Melvin groaned. 'Getting the picture now, you old cunt? he asked, taking a deep draw on his cigarette, then shrugging off his coat and looking for a relatively clean place to put it. He settled on the door handle, to keep it off the shitty, pissy floor. 'I tell you what, Melvin,' he said conversationally, 'it's nice and fucking warm in here mate, isn't it? Well, I don't know about you of course, but I'm fucking sweating buckets!'

Melvin groaned again, and tried to lift his head and shoulders off the mattress.

Vinnie leaned in close. 'What was that, old feller? You got something to say?' He cupped his hand behind his ear and waited. 'Only, if it's a priest you're wanting for your last rites, you're out of luck, mate. I've just left Father Henry, see,' he said, nodding towards the window, 'having a double-up with Sister Agatha and the convent cleaner. Shame.'

Melvin cleared his throat again, and spat blood from his mouth. Then seemed to try and rearrange his features into a defiant sneer. 'Little Josie, eh?' he said finally, through his thick blood-stained lips. 'I almost forgot how good she was, your sister. Right little fucking goer an' all. Thanks for leaving her for me, by the way. Nice tight little snatch, she had, couldn't fucking get enough of me, that one ...'

Vinnie launched himself on top of Melvin then, pinning the man's arms under his knees. He pressed his lit cigarette into the bastard's flabby cheek and was a little disappointed that it went out so quickly. 'Is that right, you filthy cunt?' he said, leaning in close and, breathing out hard because it was actually making him retch to even think about it, took a deep, disgusting bite out of it instead. He was frenzied now, and the more Melvin bucked and screamed beneath him, the harder Vinnie laughed and continued biting.

But something in the old fucker seemed determined to continue. Perhaps these were the last rites of filthy cunts who molested children – to shout their fucking filth to the world. 'Your Lyndsey's kid's the same!' he screamed, trying in vain to get Vinnie off him. He was fucking strong though – the pain must have been indescribable, but he still continued his taunts. 'Though she prefers a finger job,' he rasped.

Vinnie could no longer see straight. Much as he was driven to extract a confession from the bastard, hearing it actually spoken was quite another thing. Reaching to his side, he grabbed his pliers and, holding Melvin's mouth open with one hand, forced the pliers inside and clamped them round his tongue. Melvin really struggled now – did he know what was coming? But Vinnie's thighs were immeasurably stronger. Clamping the old man between them, he then grabbed the knife and, in one swift movement, sliced out his tongue. He then hammered with the pliers into the gaping mouth and throat, and, finally, teeth, blood and gore splattered everywhere, Mucky Melvin stopped talking.

He was conscious, if only just, and fading quickly. He'd be losing blood at a lick now, and it would probably choke him. Vinnie stared hard into his eyes, which still stared back at him. 'Take them thoughts to the fucking grave, cunt!' he spat, slapping him back into the present. 'Oh, and don't worry about the cold. My grand finale will warm your cockles. Cunt!'

A sickening gurgle was the only sound Melvin could now manage, which turned into a cough which spewed blood and bits of flesh from his mouth. And Vinnie was suddenly aware that his arse felt warm. Lifting himself up slightly – Melvin was now well beyond bucking – he saw the large stain spreading down the front of the old man's trousers, at the same time, breathed in the smell of fresh shit.

Disgusting and gagging, he plucked the knife up from where he'd put it and began plunging it into the old man's chest. 'You dirty old fucker!' he screamed, stabbing his chest with each syllable. 'You'd piss and shit on me, you dirty fucking cunt?'

He was crying now, he realised, surprised to feel the tears tracking down his cheeks. *Crying?* He hadn't cried in fucking years! And now he'd started, he couldn't seem to stop crying either so he let them flow, unabashed, as he continued making stab holes, up on his knees now, to avoid being further contaminated by the body – and it was surely just a body now – still leaking piss and shit beneath him.

It seemed a long time, but the tears stopped eventually. He clambered off then, moving carefully to avoid touching anything he didn't want to and, as he staggered to his feet, felt a calm descending. It was a calm he'd not felt before, cathartic – a sort of cleansing, and as he took the lid off the pop bottle to start pouring the petrol, he felt a lightness he didn't expect to feel.

But there was work to do and he needed to get on and do it, so he began – pouring the petrol in an orderly fashion, first into Melvin's crotch – a good half bottle there, just for the symbolism – then in a circle of sprinkles around his body. He then made a second circuit – wider this time – and then a more general sprinkling, finishing with a trail that reached out into the hall.

That done, he gathered his bag of tools – no point in making it easy for the fuckers – and collected his Crombie from the door. He had just the one fag left and he put it in his mouth gratefully, popping the bag down for a minute so that he could strike a match and light it. He drew on it deeply, enjoying the relaxing flood of nicotine for a moment, then, holding it in his mouth, took the match he'd just used and lit the rest of the matches with it, before throwing the burning box across to the soaking mattress. He watched for a minute or two, enough to be sure a sufficient blaze had started, then let himself out and began the walk home.

It was 5 a.m. before Vinnie opened the back door of his own house, and his nostrils were immediately assaulted. *Stew!* He thought, feeling his stomach begin to rumble. Then he remembered. His mam had left him another plate of stew and dumplings. *For when you get back from the pub*, she'd said. *Put some meat back on that body*. And, keen to get to bed and set his clock, he'd forgotten.

Moving quietly, pulled the still lukewarm plate from the oven, salivating even as he transferred it to the tin tray, even though, as he did so, he saw a fleck of something pink and formless stuck to the back of his hand. Bless his mam, he thought, taking his second dinner into the living room. He ate it on the couch and, though he had a half-thought there was something he should be doing, he lay down then, his belly full, his mind empty.

He slept where he lay, numb to everything except his exhaustion.

Chapter 29

Babies, thought Josie as she trudged along pushing Paula's pram, should come with a set of instructions. All night she'd been up – she'd not had so much as a single wink of sleep – and still Paula fretted and fussed and grizzled. She had no idea what the problem was – colic? Might she be teething? Was she even old enough? But hopefully she wouldn't cry for much longer. If there was one thing she had learned since having her own baby, it was that, if everything else failed, constant movement often did the trick.

Not that traipsing round the estate at this hour, dog tired and bleary-eyed, was ever going to be Josie's movement of choice. But she felt she had *no* choice. It wasn't fair on Eddie to be kept awake all night. He was working ten hours a day at the moment – he was on a big decorating job currently – and toiling almost every weekend just to provide for them both. And till Josie went back to her machining job at the local factory, it was only fair that she do her bit and look after the baby.

There were Eddie's mum and dad to think about as well. It had been kind of them to take them in till they reached the top of the housing waiting list and though she couldn't wait till that day came and they could set up home properly, she was also mindful of what a stress it was for them having a baby in the house – not least because of the constant round of smelly nappies and crying.

Paula was settling now, at least, and judging the time to be
about eight now, Titch knew she could safely think about heading home. Eddie would be off to work soon and, with any luck,
his mam would be happy to take over the reins, allowing her to
get her head down for a much needed nap.

On the other hand, she was halfway to her own mam's place
now. Maybe she should stop by there and see if they were up.
She didn't often these days – her mam was still a bit narked
that she'd moved in with Eddie – but now Vinnie was home
she felt a pull to go round there. Yes, it was a long shot, seeing
as he'd spent two nights down the bloody pub now – chance
would be a fine thing for her! But maybe he'd be up and they
could have a cuppa and a proper catch-up. She'd hardly seen
anything of him since he'd been home, after all.

She pushed the pram across the street and turned onto
Ringwood Road, but when she did so, something prickling in
her nostrils made her stop and look around. She sniffed the air.
That was it – so she hadn't been mistaken. She'd thought she'd
smelt something odd when she'd first left the house, but now it
was definitely much stronger. She sniffed again. That was it.
She could smell smoke coming from somewhere.

Josie carried on for a bit, wondering if someone had left a
bonfire burning down by the youthy, but when she reached the
top end of Dawnay Road and turned to look down it, what she
saw made her stop in her tracks.

Shit, she thought. A house fire. And a big one, by the looks
of it. There weren't any great plumes of smoke – they'd obviously got the worst of it under control now – but there still
seemed to be lots going on. There were two fire engines, both
flashing red and blue lights, and even at a distance she could
hear the sound of men shouting to one another, as they continued to mill around the scene of the dying blaze.

She stood for a moment, watching, trying to imagine what it must be like to have your house go up in flames, and wondering if anyone had been hurt or killed. Whose house was it? Might it be anyone she knew? Dawnay Road ... why was Dawnay Road ringing bells for her? She'd head it mentioned recently, but with her sleep-deprived brain, she couldn't seem to remember what it was.

It was only when a police car reversed out of the gathering of various vehicles that the something started to resolve itself in her brain. *Shit*, it was *Sammy*. Of course it was. She shook her head to try and clear it. Yes, that was the thing she needed to remember. Wasn't the squat on Dawnay Road the place Sammy had mentioned? The place where Mucky Melvin was now holed up?

Shit, she thought again, as the police car put on its sirens and began speeding up the road towards her. Christ, it couldn't be, could it? She watched the car approach and pass her, a streak of white flashing by, and an even more shocking thought slammed into her brain. Could it be that ...? Oh, God, *please* don't let it be that, she thought distractedly. Please don't let that have happened ...

She spun the pram right around, and then broke into a run, following the car. She had no hope of keeping up with it, but at least she could still see it. And she had a sickening sense that she didn't even need to. And when she saw an indicator flash on she knew exactly which street it was turning into, and that she'd have her worst fears confirmed. 'Oh no!' she howled, increasing her speed, the pram now clattering over all the pot holes. 'Oh, no, Vinnie,' she began to sob. 'Not again!'

June was standing in front of her dressing-table mirror, nightie hitched up slightly at the back. She'd thrown it on in a flap, having been woken up by something – but what was it? She'd gone to the top of the stairs but heard nothing. And it obviously wasn't Vinnie crashing in and making a noise about it – she'd already checked his bedroom and it was empty. Probably pulled some bird down the Bull after she and Jock had left, June decided, and found another bed for the night. Well, she thought, smoothing the fabric down properly, fair enough. He did have a bit of time to make up.

It was a different sound that next jolted her out of her reverie. A sharp angry rapping on the front door.

'Jesus Christ!' she yelled to Jock, who began stirring in the bed behind her. 'Who the fuck's on the doorstep at this hour?'

He rolled over. 'At this hour? It's fucking gone eight, you stupid mare! Let's see. The postman? The leccy man? A pair of Jehovah's fucking Witnesses? It's not going to be the postman is it? He'll be fucking long gone!'

June went to slap him but just as she was about to, the rapping started up again, even louder. 'It's fucking Sunday!' she snapped instead, grabbing her dressing gown from the back of the door. 'Alright!' she yelled down. 'Whoever you are, hold your bleeding horses! You'd better have a good fucking excuse, you hear! *Christ!*'

She rattled down the stairs, doing up her dressing gown as she went, feeling her head thudding painfully with every step. *There should be a law against this*, she thought, hitting the bottom step and feeling her head swim. She clutched the newel post to steady herself. She must have drunk more than she'd thought.

And that's when she saw it. The bundle on the sofa. Except that when she looked again it resolved itself into a more human-shaped lump. And, hang on – wasn't that Vinnie's Crombie slung over it? Ignoring the door for the moment

– and, Christ, now they were banging the bloody letter-box –
she went instead into the living room to see.

The lump was stirring now.

'Shut the fuck up – I'm coming okay?' she yelled into the
hall. Then she lifted the coat and felt the blood start to drain
from her.

It was Vinnie. Christ, her *son*. That much was clear immediately. Though if you'd chanced upon him in an alley you'd
run a mile before you'd got that far. He was in such a state –
matted hair, a powerful metallic smell about him that made her
nose wrinkle – and no wonder. What the fucking hell had
happened to him? Shit, he was *covered* in blood. No, more than
that – he was caked with it, in fact. It was congealing all over
him, great sticky gobs of it. And the more she looked the more
she recoiled from it.

She poked him, terrified, feeling an almost irresistible urge
to vomit. Fuck – was he *dead*? 'Vinnie, son!' she hissed, swallowing her nausea as he moved slightly. Oh, God, thank the
lord. He was alive still. 'Vinnie,' she hissed again. 'What the
fuck has happened to you? Are you okay?'

He grunted slightly. Opened an eye and then closed it again,
scowling. Just like he used to do when he was a nipper and she
was trying to get him up for school. 'Vinnie!' June snapped
now, her terror now turned to anger, 'What the hell is going
on? Is that the bizzies outside?' She turned to look but couldn't
see into the road because of the nets. And she wasn't going to
the window and showing herself. Not yet.

Vinnie stirred again and rolled over. Then his eyes snapped
fully open. And he stared at her for so long she thought he
might have lost his senses. Then he seemed to focus, and there
was something in his expression that made her blood drain
from her face.

'Vinnie!' she said slowly. 'What the fuck *have you done*, you stupid bleeder?'

The raps on the door became increasingly urgent bangings. They'd have the door in if they went on much longer.

'Mam –' Vinnie started, rubbing the streaks of God knew what across his face.

'Vinnie, look at the *state* of you! Have you been in another fight? Christ, look at the *state* of you!'

He swung his legs around and ran his palms vigorously over his face. Then lowered them slowly and exhaled as he placed them on his knees. 'Mam, just answer the fucking door, okay?'

Josie arrived at her mother's to find the police car parked outside. They hadn't left it with the doors hanging open like they did in *Starsky & Hutch*, but you could see they'd been in a hurry because it was parked all askew, with half of one wheel listing off the pavement. In any other circumstance, she'd have found that amusing. But now she just had a horrible leaden feeling in her stomach. She turned into the path and pushed the pram along it.

The front door to her mam and dad's was yawning open. Won't bother knocking then, she thought ruefully as she manhandled the pram over the threshold and squeezed it into the hall. It was a squash but she could just about park it and squeeze carefully past it. Now Paula was asleep she didn't want to risk her waking up again.

The low voices she could hear from the living room resolved themselves as she entered. Her mam and dad, Vinnie, looking – Christ, the *state* of him! She had to blink to believe it – and two stony-faced police officers in uniform. There were no screams or shouts and when they looked up and saw her, only

Vinnie seemed to register her presence with more than a brief acknowledgement that she was even there.

He said nothing, but then he didn't have to.

Her mother did though, belatedly. 'Thank God,' she said. 'Go and put the kettle on, will you, Titch?'

Josie gawped. She was expecting her to make tea at a time like this?

'What's happened?' she asked, looking more towards her brother than anyone else. And in response, one of the officers stood up.

'Come on, lad,' he said to Vinnie, placing a hand under one of his elbows. 'Let's be having you. No point making this any harder than it needs to be.'

Vinnie stood up obligingly. He looked a bit unsteady on his feet. Josie couldn't stop staring at him. How did he *get* like that? 'Hang on,' June snapped. 'Look at him! At least let him have a fucking cup of tea!'

'He can have a cup of tea down at the station,' the policemen answered mildly. 'Come on lad,' he said again. 'Let's be off.'

'What's he done?' Josie persisted. 'Why are you arresting him? Vinnie? *Vinnie?*' She felt a lump form in her throat as he approached her. Still he said nothing. She was in the way now, and what with the pram, too, they'd be unable to get past. She stood her ground. 'What's he *done?*' she asked again.

'Can you let us get by, love?' the other policeman said, the one who hadn't spoken yet. But, still transfixed on her brother, all she did was stare.

'For fuck's sake!' she heard her mam say then. 'Just get out of the fucking way, Titch!'

Which made her start. And woke Paula up as well. She felt the tears pricking at her eyes. God, she was just so, so *tired.* 'See what you did!' she yelled at her mother. Was she just going to let this happen? 'See what you've done? I only just got her off to sleep, only just got her off to *sodding sleep*! And see what you've done?' She snatched Paula from beneath her blankets.

She felt a light touch on her arm then, just after the first policeman squeezed past her, muttering apologies. It was Vinnie. And close up, he *really* looked like shit. She could hardly even think about how he'd come to look like he did. Which was like a wild man, his face stippled with blood, his hair slick with it – a deeper red in cloying lumps among the ginger. He lifted his little finger – the only digit that wasn't red-brown and sticky – and touched it very lightly to Paula's cheek.

'Oh, Vinnie,' Titch began, before a sob racked her body. Her *stupid* fucking brother. Her stupid, idiot, crazy, fucking moron of a fucking brother!

'You'll be safe now, kiddo,' he said to Paula, his voice barely a whisper. Then he squeezed past and followed the policeman out to the car.

Josie pulled Paula close to her and moved out of the way so the other policeman could get past them both as well.

'Stupid little bleeder,' Jock was saying from the living room.

'Shut yer fucking cake-hole, before I give you a slap!' June snapped back.

Josie could imagine the pair of them looking out, the grubby net curtain lifted, and had no desire to go in there and join them. She stayed on the doorstep and planted a soft kiss on Paula's head. She was wide awake now, but settled. Perhaps it had just been colic after all.

Josie watched one of the policemen help Vinnie into the back seat before going round to the front passenger seat and climbing into the car himself. Vinnie was looking straight at her now, out of the window. So she took one of Paula's tiny hands and pumped her arm up and down.

'Wave bye-bye,' she said softly. 'Wave bye-bye to your Uncle Vinnie. Say "Safe journey, Uncle Vin! See you soon!"' She felt her tears soaking into the downy hair on Paula's head. 'He's a Canterbury Warrior, he is,' she whispered.

Then the car rumbled into life and he was gone.

Epilogue

In February 1980, Vinnie was sentenced to life imprisonment for murder. He was sent to a new prison, HMP Wymott, which had been open for less than a year and which, ironically, had a VPU – a Vulnerable Prisoners Unit, which housed the very kind of prisoners that he despised most.

Despite all the damning evidence against him, Vinnie refused to testify and maintained his innocence throughout his trial. No witnesses from the estate would testify against him either. In fact there was a queue of people willing to provide an alibi for Vinnie's whereabouts on the night Melvin was murdered.

When sentencing, the judge made a somewhat controversial statement. He told the court that, sadly, in his opinion, Vinnie was a 'product of the system'. He believed that borstals were a breeding ground for bullies and psychopaths. He pointed at Vinnie, who was grinning after hearing his 'life' sentence, and said, 'Look at this man. Look carefully, for we are all responsible for what lies under the mask. Throughout this hearing, he has shown a distinct lack of empathy and displayed strongly amoral conduct. I would suggest that if this man is not a psychopath, he is at the very least bordering on criminally insane.'

In 1981 Vinnie took part in prison riots following the inner-city riots in the UK. For this, he lost the chance of parole. He served 12 years for his crime and was released in 1992.

Lyndsey died the same year, of a heroin overdose, and her former boyfriend Robbo's whereabouts are unknown. Her son, Robbie, sadly, went on to live a life of crime and has been in and out of prison for most of his adult life. Her daughters, Lou and Sammy, however, managed to avoid their brother's fate. They both went on to have children of their own and still live just off the estate.

June and Jock both died peacefully in their late sixties, still together, but Josie is alive and well. She and Eddie are still together to this day, happily married and now with four grown-up children of their own.

After his release, Vinnie kept out of prison for a while, though unfortunately, the lure of easy money was always too tempting and he spent another ten years in and out of his second home. He did, however, settle for long enough to marry and have a family, and enjoyed many years of being a bit of a celebrity on the estate on which he'd been born. And to some, more than that even. He was – and still is – a legend.

Acknowledgements

I would like to thank my agent Andrew Lownie for this wonderful opportunity to tell my stories, and the team at HarperCollins for putting their trust in me every step of the way. I also want to thank the wonderful Lynne Barrett-Lee for helping me turn my dream into reality. Without her help, these stories would still be in the box in my garage, gathering dust.

I would like to dedicate these books first and foremost to my parents Keith and Shirley Hudson. They made me who I am today, and have loved and supported me all my life. And to my gorgeous husband Ben, who has had to endure me practically ignoring him for two years while I worked on my writing, and who learned how to cook, clean and work the washing machine while I was in my 'zone'. I also need to mention my brother Glenn and sister Paula, who have giggled along with me as I decided what material to use and what most definitely needed to stay buried, and my cousin Susan Taylor (our Nipper), who has been on hand whenever I needed her for historical accuracy or juicy snippets. All of my family deserve a mention, but they are legion and mentioning them all would fill a book. They know how much I love them.

Finally, I also dedicate all these words to my favourite ever cousin, Willie Jagger. Rest in peace, Willie. You know how much you're loved and no doubt you'll be laughing your arse off up there at the thought of me being an author. Every time I see our Pauline it makes me so happy because she reminds me of everything you were.

Moving Memoirs

Stories of hope, courage and the power of love…

If you loved this book, then you will love our
Moving Memoirs eNewsletter

Sign up to…

- Be the first to hear about new books

- Get sneak previews from your favourite authors

- Read exclusive interviews

- Be entered into our monthly prize draw to win one
  of our latest releases before it's even hit the shops!

Sign up at

www.moving-memoirs.com